Harley -

Thanks for your inspiration,
guidance and support.

Love,

Larry 7/28/94

Advance Praise for

LEADERSHIP
in a NEW ERA

"*Leadership in a New Era: Visionary Approaches to the Biggest Crisis of Our Time* is a must-read for any serious student or practitioner of leadership today!"

> — Darrell J. Brown
> president and executive editor
> *Leaders* magazine

"The business world is ready for a book like this. Those seemingly invincible institutions of family, religion, government, and education have left a void in society today—a void the business world has the opportunity, and responsibility, to fill. These essays inspire those in business to focus on long-term visions as opposed to short-term profit statements."

> — Gun Denhart, founder
> Hanna Andersson

"In this time of radical change, true leadership is called for more than ever. It is, actually, the key to a not-too-turbulent transformation into a new era. In this book, the concept of true leadership is given a thorough elucidation from a large variety of angles. *Leadership in a New Era* is the most comprehensive book on the subject I have read and I strongly recommend it to everyone in business—leaders as well as followers."

> — Rolf Österberg, former chairman
> Swedish Newspaper Association;
> former president, CEO
> Svensk Filmindustri;
> author, *Corporate Renaissance:
> Business as an Adventure in Human
> Development*

"This well-written collection of essays represents the new leadership directions of the future. Some key advocates for the future are represented among these authors. Virtual corporations, teams, empowerment, servant leadership, vision, values, trust, commitment, courage, and advocating change—if you don't stand for these, you're not a future leader."

— Rick Crandall, PhD
editor/publisher, *Executive Edge*;
founder, Community
Entrepreneurs Organization

"Anyone who reads this book and doesn't think the new emerging leadership is REVOLUTIONARY didn't get the point. When you take a whole-system perspective, if one part of the system changes, everything else has to. Although it is leadership that seems to be what is talked about, underneath is the message: The whole system is changing—and must. When you find this diverse group of authors agreeing on that point, you have to pay attention."

—Willis Harman PhD, president
Institute of Noetic Sciences;
co-founder, World Business Academy;
co-author, *Creative Work:
The Constructive Role of Business in a
Transforming Society*

"The world is starved for leadership, and this book has laid a feast of fresh thoughts that have been carefully prepared by 'new leaders.' The perspective of this book exemplifies the new leadership by feeding the soul of the reader."

—William E. Halal, PhD
professor of management
George Washington University;
author, *Internal Markets: Bringing
the Power of Free Enterprise Inside
Your Organization*

"*Leadership in a New Era* is the best yet that I've seen. Challenging. Practical. Inspirational. This book is itself a leader—in the field of management into the next century. The authors are all to be congratulated for offering more than information or knowledge, but real wisdom—from the heart."

—William Miller
author, *Quantum Quality;*
founder
Global Creativity Corporation

"What an impressive array of perspectives regarding the central issue of our personal and organizational lives and times! *Leadership in a New Era* has something to offer everybody."

— James Liebig, author
Merchants of Vision and
Business Ethics

"John Renesch has done a masterful job of assembling a collection that seriously addresses what it means to be a leader in these most challenging of times. The authors—all highly successful leaders within their own domains—share a common vision of what can be achieved by leaders who hold to high ideals and standards. Collectively, their vision is inspirational."

—J. Randolph New, dean
E. Claiborne Robins School of
Business, University of Richmond

"If it's broke, let's fix it! The signs abound that traditional approaches to corporate leadership are not working well. Here, in *Leadership in a New Era,* are to be found many insights—and, still more important, inspiration—to guide the transformation of the way we do business."

—Andrew Bard Schmookler
author, *Fools Gold: The Fate of Values in a World of Goods* and *The Illusion of Choice*

"Just when I started thinking I had it figured out, *Leadership in a New Era* forced me to start thinking it through all over again. The topic, the provocative nature of the essays, and the interdisciplinary approach to the theme, make it a *must read* for anyone planning on functioning well in the next decade."

—Alan J. Parisse
business lecturer

"The most important piece of any organization is the people who make it happen. This book helped me better understand how to lead my own organization's people into the next century. What a pleasure to learn from the best and the brightest. All future leaders can grow through an understanding of this collection."

—Kye Anderson
chairman, president, and CEO
Medical Graphics Corporation

"*Leadership in a New Era* is a book that addresses our current chaos, points us toward a new tomorrow, and gives us a compelling vision about leadership—one which takes the reader to new places that transcend current realities. It gives us a sense of shared purpose and makes us feel that we are, indeed, part of something greater than ourselves. This book is a beacon of hope for the future and for the development of tomorrow's leaders."

—Keith Darcy, president
The Leadership Group, Inc.

"*Leadership in a New Era* is a veritable feast of wisdom. You are invited by editor John Renesch to join him at a banquet whose guests clearly rejoice in sharing their food for thought. Whether you are eavesdropping in on an engaging conversation, or savoring a delicious morsel of wisdom, the experience is quite heady. You will come away spinning with new insights and new applications. Don't miss this opportunity to partake."

—Jim Kouzes, co-author
The Leadership Challenge
and *Credibility*
president, TPG/Learning Systems

LEADERSHIP
in a NEW ERA

VISIONARY APPROACHES TO THE
BIGGEST CRISIS OF OUR TIME

LEADERSHIP in a NEW ERA

VISIONARY APPROACHES TO THE BIGGEST CRISIS OF OUR TIME

Featuring essays by:

James A. Autry • Carol Sanford
Barbara R. Hauser • Ann M. Morrison
Ed Oakley • Peter K. Krembs • Charles F. Kiefer
Warren Bennis • Kate Steichen • Barbara Shipka
Tina Rasmussen • Larry C. Spears
Elemer Magaziner • Susan M. Campbell
Robert Rabbin • Margaret J. Wheatley • John D. Adams
Martha Spice • Carol McCall • Max DePree
Perry Pascarella • Stewart Emery

EDITOR: JOHN RENESCH

NewLeadersPress

STERLING &
STONE, INC.

San Francisco

New Leaders Press
Sterling & Stone, Inc.
1668 Lombard St.
San Francisco, CA 94123
415/928-1473

Permissions and Credits

The editor and publisher wish to acknowledge the following sources:

"Random Observations After Twenty-Eight Years of Managing" is from *Love & Profit: The Art of Caring Leadership* by James A. Autry ©1991 by James A. Autry. Used by permission of William Morrow & Company, Inc.
"Leadership and the New Science" is from *Leadership and the New Science* by Margaret J. Wheatley ©1992 Margaret J. Wheatley. Used by permission of Berrett-Koehler Publishers, Inc.
"The Attributes of Leadership" is from *Leadership Jazz* by Max DePree ©1992 by Max DePree. Used by permission of Doubleday, a division of Bantam Doubleday Dell Publishing Group, Inc.

Photo Credits: Photo of James A. Autry by James R. Cobb Photography; photo of Charles Kiefer by Robin Raymond; photo of Warren Bennis by Paul Goodman; photo of Larry Spears by Pannars Photography.

 Printed in the United States of America on recycled paper.

Leadership in a New Era: Visionary Approaches to the Biggest Crisis of Our Time. Editor: John Renesch.

ISBN 0-9630390-3-2

First Edition
    First Printing 1994

Table of Contents

Preface

This book contains twenty-three essays written by some of the greatest scholars of leadership in the world. This fabulous group of individuals has collaborated in this unique collection, sharing intimate parts of themselves and being genuine in the process.

These chaotic times are difficult, but they will not be improved with outmoded thinking. As Einstein told us decades ago, we cannot solve our problems with the same mode of thinking that created them.

Each of these talented authors offers a glimpse into the new thinking that will allow us to transcend the difficulties of our time and create positive, sustainable futures for ourselves and our children.

Leadership in this transition will come from many unexpected areas—people we haven't previously considered "leaders" because they do not hold a position that entitles them to do so. However, in this new era we will see many people legitimizing themselves to lead—doing what is needed.

As the most dominant and powerful human institution that humankind has ever developed, we expect that the business community will be at the forefront of this revolution of leadership—taking more responsibility for the well-being of society in the short and long term.

The authors of this book represent a variety of disciplines and perspectives in the world of commerce—from business schools to multinational corporations, from the technical to the softer industries. They offer you, the reader, a rich assortment of wisdom, insights, and practical ideas for helping your organization get in step with a transforming marketplace.

New Leaders Press
Sterling & Stone, Inc.
June, 1994

Acknowledgements

Several of the authors wish to thank those people who were particularly supportive of their efforts to generate essays for this book.

Susan M. Campbell gratefully acknowledges Jordan Paul for providing both emotional support and editorial feedback. She acknowledges her parents, Harry and Virginia Campbell, for offering a living model of Both/And Thinking in their marriage, family, and community relationship.

Elemer Magaziner acknowledges his sponsor, The Foundation of Global Wellness.

Ann M. Morrison thanks Marlene Zagon for her administrative help in preparing her chapter.

Ed Oakley would like to acknowledge his Enlightened Leadership Team, including Jonette Crowley, Jennifer Joshua, Robin Oakley, Charles Kemper, and Doug Krug for their ongoing support and the enlightened leadership they demonstrate.

Robert Rabbin wishes to express his respect, gratitude, and love to his first teacher Swami Muktananda Paramahansa and his subsequent teachers, Nisargadatta Maharaj, Ramana Maharshi, J. Krishnamurti, Jean Klein, and Poonjaji, all of whom continue to awaken, inspire, and guide him. He also expresses his appreciation to Monika Pichler, who coauthored his essay and who has been his best friend, counsel, and collaborator for ten years and through whose relationship the teachings of the mystics become ever more real.

Larry C. Spears wishes to acknowledge the following people and institutions for their encouragement and inspiration: The staff, trustees and members of the Robert K. Greenleaf Center for Servant-Leadership; the W.K. Kellogg Foundation and Lilly Endowment, Inc.; and his friends and family, especially Beth, James, and Matthew.

Martha Spice wishes to acknowledge her partner and husband, Alan Gilburg, for his support and co-authorship. Without him, her essay would not have been written. She also thanks her clients, friends, and teachers who have demonstrated the elegant principle of personal responsibility in their lives and their work.

New Leaders Press wishes to thank all the authors for contributing their ideas, experience, wisdom, and their hearts to this work. Each contributor has provided a perspective of the larger collective vision for how business can serve society in a sustainable and energizing way.

We would also like to thank all the authors of our previous books, *New Traditions in Business: Spirit & Leadership in the 21st Century, When the Canary Stops Singing: Women's Perspectives on Transforming Business* and, most recently, *The New Entrepreneurs: Business Visionaries for the 21st Century,* for what we've learned from working with each of them.

The following vendors have been particularly supportive over the past several years and we thank them with great appreciation: Barrentine & Associates; InfoCom; Jensen & Roye, CPAs; and the Sherbank Corporation.

For those vendors involved in the production of this collection, we offer our most sincere thanks. This team includes Amy Kahn, Carolynn Crandall and her team at Select Press, Jennifer Barclay, Gretchen Andrews, Connie Coleman for her cover photo, Dennis Rathnaw for his cover layout, and Lyle Mumford and his team at Publishers Press.

Editor John Renesch wishes to thank Barbara Shipka, one of the book's authors and a significant supporter of this project and other New Leaders Press projects that are underway. He is particularly grateful to his colleague Steven Piersanti, founder of Berrett-Koehler Publishers, for the unselfish sharing of his "selfness" as well as his years of experience in the publishing business.

Sincere gratitude is felt for a group of friends who have suppported him for the past five years in a very special and private way: Earl & Sheila Babbie; Donna Balsamo; Diane Behling; George Fritz; Ben Hidalgo; Jim Hodge and his partners at Sheppard, Mullin, Richter & Hampton; Tom Jackson; Alice Jensen; Kris Knight; Carol Lerner; Diane Levine; Barbara Musser; Donald Weck; Alan Parisse and Bettina Herbert; Jim and Muriel Ray; Jerry Richardson; Bob and Fran Ruebel; Mac Suzuki; and Peter Turla.

The publisher also wishes to thank Jenny Bent at the Raphael Sagalyn, Inc. literary agency who represent James Autry for her help in facilitating the permissions process as well as

Debbie McCarroll at Mr. Autry's office. Special thanks are also due to Max DePree's agents—the Sandra Dijkstra Literary Agency—for their cooperation.

For those who took the time to review early drafts of this collection and provide their feedback and comments, verbal and written, everyone involved with this book thanks you all. Our appreciation goes to Kye Anderson, Darrell Brown, Rick Crandall, Keith Darcy, Gun Denhart, William E. Halal, Willis Harman, Jim Kouzes, Jim Liebig, William Miller, J. Randolph New, Rolf Österberg, Alan J. Parisse, Michael Ray, and Andrew Bard Schmookler.

Finally, the advisory board of New Leaders Press/Sterling & Stone, Inc. has been invaluable as a resource and we wish to acknowledge each of them: Pat Barrentine, David Berenson, William Halal, Willis Harman, Paul Hwoschinsky, Jim Liebig, William Miller, Shirley Nelson, Christine Oster, Steven Piersanti, Catherine Pyke, James O'Toole, Michael Ray, Stephen Roulac, Jeremy Tarcher, Peggy Umanzio, and Dennis White.

John Renesch
is editor and publisher of *The New Leaders*, an international business newsletter on transformative leadership, and managing director of Sterling & Stone, Inc. He also serves as publisher for New Leaders Press, producers of collective works such as *New Traditions in Business*, which he also edited, *When the Canary Stops Singing, and The New Entrepreneurs*, which he co-edited with Stanford Business School's Michael Ray.

His career includes a wide variety of business experiences: real estate, financial services, event promotion, public relations, and publishing. He served as managing director for a real estate investment firm and was the founding CEO for a secondary market real estate securities brokerage firm in the mid 1980s.

Renesch was a founding trustee of the World Business Academy and received its Willis Harman Award in 1990. He is a member of the advisory board for the World Future Society's World 2000 project and speaks publicly on transformative leadership in business.

Introduction

A Commitment to a Change in Context

John Renesch

In these days of constant and profound change, a new brand of leadership is called for. New approaches are being demanded, requiring people in existing leadership roles to significantly adjust styles and attitudes or become part of an extinct breed. People previously seen as followers will need to develop new self-images and new skills in order to accept more leadership responsibility than they have in the past.

These new leaders will be men and women who inspire rather than control—who are challenged by changes, not threatened by them. This new leadership must emerge from all levels of our organizations if they are going to survive the challenges and the transition into the next century.

Leadership has been redefined several times in modern history. Many of these redefinitions have taken place only at a superficial level, however. A Western tendency has been to adapt—to take on the form, the semblance of change—without embracing the underlying principles. We have a habit of taking on the appearance of doing it right without committing ourselves to the substance. This new brand of leadership will require a deep level of commitment—a new context—a change in the very essence of what it means to be a leader.

This contextual shift requires greater numbers of people to accept responsibility whenever it is called for—to be leaders whenever it is appropriate. This new context is based on individual freedom, trust, and intention. It will require great courage, wisdom, and compassion on the part of those who are up for it.

This new leadership does not rely on titles or positions of power to make a leader. It does not require external authority to legitimize a man or a woman as a "designated" leader. It relies on one's inner strength and character—the source of one's true power. This new leadership requires individuals to have genuine dominion over their reality, not the forceful domination or manipulation of people or circumstances.

What's an example of a change in context versus a change in content or form? Take the coaching styles of Vince Lombardi, a legendary coach from the 1950s and 1960s, as compared to Bill Walsh in the 1980s, as an example. Lombardi had a way of getting his players motivated to play excellent football that was, by most opinions, the best of the era. He was very good within the conventional wisdom of the day. The style that he epitomized, however, was rooted in insecurity and fear. Players performed largely because they were afraid to fail. Walsh's style, on the other hand, was rooted in a whole different context—inspiring and encouraging players to play their best—a more positive style in view of the current culture, a generation later.

These two great coaches were operating in different contexts. The form or content of their professions was pretty much the same—gameplans, practice, workouts, strategies, and playbooks—very useful stuff if you want to win football games. But the two contexts are miles apart in how basic motivation and performance are achieved.

Another relevant example of a contextual difference is thinking of management as a "science," as popularized by Frederick Taylor earlier this century, or as an "art," as described by Max DePree, while CEO of Herman Miller, Inc. One context is based in control, linear thinking, and mechanistic process while the other is more innovative, intuitive, and spontaneous.

More and more of the current wisdom suggests that companies cannot change long-established cultures unless their leaders also change. The modern business books are full of attempts to transform organizations without any material change by the chief executive or other senior people. These case histories nearly always end in disappointment. The leaders of tomorrow must be willing to be personally transformed—that is, to have a transcendent change in how they think and feel, not just have a change of attitude about some part of the operation.

All too often, the term transformation is used synonymously with change. By transformation, I mean a core shift in how a person exists in the world. Leaders of tomorrow must be willing to undergo deep personal, psychological, emotional and even spiritual change if they expect their followers to be open to change. Leaders can no longer ask everyone to change except themselves.

Business practitioners, consultants and professionals are sitting on enormous responsibility, whether they like it or not. Business is the locomotive pulling the train of society worldwide. Everyone in business—the small enterprise owner, the manager, the Fortune 500 employee—is responsible for the impact business has on society. Each person in the business community has a responsibility to be a new leader.

The other side of this responsibility is an opportunity. Every chance to take responsibility is accompanied with an opportunity to be a pioneer in "new business"—a chance to thrive, to innovate and succeed, in ways only dreamed of previously. The brutal truth is that those who don't take responsibility will miss the opportunities that lie ahead and, possibly, will fail to make the transition to a new way of being in business.

It is important, in these days of constant and unprecedented change, that people in positions of power are not threatened by the need for transformation. This kind of challenge will require great courage—to accept change without feeling threatened.

The new leaders will be people of vision, who inspire others to become part of that vision. They won't convince or manipulate to recruit other people to join them; they will attract them, like a magnet. These new leaders will not monitor trends or join in fads. They will create trends, building new futures in collaboration with other like-minded men and women.

New qualities are needed for these new leaders—qualities that have not been traditional characteristics for the scientific model of the past. One of the essential qualities of new leadership is the willingness to see oneself as part of the existing problem, as one element in the system that needs to change. When an organization undergoes major change, everyone and everything affected will need to change as well. Some will require big change—perhaps as much as complete severance from the whole. Others may only need to change slightly—but every part of the system will change in some way.

These new leaders will need courage—not the Audie Murphy variety of fearlessly advancing into the enemy's gunsights but a compassionate, spiritual courage—to question the unquestionable, to reexamine the sacred cows, to challenge the status quo. It includes a willingness to risk peer disapproval or ridicule. A new brand of commitment is also needed in these new leaders—not commitment to work long hours or to sacrifice one's family life, but a commitment to act as one believes he or she should. "Doing the right thing" because it's right, not because "that's the way we do things around here" will become the rallying cry of the new leaders.

Compassion for one's fellow workers will replace blame in corporate affairs. Systems thinking will be the technology for rationale of the new leaders, wherein organizations are seen as interdependent parts of larger social systems and people are interrelated within all these systems. A compassionate understanding for how all the parts relate allows the new leader to drop the "blame game," eliminating the need to attack, defend, or engage in destructive politics at work.

Each of us can become our own leaders by living congruently—matching what we think and feel with how we carry out everyday duties. We can't change other people. All we can do is change ourselves. This is a time for "authentic leadership" from everyone, especially in business.

This collection of essays has been produced to address the issues facing business leaders of the future—the "new leaders." Matters of the heart and soul are being included in business essays that have traditionally excluded such "soft" topics. The authors who have contributed to this collection are all breaking new ground—discussing what has been previously "undiscussible" in business books.

Starting with *Love & Profit* author James A. Autry, Part One contains seven essays. Additional chapters are written by author and corporate consultant Carol Sanford, *Breaking the Glass Ceiling* lead author Ann M. Morrison, *Enlightened Leadership* co-author Ed Oakley, attorney Barbara R. Hauser, co-founder of The Women's Leadership Forum, consultant Peter K. Krembs, and Charles F. Kiefer, a contributor to the *The Fifth Discipline Fieldbook*.

The new leader's new responsibility is a common theme for Part Two, featuring USC's Leadership Institute chair and popular author Warren Bennis (*On Becoming a Leader* and *Leaders*), leadership and creativity consultant Kate Steichen, organization consultant Barbara Shipka, and Nestlé executive Tina Rasmussen.

Four authors examine the emerging "age of paradox" in Part Three which contains the writings of Robert K. Greenleaf Center executive director Larry C. Spears, consultant Elemer Magaziner, author/consultant Susan M. Campbell, and clarity coach Robert Rabbin.

Part Four focuses on new thinking—starting with Margaret J. Wheatley, author of the successful book *Leadership and the New Science*. Original essays by John D. Adams, editor of *Transforming Leadership*, executive coach Martha Spice, and leadership trainer Carol McCall are also included in this segment of the book.

The final segment of this book, Part Five, consists of three essays—best-selling author and corporate chairman Max DePree, publishing executive Perry Pascarella, and Stewart Emery's essay, including his interview with TV genius Norman Lear.

As you read each of these essays, I urge you to be as open-minded as you can and be reminded that the new leaders are those who feel drawn to accept responsibility at any particular time, not necessarily those who are elected, appointed or self-anointed to leadership positions. Each of us has a leader inside of us. Is your "leader within" ready to accept responsibility?

PART ONE

Difficult Issues: Challenging Times

Indeed these are difficult times. Even chaos has earned the right to have its own "science" or discipline of inquiry—chaos theory. Unprecedented in human history, the present levels of change are going far beyond our ability to predict. Most organizations are holding tight and praying for the "good old days" to return. They never will.

A new era has been dawning for several years now and new breeds of leaders are being called for. This first part of the book offers the keen perceptions of seven of our authors, dealing with specific issues which are at the heart of much of this chaos. Management styles, diversity issues, teams, technology, gender distinctions, ethics, and motivation are all addressed in the opening portion of this collection.

Publishing executive James A. Autry (author of *Love & Profit: The Art of Caring Leadership*) opens with his reflections as a corporate manager with nearly three decades of experience. Consultant Carol Sanford, a co-author of *New Traditions in Business: Spirit & Leadership in the 21st Century*, examines the ethics and practicality of traditional motivation practices in the emerging new era.

Women's Leadership Forum co-founder, Barbara R. Hauser, challenges the stereotypical behavior of males and females in a compelling essay written for both genders. Ann M. Morrison, lead author of *Breaking the Glass Ceiling* and, more recently, author of *The New Leaders* book, writes about diversity and leadership. Consultant Ed Oakley, author of *Enlightened Leadership*, addresses this very topic in his original essay.

Engineers and scientists will enjoy reading about leadership in the technical field, a challenge accepted by consultant Peter K. Krembs in his essay. Consultant Charles F. Kiefer addresses an important aspect of organizational leadership—the executive team.

Each of the issues addressed by these seven authors is strategically vital to the present day enterprise and its prospects for succeeding in the years ahead.

James A. Autry
is a former Fortune 500 executive,
an author, poet, and consultant
whose work has had a significant
influence on leadership thinking. His book, *Love and Profit: The Art of Caring Leadership,* won the prestigious Johnson, Smith & Knisely Award as the book which had the most impact on executive thinking in 1992. He received considerable national attention when he was one of the poets featured on Bill Moyers' special series, "The Power of the Word," on PBS. He is also featured in a video, "Love and Profit," produced by The Excellence in Training Corporation in 1993.

Before taking early retirement in 1991 to pursue his present career, Autry had a distinguished career at Meredith Corporation where he was senior vice president and president of its Magazine Group, a $500 million operation with over nine hundred employees.

Autry has been instrumental in shaping the field of service journalism and has worked to establish service journalism chairs at the University of Missouri and the University of Mississippi, where he was named a Distinguished Alumnus and was elected to the Alumni Hall of Fame. He holds three honorary degrees and has just published a new book, *Life and Work: A Manager's Search for Meaning.* This essay is excerpted from *Love and Profit* and is used by permission of the publisher.

Random Observations After Twenty-Eight Years of Managing

James A. Autry

There's an old saw about management that gets a lot of us off on the wrong foot. It says that if all the employees did their jobs well, there would be no need for managers.

I've heard it, and you've heard it. For many years, I accepted it without stopping to think about what it was saying and how it was forcing me to behave.

If my job as manager depends on at least some employees not doing their jobs well enough, then you can be damned sure I'll find employees who aren't doing their jobs well enough. And you can be sure I won't be putting my efforts into creating an environment in which people can do a good job better. Which, of course, is the real job of management.

A work group, whether you call it an accounting department, an editorial staff, or a sales group, or an orchestra, cannot operate as a collection of people who simply do their jobs well. To believe that is to disbelieve the power of the group to become more than the sum of its separate parts.

And to believe that the manager's job is only to assure that people do their jobs well is to return the manager to the old role of overseer or supervisor.

Staying Balanced

I know managers who cannot stay away from the office; it is as if they become insecure if they are not working. I'm not talking about those times we all have when things pile up and we have to take a Sunday and wade through the stack. I know people who come to the office when there are only the most routine things to deal with.

I also know managers who come in, read *The Wall Street Journal* and *The New York Times*, make some phone calls, dictate a few letters, have lunch with a crony, spend another couple of hours at the desk, leave in time for the 5:11 train, and think they've done a full day's work.

Neither work style says anything about commitment; the workaholic is no more committed than the lazy worker. Commitment has more to do with the quality of effort than with the number of hours in the office.

The balanced life lies somewhere in the middle, as it always does. The middle changes from time to time, depending on the work load, or perhaps the newness of the job.

Finding the middle is the tough part, but you have to keep at it. Otherwise you'll find yourself one day without resources.

Even workaholics retire. Sooner or later, they will lose the job that so preoccupies them. Then what?

At the other end of the spectrum are those who may lose the job because they are so preoccupied with everything but the job. Then what?

My advice for finding the middle is very simple. Consider everything of equal importance: job, family, friends, church, clubs, volunteer work, exercise, sports, hobbies, and killing time.

Walk the balance board and make time for it all. Otherwise you'll face that inevitable moment of truth when you'll wonder where the hell all the time went.

Chief Cheerleader

About twenty years ago, I became manager of a department of people who were overworked, underpaid, and generally demoralized. Nonetheless, they worked hard and produced good work despite their problems. But it was only a matter of time before we would face heavy turnover and a debilitating disruption of work.

It was one of the happiest experiences of my career. I had but to take off the harnesses and let them run. We brought their salaries up to date. Then I made time each day to reassure every person that mistakes were okay and I was not waiting to beat on them.

One day, one of the senior people asked, "You know what some of the people are calling you around here?"

"No," I said. "Should I want to know?"

"It's not bad. They're saying you are the chief cheerleader." Not bad indeed, I thought. In fact, I later told my boss that I thought of that label as part of my job description.

After not many more years in management, I began to think of "chief cheerleader" as part of every good manager's job description.

Drawing the Line on Mistakes

It is important to make mistakes, and it is important to let your employees make mistakes. It is so important, in fact, that most of the popular management books of the past few years have made a big subject of it.

What few seem to address, however, is when to stop a mistake before it gets made.

It is a given that a good manager frequently sees an employee headed for a mistake well before the critical point comes. So when should the manager act to avoid the mistake?

I think of this problem like a flight instructor. It is also important to let student pilots make mistakes. Obviously, though, the instructor cannot permit the student to crash and burn, so he waits until that critical point at which the student realizes the mistake but when the airplane can still be controlled. *And he never permits the mistake that can be made only once.*

Not a bad guide for managers. As long as people can learn from mistakes, encourage risk taking. But do not allow any mistake that threatens the operation's survival.

Sharing Ownership

How many times have you read about this in the past few years? Plenty. Some CEO is always saying, "We get everyone to buy into the vision; we try to instill our employees with a sense of ownership."

Sense of ownership, hell! How about some real ownership? I think the subject of ownership deserves more examination by management as well as by the employees. There are plenty of examples that employee-owned businesses can create real advantages for themselves. How, then, can some kind of employee ownership be accommodated within the context of a publicly owned corporation or a large private corporation? But ownership, as we know, is not just a matter of dividing up the rewards. How, also, can the problems and responsibilities of ownership be shared and felt?

Share it all, I say. Adjust the compensation systems so that employees get a piece of the business. Institute performance-based bonuses. Include stock awards throughout a career. Let employees feel the pride of knowing they are providing for the welfare of themselves and their families.

But let them also feel the frustration of rising medical and other benefit costs, escalating taxes, shortages of resources and materials, price pressures, share struggles, and increasing global competition. I think the full experience of shared ownership— the pain as well as the joy of it—can hold more potential for the reinvigoration of a business than any other single factor.

Decisions, Decisions

If ever a manager can say, with absolute certainty, I made that decision, then something is wrong with the operation.

The day of the single decision-maker is gone, if ever it existed. Even the entrepreneurs who so pride themselves on being one-man bands realize at some point that their businesses will be limited by their unwillingness to let other imaginations and judgment get into the act.

One More Thought About Firing

No one ever believes he or she is justly fired. There must be some sort of immune system that protects us from facing the reality of our own failures.

So what can a manager do but try to determine what he or she wants that fired employee to come away with? What understandings? What lessons? And what hopes?

I want people I've fired to know why and to decide for

themselves what might have been done. I want them to learn what to do next time. And I want them to realize that they still have a future, and they will grow enormously in embracing that future.

But I don't expect to convince anyone of that. And when a person I've fired does learn and grow and make a better life, I don't expect to be thanked.

Nonetheless, I have the satisfaction of knowing that only one or two people did not go on to better things after I fired them. The rest of them have done well.

The nagging question, of course, is, if they've done well somewhere else, why didn't they do well for me?

It's a question that can keep me awake nights.

The Bell Curve is for Dumbbells

Dumbbell managers, that is. And there are still plenty of them who believe that, in a perfect world, worker performance will be distributed on a bell curve throughout the work force.

What nonsense. On the one hand, we speak the glowing phrases. We talk about motivating people to rise above themselves, about creating environments for quality work, about building a passion for excellence. Then, when we want to set up appraisal and compensation systems, we cannot accept that perhaps—*just perhaps*—we've been so successful as managers that there is no bell curve, that the distribution of performance and abilities is distorted toward excellence.

The bell curve is management for statisticians, not performers.

Managing as Parenting

A touchy subject, this, but one that all managers come to understand at some point in their careers. Part of the touchiness comes from the old paradigm of the boss-as-father with his paternalistic indulgence on one side and harsh judgment and disapproval on the other. This has become the symbol of bad management, and for good reason.

But there is another way to look at manager as parent. Patricia Pollock, managing editor of a custom publishing department at the Meredith Corporation, wrote, as part of a guest editorial for the company's management newsletter, "I've also learned a lot from raising children. I spent a lot of time with the kids trying to solve all their problems for them, and along the way I realized that this was not what I was supposed to do. I learned to create an atmosphere so they could learn how to cope with a problem and solve it themselves.

"In the same way, as a manager, I don't believe in being the provider of answers—people need to learn on their own. This turns out to be trusting people."

What a perfect expression of the manager as parent. And it is appropriate that a woman manager wrote it. Few men managers would be that open, that guileless, and that willing to be credited (or blamed) with such a thought in print.

Yet I hear many managers express these parallel concerns about kids and employees: how to pay attention and lead and teach without doing too much for them; how to encourage individual risk-taking while making sure they don't go too far; how to reward and recognize the accomplishments of one while still caring about another who does not do as well.

As a "parent" in the workplace, the manager must give daily expressions of pride and satisfaction in both the professional and the personal accomplishments of employees.

And those expressions must be sincere. You can't fake it. Part of a loving and caring environment happens because of the manager's commitment to grow from a genuine interest in, and concern for, the growth of his or her employees.

Exactly the same is true of parents.

The Myth of Being Overqualified

I've never turned down any job applicant because I felt he or she was overqualified, and I wonder about managers who do.

The "overqualified" label means one of three things:

1. The manager is afraid that the applicant has been around so long that he or she has a lot of bad habits, but the manager won't make the effort to find out.
2. The manager is intimidated by the applicant's qualifications and feels threatened or not qualified to manage him or her.
3. The manager is playing God and deciding whether the applicant will be happy in the job or not.

I don't believe that any good manager, with five minutes' reflection, could make a case against hiring the most qualified person possible in every job, whatever its level.

The only issue should lie with the applicant: Does the person understand fully the limitations as well as the responsibilities of the job? If so, I say let 'em at it.

Communion of the Saints

In the old-time religion of my youth, we believed that, through the ritual of what we called "the Lord's Supper," we communed with the saints, with all those who had gone before.

I was struck with this old image at a retirement dinner as the retiree invoked the names of company people long dead and spoke of them as if they were just on some kind of sabbatical. He talked of what they had taught the people who had taught him, and how he had tried to teach others who were now teaching the beginners.

As he spoke, we realized that a true community has no limit in time. He made us feel the extension of our community of work, into a time long before us and into a time yet to come. As if the work exists in and of itself, and we come and go from it in a kind of continuum of endeavor, in a kind of communion.

Good News/Bad News

There was a time when I had great doubts about my abilities and about my career. It was a time of personal trauma and a huge job change.

A close friend sent me a letter with a single sentence.

I now share it with every employee or colleague who's suffering from a lapse of self-confidence. One of these days, I plan to get a calligrapher to do it up right, then I'll frame it and hang in on the wall of whoever needs it at the time:

THE ORIGINAL GOOD NEWS/BAD NEWS:
YOU ARE AS GOOD AS YOU WERE AFRAID YOU ARE.

Judging What's Important

I'm always getting surprised by the gap between my perception of the importance of an act and the perception of the other person involved.

A few weeks ago, I had dinner with a colleague, a person who reports to me. The dinner was squeezed into a busy travel schedule, but there had been a recent death in his family, and I felt somehow moved to make the time.

The dinner was pleasant though unremarkable, yet in a few days I received a letter of profuse gratitude for my having taken the time. I was stunned and a bit ashamed for not having imbued the evening with nearly the importance my colleague gave it.

On another occasion, I turned on my computer to find an updated word-processing program installed. I was irritated because, having only a few years ago given up my old manual typewriter, I was just getting used to the old program. I was peevish about the change, and asked that the old program be reinstalled.

Only later, after the damage was done, did I realize that the programmer who installed the new software surely was very hurt. She had worked hard to get the new program in while I was on a trip, thinking I would be delighted by it. Far from being thanked for the effort, she had to do double work.

I could have kicked myself.

We managers just have to realize that what is important to employees is what they think is important, and we have to measure our impact on those matters. Too often we forget that our words and actions carry weight out of all proportion with the import we may have intended.

Volunteer and Learn

If, as a manager, you think it is difficult to get results through people over whom you have some authority, imagine how it is to get results through people *without any authority over them whatsoever.*

That's the description of volunteer work.

There is no better place to learn the subtle points of management than as an officer of a volunteer organization, be it a volunteer health agency or the board of an educational institution or the Boy Scouts or the PTA.

I have heard people describe these jobs as "thankless" and without reward.

Not true. Most of them are involved with doing good and doing good work, reward enough in itself. The people I know who volunteer regularly are richly rewarded.

Beyond the spiritual reward is a management learning experience beyond anything they could dream up in business school.

As a member of, and then president of, the board of directors of a national voluntary health agency, I was involved in a near-bankruptcy situation, a complete reorganization, the hiring of new staff, restructuring the board, redoing the fund-raising apparatus, introducing a new planning process, lobbying for congressional action, leading national conferences, and participating in the successful merger of two national organizations.

All that was accomplished without benefit of *authority*. All of us on the board were driven only by our concern for the cause to seek consensus and workable solutions for every nasty problem.

I learned about influence and quiet persuasion, about good committee work, about getting the best possible work from people who were sincere and well-intended but not very qualified for the tasks for which they had volunteered. (You can't "fire" an incompetent volunteer.)

This experience has served me countless times in my business life.

I encourage all my managers to find a cause, to volunteer, to learn, and to grow.

The Internal Job Description

People do well what they want to do, and they do not do well what they do not want to do.

It's as true of managers as of anyone.

So do a check once in a while to make sure your job description on paper matches the one in your heart.

If not, it's time to change the one on paper.

The Willingness to Care

There's a problem with creating what I call the loving and caring workplace. It is that no one person can love and care for all the employees all the time. The daily act of caring is very hard work.

So you have to choose other managers who have the

willingness to care. You have to focus on nurturing your good, close managers, then teach them to pass it along.

Spread the caring, spread the work.

Empty Threats

Remember this: People who consistently threaten to leave do not want to leave. They want you to ask them to stay. They need to hear that you care about them and that they are valuable in your eyes. One of the young managers in my group came to me about a good creative person who, every six months or so, threatened to leave. "What are the issues?" I asked. "Pay?"

"No," the manager said, "that's what makes it so damned frustrating. He doesn't demand anything; he just says this place is getting to him and he's going to quit."

"So what have you told him?"

"I've been telling him that this is a good place to work and that he won't do better anywhere else, but if he has decided to leave, that's his decision."

"And he stays."

"Yes, but next time, I'm going to tell him I'm tired of being threatened and he should just leave."

Well, yes. That is the temptation, I admit, because I've felt the same way.

But I said, "Lighten up and try this. Just look him in the eye and say, 'Look, I really want you to stay. Your work is very good, and you are a valuable part of this department. I've been worried that you're going to leave, so I'm asking you to tell me you're going to stay so I can stop worrying.'"

"But that's like begging!" the manager said, red in the face.

"So," I said, "is it so bad if it solves the problem?"

Not only did my advice work, but it changed their relationship and changed the atmosphere in the department.

Old-Fashioned Employee

I once heard a speaker make the point that ninety percent of the men of my generation profess to want an "old-fashioned wife."

He asked for a show of hands. "How many of you men would say 'Aren't I lucky' if you had a wife who says she wants to satisfy

"The marketplace is driven by greed," he said. "Take it or leave it, that's the way business is."

Unfortunately, I bought into that statement for a long time before I realized that, like many simple statements, it requires a lot of definition.

By greed, did my mentor mean self-interest or selfishness?

If, indeed, the marketplace is driven by the greed of selfishness, then the marketplace by its nature is hard on the human spirit. It is all the things its critics say it is.

If, on the other hand, the marketplace is driven by an enlightened self-interest in which our self-interest is served as we serve others, then it can help ennoble the human spirit.

If the marketplace is hard on the human spirit, how has it survived in the world of humans?

Or could it be that those who believe in the greed of the marketplace have just found a convenient excuse for their own greed or for their own unwillingness to concern themselves with the human spirit? Maybe they hide their self-serving ambitions, their willingness to do harm, their disregard for humanity in the workplace, and their harsh management techniques behind the more abstract concept of the "marketplace."

I do not doubt the presence of greed in the marketplace, because I do not doubt the presence of greed in people.

But I also do not doubt the ennobling aspects of work, of the workplace, of the community of endeavor, of the marketplace.

So I choose to believe that most of the marketplace is driven by people who want to do good work for others and for themselves.

The Manager's Little Piece of Immortality

A while back, I received an invitation to a reunion of the 48th Tactical Fighter Wing that was based in Chaumont, France, from the early 1950s until 1959. The invitation was specific: It was not for all former 48th people, just those who had served in Chaumont.

I left the air force in 1959, and much has happened in my life since then. Why, I wondered, would I be so tempted to join this group of people, most of whom I no longer knew? What would we have in common? What could we talk about?

Days in Chaumont, of course. Flying. Partying. Cutting the

tie off the new wing commander his first night in the club. Mock dogfights with the French out of Saint-Dizier. Bombing on the range in Libya. Flying low over the rivers and canals and vineyards of Burgundy. Crashes. Death.

Nothing special as military experiences go, except to the extent that the intensity of the experience itself made it special. And except to the extent that being isolated in Chaumont, where the living was fairly primitive, made it special. And except to the extent that our bonds as members of a community made it special.

Every year, former military people gather for reunions of their old units, many of them from World War II, meeting once again after forty-five or fifty years to relive times made special by the intensity of the experience.

If nothing else, it is proof that the most lasting friendships, the most enduring memories, are those born of intense relationships in a community of mutual endeavor, temporary though it may be.

A few months before receiving the invitation to the 48th reunion, I attended a retirement dinner for a colleague who had been with our company for thirty-five years or so and with whom I had worked for twenty of those years.

In but a few minutes, she recalled the years, telling anecdote after anecdote, the silly stuff, the complaints, the jokes, the hard work. She reminisced about people now retired or dead and told how they had shaped her life and career. Each department she had worked in became its own experience within those thirty-five years. It was clear that she did not think of the years as a whole, or remember them as one continuing jumble of professional experience.

It was as if her career were divided into eras.

Not long after that dinner, I attended a sales conference at which a retiring senior manager was honored.

He spoke eloquently, and his themes were the same. He told us the stories that have become part of our corporate mythology, even as he was recognizing, and taking, his place in that mythology.

His final remarks were for the young people, the sellers now out there doing the everyday hard stuff. He told them he knew the world is different now, but he asked them not to think of it as all that different, because, he said, the important things endure: honesty, integrity, hard work, service, courage.

Then he asked those young people to look to all the good salespeople who had gone before, those he had cited as influencing his life. "You'll never know them," he said, "and I'm sorry you won't, but I've tried to teach you what they taught me."

I thought, of course they *do* know these people whom they never met. They know them through you.

Within another few weeks, there came a third retirement party, this time for a personnel director, a man I never thought of as being particularly good with words and until then would never have described as eloquent.

Among his comments were these: "I have worked the last twenty-two years for a company that cares about people and expresses that concern by action. I have been a part of that, so I know what *success* is....

"I have not fulfilled all my objectives, my hopes, my dreams, so I know what *adjustment* is....

"And because I have known all these things, I truly know *contentment*."

It would be easy to write off these reminiscences as simple sentimentality. After all, it's pretty easy to be abiding and loving about most any experience when you're leaving it forever. Even prisoners have expressed nostalgia for the penitentiary.

It would be easy also to say that business has changed: Almost no one these days expects to stay with a company for decades and then retire.

But to ignore what these retirees said is to ignore a major lesson for management. The lesson has to do with recognizing that our careers, like our lives, somehow divide themselves into eras, into distinct periods involving distinct kinds of experiences. People come and go and are identified with these periods. And the success of the enterprise frequently rides on the ability of the people to create a community of effort within each era.

At the center of it is the manager. One way or another, the manager will become part of the mythology. He or she has the opportunity to create an environment in which the experience of mutual enterprise is so intense that the people who participated in that time and that place want to recall it forever. Whether those people stuck around the company until retirement or moved on to another company is irrelevant to the intensity and the memorability of the experience.

Think of the eras of your own life. They could include school years and the first job and, as in my life, an intense military experience. Never mind that all the people who served at Chaumont in the fifties went on to other lives, other experiences, some of which were just as intense and binding. The point is that those years are set in our memories for all time, transcending whatever happened before or after. Nothing can change it, and nothing can take it away.

Those same kinds of experiences and feelings happen in business day after day and year after year, more than any outside observer would ever guess. And when they happen, the manager's place in the shared history is passed along for generations, as each person who lived through those eras retires and makes the speech we all hope to get to make someday.

What more could a leader/manager/mentor/coach/friend ask for in this world? It's as close to immortality as a businessperson ever gets.

Carol Sanford
works in North America, Western
and Eastern Europe, Africa, and
Asia with global corporations who
seek to access untapped potential in their people, product offerings,
technologies, and raw material transformations. For over 15 years, she has
worked as a resource for business, organizational, and human development, helping business teams design developmental work systems and
businesses, develop strategic leadership capability, and integrate the
business with all its stakeholder constituencies.

She is co-creater in research, development, and learning processes
at the Center for Developmental Systems and SpringHill Publications. Her
work, which has been translated into ten languages, emphasizes continuous development of the intellectual capacity and thinking capability of
individuals and teams, and of their ability to realize a meaningful
contribution. Its theory base is drawn from interdisciplinary research in
science, philosophy, systems theory, and psychology.

2

Leadership of Motivation: The Ethics and Practicality of Incentives

Carol Sanford

Probably one of the most erroneous notions sold to American business leadership today is the idea that incentives are the best medicine for improving low productivity and bottom line return. Incentives are those experiences we have that generate in us the fear of punishment or the expectation of reward, thereby inciting us to action or effort. For the last forty years, increasing refinements and enhancements have been made to incentive programs with the belief that incentives are the foundation of motivation. In fact, this belief is so prevalent that incentives have become the cornerstone of a culture themselves, an "incentive culture," so to speak.

The American Dream: A Systematic Erosion

Many businesses today are seeking to move toward becoming self-reliant organizations where individuals and teams can be counted upon to use their own judgment. What is "right" for the whole of the business is to be the guide for behavior of employees. "Full Business Partners" implies a workforce that is continuously learning, developing, and taking on bigger and riskier challenges in service of the business. Companies which have workforces that routinely behave this way are unbeatable from a competitive standpoint. Business leadership wants the workforce, in short, to have the same level of commitment and value for the business, its resources, and its future among workers, as though the workers owned the business themselves.

As a society, we want our young people to grow up to be contributing and forthright citizens who represent the stalwart, honest, and determined nature that is idealized, and maybe romanticized, as a legacy from our founding fathers. We want leaders of our communities and nation who care more about the welfare of the whole than their own self-interest or that of a special interest group. We want a society in which uniqueness can be discovered and expressed and every person, from birth to death, is continually learning, developing, and contributing this personal evolution toward enabling a better society.

Incentive-based cultures are the antithesis of such dreams, not just from poor implementation or design of such programs, but in the scientific, economic, and psychological premises from which they are drawn. Alfie Kohn in *Harvard Business Review* points out that we have spent so much of our energy on refining and tinkering with incentive plans that we have forgotten to assess whether incentives are the right approach at all.

Incentive Culture: A Flawed Theory Base

An incentive culture is one that has embedded incentives so deeply in its way of working that people can no longer see any other way of viewing the world and every program and plan has the premises behind creating incentives built into its design. *Examples:* programs that rate and rank employees against one another, or managers who buy pizzas, hats, or jackets for the workforce for a job well done. It is those who post their "employee of the month" for safety, service, sales, or "whatever" on the bulletin board. It is paying for the pieces of work produced or the achievement of production goals or sharing the "gain" with the employees. And even seeking motivational speakers to inspire people with "a better way." By now you are probably feeling like a challenge is being made to the American way, and apple pie. Looking behind these programs provides a better understanding regarding why incentives are giving us something akin to our worst nightmare, instead of the American Dream.

For an incentive culture to be effective, it needs people to be highly susceptible to the wishes of others, to focus on specific prescribed behaviors to the exclusion of other behaviors, without necessarily producing any understanding of the implications of such choices to the whole of which they are a part or any secondary negative impacts. These people need to be concerned with direct personal benefit for one's efforts, and to compete with one's own colleagues and peers to an end where some and maybe most others become losers. The culture requires that others determine the merits of our work compared to those of our co-workers. This culture is based on the assumption that higher organizational levels know the "right" answers in the same way parents and teachers do.

The development period of the incentive approach to motivation covers about three hundred years of evolution and can be found in the tenets of scientific, economic, and psychological thought, much of which has been rejected by modern thinkers as incomplete or misapplied. During its evolution, the incentive culture has been woven from the premises of Adam Smith, the Father of Economics; Charles Darwin, whose many followers created what has come to be called Social Darwinism; John Watson, the founder of Behavioral Psychology and his student B. F. Skinner; and Sir Francis Bacon, the English philosopher and scientist. The core incentive premises might be stated as:

- The essential nature of human beings is one of self-interest versus sacrifice for the common good (Adam Smith's main economic postulate).

- Humans are driven by stimulus-response mechanisms without the presence of consciousness or free will with which to override the mechanical choices.

- Humans are the product of competitive forces with a natural tendency to try to win based on the laws of survival of the fittest, incapable of operating from purpose (Darwin principles adapted to social settings).

- Humans will seek to imitate that which is offered and rewarded as a role model (behavioral psychology).

- It is possible and desirable to predict and control nature and therefore men as beings of nature.

Human Nature: Altruistic or Self-Interest? YES!

There has been a long-standing debate about whether humans are, at their core, purely interested only in themselves or whether they are altruistic. The intensity of this debate seems to be based on the often held assumption that things must be one way or the other with, maybe, on some occasions, a compromise. As a result of this dualistic way of resolving philosophical questions we frequently settle for partial answers, which is the case with motivation. Motivation, when viewed non-dualistically and less simplistically, provides a richer source of leadership ideas .

Several Eastern and Western traditions see motivation as a triadic phenomenon that can be understood as a developmental process. The three natures move from a lower to higher order, each encompassing the lower. *Order* here is not meant in a pejorative sense, relating to relative value; it is meant to describe the ability to organize thinking about increasingly complex situations and matters. Modern psychology includes non-dualistic systems developed by human behavior scientists, the most well known being Abraham Maslow. Maslow's theories are frequently used, or at least referred to, in the same organizations embedded in the incentive culture, without ever noticing the potential for inconsistency. The theoretical constructs of both Maslow's work and older philosophical traditions add dimensionality to people and see them as having several levels of needs, motivations, or elements of drive. It is helpful to take these into consideration when observing behavior and, as a leader, when seeking to understand the potential and the complexity present in the make-up of human beings.

Behavior and Motivation: A Triadic View

If we reflect on our own and other's behavior we can detect that we engage in a three-fold set of behaviors and have experienced each of the three over a period of time, even in the same situation. At the first level, we find ourselves being *reactive* to a stimulus that comes toward us. A response is produced that seems to come without thought or reason. This is the same level of behavior that the Behaviorists presented as cause-effect or stimulus-response, and as the sole source of learning and motivation. A triad view holds this as one element of our psychological make-up, but with a lower *ordering* quality. Our reactive nature is conditioned by our environment and by others interacting with us. It is not, however, our only mode of behavior.

Triad of Behaviors

On another level, we experience ourselves as able to respond to nuances surrounding us, to override a reaction by choosing to be sensitive to particular needs in a situation, including personal needs. This behavior comes from a higher *ego* strength or self-esteem—an ego-managed behavior. In these situations, our ego takes control of our reactive or impulsive self and works to produce a desire end. It is this behavioral attribute that allows us to be an acceptable member of society. We use our ego self to manage the reactions that are in our lower nature.

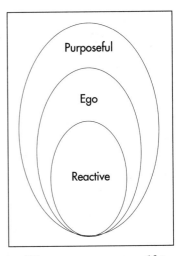

Beyond the ego resides another level of behavior which again must be guided by us if it is to be active in a situation. This behavior is referenced in ancient and modern literature as *purposeful* behavior—or the teleology of human nature. We will-fully bring this behavior to bear on a situation when we make ourselves conscious of a higher purpose that has meaning and significance to a greater whole of people or entity of which we are a part. Purposeful behavior can take control of and manage the reactive and ego behaviors. This behavior requires development and is not well understood or developed in our industries or as a society.

When we are able to enable our purposeful behavior, we can manage the role our ego plays in any situation. We will find that situations that might be threatening in a reactive mode do not capture our energy and attention or divert us from a path we see as critical to the achievement of a purpose. Thus, our behavior comes under our own management.

Incentives are working with the lowest nature of human behavior and invite workforce members into a cycle of environmental stimulus, with the hope of a predictable response. Just as with animals in research studies, the reactive behavior of humans becomes focused on the reward or as also happens when the animals cannot determine how to achieve the reward, they stop trying and "die" (in spirit in the case of the factory worker).

A 1993 survey of employees by *Inc.* magazine found that the highest response to the question "What was the single most important long-term motivator?" was "a sense of mission and purpose," with "bonuses" second from last just above "profit sharing." Second was "feedback and communication." Number one and two are highly correlated to a purposeful mode of behavior and our ability to realize it at our place of work. Even in organizations that develop purpose and mission statements, the incentives tend to absorb the greatest attention. Incentives are frequently used to show how the mission statement of the organization is merely platitudinous.

Values Behind our Behavior: The Triad Deepens

Each of these behaviors is nurtured by and nurtures in return a particular set of values that enliven and inform motivation. To understand the value base provides enlightenment regarding the triadic processes of behavior.

Triad of Values

The first level of value to which we may be drawn in a situation, at least as an initial response, is one where the ability to realize *self-preservation* or *self-gratification* is sought. We will initiate or respond to causes that nourish this basic value of being in ourselves. We tend to be reactive in these situations, particularly if we feel ourselves threatened—whether the threat is actual or imagined. Beyond that we have a level of value, *belongingness,* that responds to a need or desire to belong to a social group, and to feel welcome and valued—i.e., a part. Here we respond to causes that nourish the level of self that wants to avoid alienation and rather feel identity with a peer group. This need is frequently realized by being on a team, or joining a club or union. The third level of value might be called the need to make a *contribution,* or sometimes on a grander scale, to "make a difference" with our lives. These three levels of value are always seeking a place and a way to be realized.

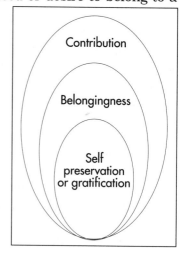

There is an inherent hierarchy in these levels, one that clarifies the distinctiveness of each but also the potential relatedness. For instance when we join with or become a true part of causes that help us realize a *belongingness* need, such as a team in the work place, we are able to realize a self-preservation value by having others "in it with us." When we are part of a contribution opportunity, such as a charity campaign, we have a feeling not only of belonging with any co-campaigner, but also with a larger community of receivers of charity or beyond. We also feel a sense of self-satisfaction or self-gratification from the camaraderie we find.

On the other hand, when we evoke the *drive* in people to attach themselves to the level of motivation that helps them realize a self-gratification need, such as "service employee of the month," we may—and frequently do—work against the other needs being realized. How often have you seen conflict and disagreement among others when a person wins over others or is recognized over others; this *divisiveness* may happen even though it is imperative to the success of the organization that everyone feel a part of the same team and further to make a contribution of their unique talents.

We cannot work to satisfy lower needs by working on them directly, but rather by an approach that works from the highest order of contribution being enabled. This approach provides the context in which higher order motivation can be realized. An incentive culture is by its nature divisive since everyone is "working the system" with their own agenda—either to win, or prove the system is unfair. Uniqueness of contribution is also aborted when some people are seen as "higher performers" than others.

The Enabling or Limiting Factors of our Brain: The Triad of Intelligence

A team of researchers led by Paul MacLean at the National Institute of Health has synthesized the work on the brain done by themselves and several major research centers. They have developed a construct of three brains or neurological systems in humans that act vertically *and* as an integrated unit similar to the interaction we have already seen in our behavior and value structures. Charles Krone has developed a set of intelligences and processes for developing them that correlate directly to these brains. These structures gives us a scientific, psychological, and even physiological base for understanding the functioning of our behavior and values.

Triad of Intelligences

Our brain is composed of three parts, literally organized in three segments. Part of this triune design of our brain structure is shared with reptiles, and part with mammals. The third part is shared partially with higher mammals, e.g. primates, but within the third part is a smaller though distinctively important part that is unique to humans. All brains and intelligences are working all the time, primarily outside our control and awareness, therefore not to their full potential. It is critical to develop

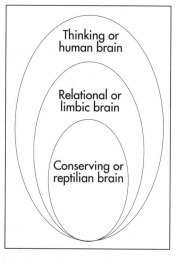

the capacity of the higher intelligences, because without this development, the lower brain and intelligences usurp the higher capacities into the service of the more primitive "defensive and territorial systems" of the reptilian brain. With development, the higher intelligences and more human sections of the thinking brain automatically integrates the lower brain and associated intelligences into the thinking brains service and employs all thinking processes to their best advantage.

The *reptilian* brain is conservative by its nature and seeks habituation, permanence, and stability. It correlates with the stimulus-response mechanism that is studied by the behaviorists when they look at animals. Their extrapolation to humans is correct as far as our reptilian brain is concerned. However, even these stimulus response mechanisms can be guided, directed, and modulated when put into the service of the higher intelligences.

The middle brain, or *limbic* brain, maintains all relationship at the physical level of the body as well as the emotions bonds between individuals, families, and societies. This brain also has responsibility for dreaming, visioning, and intuition. It can help the lower brain determine whether there is a true emergency or threat and develop appropriate action. It can help individuals

overcome their competitiveness in settings where this is inappropriate and to design cooperative efforts where needed. If it is not
well developed, the lower brain will use its emotions to bring an
emergency to a fever pitch and to become carried away with fear
or other intense emotions. The middle brain has functional
aspects of its own and it can provide the reflective intelligence
needed to make best use of the sensory motor and physical
processes of our lower brain. Since the middle brain can scheme,
and figure out ways to predict and control our environment and
other people, be philosophical and poetic, inventive and emotional, it is a powerful force when co-opted by the lower brain or
a potent manager when developed as a guiding force of the lower
brain.

The *thinking* brain, or neo-cortex, can radically alter the
potential of both the other brains if developed. It instantly
incorporates the learning of the two other brains. Most importantly, it can use them for higher purposes. Managing the lower
brains takes only a small amount of energy from the neo-cortex
because it is designed for constantly evolving and intervening in
the constructs we hold of the universe and reality itself. When the
neo-cortex brain is undeveloped we tend to get stuck in defensive
or emotional postures and the higher system is forced to focus on
the needs of the lower system. Since this takes very little effort,
the higher system is simply put on idle until such time as the
coast is clear. If this happens often enough for long enough, the
highest system tends to atrophy and this brain becomes dor-
mant.

What does this suggest for leadership? It is not merely a
matter of putting the minds of our people to work-using the
potential of people. People will tend to put to work the reptilian
brain, particular if the involvement of people is accompanied by
incentives of any sort. The upper brain and its corresponding
intelligence is not developed in our culture through families or
schools, or work environments with so few exceptions that we
can only use this brain in the service of our self-preservation and
belonging values which tend to be ramrodded by our lower and
maybe middle brain. Most organizational work designs today
provide lots of food and fuel for the reptilian brain and intelligences. Some new work designs are initially nourishing the
middle brain without really developing it and giving the guiding

capability needed to manage a now unruly and quite strong lower brain. The higher brain is not yet considered in work designs for any level of system—educational, or business, or societal. Think of the potential of a nation, or an industry, or a leader who has all three brains/intelligences developed.

The design and implementation of incentive programs impact almost exclusively on the lower brain, even though most managers would say they are working on the qualities we have spoken of for the middle brain and even some of the higher brain. The programs are intended to get a specific predictable response that produces some habitual result in the organization. Even though designers hope to provide encouragement and self-esteem to the winners or recipients of such programs, the lack of relationship to purpose, the production of "losers" (i.e., those who did not "win") tends to trigger the lower brain sensing threat among the majority of the members of the organization. An organization that works on the development of all three brains and the intelligences that go with them, is creating a culture that will enable the full development and expression of a full value base. This makes possible a whole set of behaviors guided in their execution by the thinking brain that has the potential for creating development and evolution of us as businesses and nations.

The Bottom-Line on Incentives

Some of you, at this point, will think you now see a way to make incentives work by trying to appeal to and provide incentives to higher values, and mental capacities. Rest assured, that the nature of incentives themselves works to make this impossible. Incentives have the effect of conditioning, just as Pavlov's dog was conditioned by the ringing of the bell for food. Because incentives are environmental stimuli, we are nurturing the lower reactive self that seeks self-preservation and gratification. Buyouts of such programs are frequently necessary. Because these programs initially engaged the conservative reptilian brain they are confronted with the conservative brain throughout implementation and even cancellation. The behaviorists are right about it working—at least to some degree; we may be effective in producing the expected response in some, but then it is necessary to accept the trade-off of activating the lower nature of human psychology that does not use judgment. This mindset is the same one that leads some people to see society as "owing them." This is becoming even more pervasive since the practice of incentives has also invaded the home and schools where children are taught from a young age to expect rewards for efforts or in many cases to see themselves as never able to achieve the rewards.

Incentive cultures cause us to look to others for thoughts about what is best to pursue and even the worth of our efforts. We slowly lose the ability to assess our own actions and their appropriateness, and to test and upgrade our own thinking. We are not enabled to develop critical thinking skills. Even if these skills are being taught in training courses the value for them is expressed principally by leadership actions. Thinking skills are not seen as the highest priority since the workers become focused on the incentive programs. It is just an adult version of peer pressure and as sophisticated adults we learn to work the system and keep our own values and thoughts to ourselves. Over time, this nature of intervention, encourages people to listen only to a part of themselves, and not to the whole of their values and intelligences.

Incentive cultures tend to produce homogenization of approaches and ends rather development and expression of uniqueness. The role model is what we are to emulate, not the finding of an inner source of creativity which can be put forward and from which the whole can gain.

A society cannot sustain health when its citizenry limits itself to conserving the past, the habitual, the non threatening, and to seeking self-gratification. A business can not serve its stakeholders with a workforce waiting for the next set of incentives to be articulated or experiencing failure and loss of spirit from an incentive program. Business leadership can lead in the development of a society and the success of a business by working to develop the full intelligence and critical thinking skills of its workforce by designing work systems that enable the higher values of uniqueness and contribution to be developed and expressed. Through this development and expression of higher order process, lower order values are satisfied. Organizations that move in this direction—Developmental Organizations—are not only incredibly successful as businesses, they are also the most exciting places on earth in which to work.

Barbara R. Hauser
is a partner in Gray, Plant, Mooty,
Mooty & Bennett, P.A., a Minneapolis law firm. She is a member of
the International Bar Association, the Union Internationale des Avocats,
and the International Fiscal Association.

Hauser has received degrees from Wellesley College (BA), the
University of Illinois at Chicago (MA, Philosophy), and the University of
Pennsylvania Law School (JD), and has clerked for the U.S. Court of
Appeals and Justice Potter Stewart at the United States Supreme Court. She
is Vice Chair of the American Bar Association Section of International Law
and Practice, Committee on International Property, Estates & Trust Law, and
is a frequent speaker on a variety of topics.

She is a co-founder of The Women's Leadership Forum, a past
Commissioner on the Minnesota Humanities Commission, and a past
Board member for the Guthrie Theater.

3

Cinderella Can be Tough, John Wayne Can Cry

Barbara R. Hauser

We would have more women leaders if Cinderella had *taken* the ball, instead of attending it.

We all grew up with fairy tales, but all the fairy tales weren't very grown-up. In particular, Cinderella has caused a lot of problems. For those of us who grew up with her, developing leadership skills has been a stretch. There is something wrong with the popular opinion that "women lead just as well as men do; they just have a *different* way of doing it." It's beginning to seem clear that Cinderella and her glass slippers lead right to the "glass ceiling."

Cinderella was not a good role model for leadership. To become leaders, we have had to learn a lot of adjustment skills. Some of those are not good skills—no one should be learning them. Others, though, do have value—and we should share what we have learned. I also think the same is true, although to a lesser extent, of the stereotypes that men have been raised with. Some of these leadership skills are valuable—and should be shared with us. Some are simply a result of power and authority, not leadership—and no one should be learning them.

I think we all need to learn to collaborate more—to participate and share our experiences and our strengths going forward. We need a truce in our gender wars, to culture hostilities and country battles. After comparing the traditional men's leadership model of the "warrior king" and the new women's style of the "caretaker princess," I offer a synthesis of strengths I call the "interpretive guide model." I have arrived at this from my personal experiences.

Why do I care? Why have I spent all these hours at a small computer screen writing this essay? It sounds odd, but at some level I feel I have no choice. Like the women in all the recent studies, I grew up supremely confident as a youngster and became timid and quiet (and angry) as a teenager. Becoming a wife and mother was a lesson in second class status. Then I went to law school, with fierce determination, and learned how to achieve success in a law firm. Along the way, I continue to see issues of women and leadership everywhere I go. I do want to change the world—especially for women.

Returning to Cinderella, we could compare her job to the pink collar ghettos, to the fact that we still keep track of how many cents it is that a woman earns to a man's dollar, to the slim numbers of women in management, and so on.

Cinderella, of course, lived happily ever after. Being chosen, for her beauty and small feet, meant that she had no more chores. She would be taken care of, by the Prince, for the rest of her life. This was the happy fairy tale ending. I know many women who are still trying new dresses, new shoes, hoping to find and then be chosen by another Prince Charming.

Lessons From Cinderella

Leadership involves confidence and courage. A leader is in front, sees a goal, provides motivation and moves a group forward. What leadership skills, good and bad, have we learned from Cinderella?

The most valuable trait learned from having a caretaker's perspective is the ability to understand and anticipate needs of the bosses. This is very valuable to have learned, even though it's hard to imagine anyone choosing to have to learn it.

Now, I work often in Japan. My success baffles the men at home. Sooner or later they ask for confirmation that it's hard for a woman to succeed in Japan. I explain that the skills I have developed as a woman are actually an advantage there.

Cinderella wished for change.

It's okay to hope for change; all leaders do this. What's not okay is to feel helpless about it, as did Cinderella. The classic fairy tale teaches that appearance is nearly everything. A sense of beauty can enhance our corporate life—from office decorations to annual report covers.

Cinderella's chance for success is a passive one; her only "hope" is to be chosen. Then she will be taken care of, and live happily ever after. To become successful in today's organizations also means being chosen by the men in power (e.g., the prince); those who aren't chosen are understandably jealous. It's hard to find a positive leadership trait here. Patience is the only one that comes to mind. The prototype leader is much more of a "take charge" type. To choose change and to create change are critical leadership skills. Within that context, patience is one valuable lesson we have learned from Cinderella.

Women's Leadership Debate

Today everyone is taking sides on "women as leaders." The popular position is that women have different ways of leading. Just last week a male partner of mine explained to me that "women have different ways of managing—they're more inclusive and participatory."

The debate he and others are eager to begin is whether or not this women's style of leadership is better than the traditional men's style. I have become impatient with this debate. I think the wrong assumptions are being made. We should look harder at the skills women in management have developed, and at the options they had or thought they had, before we begin evaluating an assumed free choice of style. I think there is an unfortunate but clear connection between Cinderella and the glass slipper and today's Cindy and the glass ceiling.

An energetic debate is taking place, which will continue to separate women from men. The issue is framed:

Do women have a different leadership style which has "better" traits than the men's style?

Before answering that question, we need some background on the men's leadership style. The traditional model is of a warrior/king. The American CEO is "the head of" the organization. The traditional view of the strong rugged (male) individual fits with the image of force and "take charge." The model is the warrior, who "is always stirring up some war or other, in order that people may require a leader," according to *The Republic*. This model is based on, and perpetuates, male stereotypes.

A second model is the leader whose role is to take care of everyone, to keep the community safe. This can be referred to as the caretaker/princess. This model is based on, and perpetuates, female stereotypes.

The third model, the one I want to promote, is the guide/ interpreter. In this model, there is an assumption that there is a "way," which is what the guide knows, and shows to others. Part of knowing the way and bringing others along is an ability to interpret. This is a new model, and one we can and should collaborate to develop.

Warrior/Prince: The Old Model

The warrior is a model of traditional successful leadership. Since U.S. businesses are run almost exclusively by men, the warrior model of the powerful leader who rules by fear has been adopted. This stereotype explains that the men's style of leadership is based on linear (left-brain) thought and rigid hierarchies. Accordingly, men are linear, strong, independent, individualistic, competitive, and confident leaders.

Linear. The linear, left-brain stereotype gives to men the field of logic, reasoning in an orderly, "linear" manner, and structure building, as in constructing organizational charts and strategic plans. There is orderly goal-setting and rational selection of the methods to achieve those goals. Speaking as someone who used to teach logic, though, I can tell you that in practice the men in charge don't quite fit this rational image. At one planning session, the consultant asked if "we" (the men and I) thought our client fees would be decreasing as a trend, and all hands went up. The next question was whether we thought our own incomes would continue to increase, and again all hands went up (except mine)!

Strong. Growing up, these men were raised to be "tough," to "act like a man," not be a "sissy," not to cry, etc. The most important body characteristics were strength and large size. Now we have a President who will hug and cry (and appoint a tall, strong woman as Attorney General). One of our political hopes for change, Senator Paul Wellstone, refers, in a talk, to "one of those big guys, although most guys look big to me." It's refreshing. Can we women quit wearing high heels? The glass slipper was not designed for confident strides along the leadership path.

Independent. These men were also raised to "stand on your own two feet," ridiculed for being a "momma's boy" or "tied to her apron strings." The "real man" doesn't need help. We all know "it's lonely at the top" but everyone is climbing up there. How do we reconcile this with the new wish for work "teams"? Is the captain on the team? Or is he the coach?

Individualistic. These were the expressions like "you can do it," "be the star," "pull yourself up by your own bootstraps," "be the hero." These are the merit badges, the individual awards and recognition. (I think I still have my series of bars and pins from that Sunday school attendance.)

Competitive. Here we have: "it's a dogfight out there," where "it's every man for himself" and "may the best man win." A top scientific company recently ordered its inventors to work as a team, but the individuals who claimed personal credit for the most patents were still paid the most. The company couldn't figure out why they weren't cooperating. (I think a consultant has now explained it to them.)

Confident. This is actually the end result of the preceding training. It is the "you can do it" attitude. It's what Cinderella never had. Without both the fairy godmother and the prince, she'd still be sweeping other people's cinders. She even had trouble remembering her deadline for the pumpkin.

Caretaker/Princess: New Model

The caretaker is a model of "softer" leadership. According to this stereotype, women are round, gentle, cooperative, group-oriented, nurturing, and hesitant leaders.

Round. If men have the "left-brain," then women have the "right-brain." This means an ability to see the whole, to apply creativity, to reason by intuition, etc. There is a more "organic" approach to institutions and to the world. Instead of hierarchies, there is a preference for circles, the "round." Put another way, it's okay that women aren't too good at thinking logically; we have "intuition."

Gentle. We women were raised to be quiet and kind. Children should "be seen and not be heard," little girls are made of "sugar and spice and everything nice" and should "act like a lady" and "mind your manners." Acting like a "tom-boy" was not tolerated after a certain age. A recent newspaper article showed a girl in tears at the school playground, because when she tumbled around, in her dress, the boys would chant, "I see London, I see France, I see Susie's underpants." I thought, "I remember that." I used to wonder if I would raise a girl in dresses. Having no daughters, I gave my nieces lots of books instead.

Cooperative. Women were raised to "help out" around the house. The childhood games (skipping rope, playing house or with dolls) involved taking turns. To be a "momma's little helper" was to be good. My mother will have to laugh here—I was famous for avoiding household chores. My main protest at Wellesley was objecting to the Dean about our weekly inspections for "beds-made/room-clean." I was told I was free to go to another school.

Group-oriented. For young girls, there was an emphasis on being liked, by as many as possible. To be the most popular was the goal. To stand out was to be criticized as a "prima donna." To think of oneself was to be labeled "selfish." A delight in "winning" earned the label "show-off."

Nurturing. Florence Nightingale and playing mommy to dolls reinforced the importance of nurturing. Taking care of other people's children was often the first job experience. Taking care of the difficult lawyers in a firm even became my job for a while. As he left the firm, one man said to me "Barbara, keep taking care of the boys." That's when I realized the role I was playing. That's when I quit doing that and put all my energy into my own development instead. Not everyone liked that change.

Hesitant. The end result has been a hesitancy in girls as they grow up. They are increasingly less likely to speak up in class, to question authority or to stand up and "take charge." This is not changing either. Extensive studies continue to show the same thing. Girls quit doing as well in math and science, they are called on less often by teachers, etc. At Wellesley, there were no boys to be called on. I remember when one visited our freshman lecture class: he kept speaking and volunteering and commenting (the rest of us were usually quiet and took a lot of notes). And he was just a visitor! And Wellesley graduates a disproportionate share of confident women.

you completely and sacrifice her own ambitions and just let you grow and develop?"

With some laughing and some overstatement, I suspect, there were a lot of hands in the air.

Then the speaker asked, "How many of you would accept that same kind of love from your children?"

There were no hands. And the point was made that one cannot sacrifice one's own growth and call it love. Conversely, it is not love to accept another's sacrifice of growth, because love is about growth.

Which begs the question about the self-sacrificing, ever-loyal, do-anything-for-the-company employee.

Yes, I believe in loyalty. Yes, I believe in love in the workplace. Yes, I believe there are times when we must give beyond ourselves for the good of the group and the achievement of the goal.

But it is not giving of one's best self to be constantly sacrificing one's own opportunities for "the good of the company" or out of loyalty to the boss.

And it is *terrible* management to either demand or accept an employee's sacrifice of advancement or opportunity or growth and call it "loyalty" to the manager.

Think about it this way: You wouldn't accept that from your children.

The Bag of Tricks

Face it. We have our bag of tricks. All managers do, and those tricks can be both valuable and limiting.

A lot of managers think themselves lucky to have changed jobs just as they had done all the obvious things they knew to do.

The luckier managers, by far, are those who had to stay with a job after the bag of tricks was empty and who had to start inventing the job fresh every day.

Then, and only then, does growing begins.

A Note About Greed

One of my early lessons in business was taught to me by a man who thought he was doing me a favor.

The Debate

Even though the traditional preference has been for the men's traits (which successful women have traditionally studied and copied), the new debate is framed around the assumption that, not only do women as a group have a different leadership style, but also that it is a better one. This means that women are, by their nature, deserving of not just "equal" treatment and representation, but are really entitled, "by their nature," to superior treatment. But this conclusion is based upon a background assumption that, if there are two styles, one will be better. It will be the "winner."

This debate began with an article, "The Debate Over la Difference," in *The New York Times* on August 15, 1993. The genesis was Carol Gilligan's view, published in 1982, that girls solve problems differently than boys do, based upon psychological development studies. This led to beliefs that women who do not show the same leadership traits as men do are not deficient; they are just different.

In 1990, Judy Rosener wrote "The Ways Women Lead" in the *Harvard Business Review,* saying that men were more "take charge" and transactional, and women were more "transformational." Men were said to use the power of their position; women would rely on interpersonal skills.

Every time I hear this, I laugh. It is stated as if women chose this style, in lieu of using the power of their position. In fact I'm convinced that these skills have been developed to make up for not having any power of position. Instead of "command and control," the Rosener theory is that women use "interactive leadership." Again, I wonder how many opportunities there were for command and control.

Rosener explains: "I call their leadership style "interactive leadership" because these women actively work to make their interactions with subordinates positive for everyone involved....[They] encourage participation, share power and information, enhance other people's self-worth, and get others excited about their work. All these things reflect their belief that allowing employees to contribute and to feel powerful and important is a win-win situation—good for the employees and the organization."

I don't disagree with this. Women generally have more

experience with how it feels to be commanded and controlled. To organizations eager to change and improve, this often sounds as if there would be benefit from learning how women lead.

Accordingly, there has been a fair amount of interest in whether women do have a different way of leading, which clearly seems to be superior. In fact, a case-study approach of women leading differently was used by Sally Helgesen in her book *The Female Advantage* about such superiority.

In my experience, anyone who has a taste of formal authority would covet it nonstop. It is the way things get done. As far as learning to lead without authority, I'll just add that many great, and some not-so-great, skills have been developed to get around the lack of authority, but, in the end, the lack of authority does equate completely with no leadership.

One reason this debate exists is that there is so little information about how women lead, because there are hardly any women in leadership positions in big businesses. In 1990, a survey of the highest paid executives found that 0.5% were women. The organizations reflect the leadership styles of the men who run them. The few women who are successful in those organizations have had to be judged favorably by the men in charge. This realization has lead to more recent books with titles like *Hardball For Women,* in which Pat Heim argues that, as long as the institutions are male-run, women had better learn to play their game if they want to succeed, after which they can revert to and exert their women's style of leadership.

While the debate continues, women who did aim for the "top" in business are dropping out of the struggle. Studies acknowledging the mysterious but impenetrable glass ceiling are having widespread effects on the aspirations of younger women, who are beginning to opt out at very early ages.

If there were more women leaders, would we see a "women's style"? We do not know. As telling comments on the men's vs. women's leadership debate explain, we do not have enough data about women leaders. The anecdotal surveys include a wide range of styles that have worked: the nurturer, the queen bee, the tom-boy, the has-and-does-it-all superwoman [believe it or not, the spell check-program for my computer reports "superwoman" is "not in the dictionary" and suggests "change to 'superman'"], the replica man, the company cheerleader, the mommy-tracker, the dedicated spinster, the PR beauty packager, the HR mother of many. These women are told they have the superior caretaker style in common, and that they share a concern for the flock, not for power.

In practice, these women leaders do have a lot in common. They share feelings of exhaustion, isolation, and loneliness.

Interpreter Guide: The Needed Model

There is the third alternative that I wish to promote—the "interpreter guide." I want us to begin talking a lot about our differences as men and women, to begin to understand each other, and to contribute our joint strengths. The world has very few concrete stereotypes walking around: Cinderella can be tough and John Wayne can cry.

How do we do this?

We have to treat each other as both foreign and different. We cannot continue assuming that we already understand each other. To paraphrase William James, we need a "willing suspension of belief." We could also chuckle over (we all need a lot more humor here) Katharine Hepburn's comment that, "Sometimes I wonder if men and women really suit each other. Perhaps they should live next door and just visit now and then." Or we could listen to Gloria Steinem describing women as "the only oppressed group that doesn't have a nation, a neighborhood, or usually even a bar." Achieving the interpreter guide model is a three-part process.

Begin with Respect

The first part is respect. A person, a point of view, must be treated with genuine respect. Respect means, "I will regard you and your opinions as having value" and "I will do this even though I may not understand you at all." In fact, it is quite helpful to assume at this point that there is no understanding of each other. Men and women may, in fact, not understand each other well at all. Nature aside, most women have been raised quite differently from most men.

Interest

The next part is interest. With respectful interest, real communication can begin. Let us listen to each other, with respect and interest. Let us learn more about each other, from listening to each other.

This isn't easy to do, at either end. For the speaker, we have to be vulnerable, to share our thoughts and different attitudes. This risks that the other will either laugh or be bored.

Until recently, I have discussed women's issues only with women. I know that this was, in part, based on an assumption that men would not be interested (the other assumption was that they wouldn't understand). Two events stand out for changing my mind.

First, I spent a weekend in the home of a male colleague and got to know his wife. Larry and I continued our usual talks, of law firms, tax codes, and so on. His wife, though, continually raised women's issues which he always seemed to listen to carefully. Her work involved feminist issues, her hobbies were on feminist issues, the mystery writers she shared with him had to be women, and so on. All of the conversations the three of us had would include feminist discussions. Finally, as he drove me to the airport I was able to ask what he thought of how often his wife talked about women's issues. He said it was wonderful. He said he was learning so much. He said he had no idea how widespread the discrimination was. He said he wished all men were able to hear and learn more. They are quickly becoming one of my favorite couples.

Second, I attended a full-day session on the status of women at the annual meeting of the Union Internationale des Avocats. The first surprise was that the majority of attendees were men. I found out that the invitation letter, from the woman chairing the project, included an appeal to the chivalry of her male colleagues to attend, and to come to the assistance of "woman," "the being who embellishes your life." In any event, the men were there, and they were clearly interested. Even on the extremely female subject of clitoris removal, the presenters were a husband and wife with equal passion. This also is a group I'm going to stay with.

In writing this essay, my first draft contained no personal information. Changing it the way I did felt risky and unfamiliar. I have become persuaded, though, that our personal stories can explain more than lots and lots of surface words can. At least it's worth a try.

Trust

The gradual insight that develops from real communication leads to trust of each other. Trust is the cement of our social relations. It develops over time. A current analogy is that we make deposits in each other's trust accounts. The larger our deposits, the more easily we can make withdrawals.

Trust is earned by kindness and reliability. If there is a background of trust, surface disputes disappear. The explosion of sexual harassment litigation is distressing on a human level. Of course I understand the injustices leading to the litigation. I also regret the increased tension and suspicion. My wish is to create a commitment to working together. My big dream is to thoroughly enjoy working together.

Gender wars need a truce. We need to find guides who have a vision of working together, cooperating, and enjoying each other. We do need to rely on each other as guides. We all know different ways to different goals. A woman from Cameroon criticized me (and American women) for lecturing to women from Africa about how to be stronger leaders. She said there are some things we could learn from them, too. In fact, thinking back, one of the things she suggested was "include the men."

I have learned a lot from men about risk, courage, and efficient decision-making. I am also teaching men in workshops about negotiating more "softly" and politely, with more "bottom-line" success. I can sympathize with the Japanese businessmen I know when they complain (very politely of course) about the blunt, hurry-up-and-get-down-to-business approach of the U.S. businessman, as I sit with them for hours, having tea, sharing family photos, and nodding.

Many women practice leadership in the non-profit sector, but many of those organizations are failing due to a lack of strong decision making. I was on the first board of a women's art collective. The women didn't like granting decision making authority; others weren't comfortable receiving it (women don't grow up used to power, at least of that kind). The organization is now bankrupt.

At our most recent firm retreat, we had an excellent presentation on cultural diversity which focused on reassuring the predominately white male audience that they had not purposely ever excluded anyone, etc., but that they all had the benefit of an unconscious "white privilege" which black people did not have. The black presenter gave many examples of how different life was without that privilege. She explained teaching her sons to fear for their physical safety if they were in a white neighborhood at night, told her boys some people would never respect them without even knowing them, and so on. (These are familiar themes to women.) It intrigued the men and made respectful interested conversations possible.

We need to do the same with our gender differences, to be able to guide each other and to share leadership. We can leave Cinderella with her pumpkin. There's much more interesting work to be done. We have a lot to talk about. With respect, interest, and trust, we can go anywhere.

I do believe that the times, they are a-changin'. On the same day, a newspaper printed an article about a 17-year-old girl in her football uniform wearing her homecoming queen crown, just a few pages away from the new cowboy style of "gentling" colts, instead of breaking them.

For my part, our Women's Leadership Forum newsletter, *Voices*, will include voices by and to men—a new idea. The intention is to get away from Cinderella. Women need stronger leadership training than she had. We can do this together with men to the extent that we listen to each other with respectful interest. We can be each other's interpretive guides. If we can do that, we can be interpretive guides for the world.

Ann M. Morrison
is the founder and president of the
New Leaders Institute and author
of the 1992 book, *The New Lead-
ers: Guidelines on Leadership Diversity in America.* Her work in diversity,
leadership, and executive development has been published and presented
throughout the world. She is lead author of the 1987 book (revised in
1992), *Breaking the Glass Ceiling: Can Women Reach the Top of
America's Largest Corporations.*

    She is an honorary senior fellow of the Center for Creative Leadership
and co-author of the 1988 book, *The Lessons of Experience: How
Successful Executives Develop on the Job.* Clients for her work in leadership
development include companies such as GE, IBM, and Eastman Kodak,
as well as public-sector organizations.

    Morrison's articles have appeared in *The New York Times, The Los
Angeles Times, Small Business Reports,* and *Working Woman Magazine.*
She holds an MBA from Wake Forest University and an MA in psychology
from Bucknell University. This essay was adapted from a chapter in *The
New Leaders* and an article written for the Center for Creative Leadership's
newsletter, *Issues & Observations.*

4

Diversity and Leadership Development

Ann M. Morrison

A major goal of many organizations is to find and develop
future leaders, those talented managers who will help the organization prosper. As diversity within our society increases, this
goal involves enlarging the pool of potential leaders by including
more nontraditional managers. It also involves improving traditional methods of preparing people for leadership. Better methods of leadership development applied to a larger pool of candidates, it is argued, can enhance organizational productivity,
profitability, and responsiveness to business conditions.

The prospects for effective development are too often affected by a manager's sex and ethnicity. Nontraditional managers (such as people of color and white women) may not be well
served by the assumptions and techniques used for years as a
development approach in organizations. Our research for *The
New Leaders* suggests a model for leadership development that
includes a balance of three components—challenge, recognition,
and support—which work together over time to provoke and
sustain growth. This model assumes that to sustain development
over time, all three elements need to be provided in roughly the
same proportion. The *challenge* of new situations and difficult
goals prompts managers to learn the lessons that will help them

perform well at higher levels. *Recognition* includes acknowledgment and rewards for achievements, and the resources to continue achieving, in the form of promotions, pay, and awards. *Support* entails acceptance and understanding, along with the benefits that help managers incorporate their career into a full and fulfilling life.

Typically, the element of challenge overwhelms the other two elements. Our research indicates that some aspects of challenge may be overlooked, recognition may be slow, and traditional support systems may be inadequate. The barriers confronted by many nontraditional managers, which were identified in our study, contribute significantly to this imbalance. The consequences for high-potential women and people of color, and sometimes for white men as well, can be exhaustion, repeated failures, or opting out of a debilitating work situation. To prevent this talent drain, some of the most progressive organizations in this country are exploring ways to restore balance in their leadership development efforts.

Challenge

One of the most important methods used to prepare people for executive jobs is a planned sequence of assignments that provides individuals with continual challenge. The practice of changing or rotating jobs every year or two is commonly used as a "fast track" for aspiring executives. Ideally, job rotation not only exposes managers to the workings of an organization, but it also puts managers into situations that require new or better skills than the previous assignment. Research done at the Center for Creative Leadership and reported in the 1988 book, *The Lessons of Experience*, identified developmental assignments that have figured in the success of the white male managers we studied. These assignments include promotions with dramatically increased responsibilities, transfers into staff functions at corporate headquarters, serving on task forces, troubleshooting stints, and start-up experiences that often involve time overseas. These assignments partly overlap with those found at the Center to be important for white female executives, described in the book, *Breaking the Glass Ceiling*, and in the Center's technical report, *Gender Differences in the Development of Managers: How Women Managers Learn From Experience.*

These assignments are important because they force managers to broaden their perspective and learn a range of skills that will presumably help them be effective in executive-level posts. They are valuable because they demand a great deal from the incumbents. They provide the *challenge* for people to learn, to grow, and to develop to their fullest potential.

As reported in *The Lessons of Experience,* these assignments provide challenge because they appear to share eight common characteristics. These characteristics may represent the key ingredients of challenge for traditional (white male) managers. They are:

1. *Dealing with the boss.* Challenge arises when the boss is inexperienced or indifferent. The boss may also have a difficult style or even serious managerial flaws.

2. *Dealing with staff members.* Challenge also arises when the staff is inexperienced, recalcitrant, or incompetent. Some staff members may hold a grudge against the manager for being promoted over them.

3. *Other significant relationships.* Presenting to senior executives, negotiating with outsiders, and collaborating with people from different backgrounds and functions or regions of the organization all create challenge.

4. *High stakes.* Challenge is created by the extreme visibility of certain assignments, especially with top management. Tight deadlines and financial risk add to the challenge.

5. *Adverse business conditions.* Often seen in overseas assignments, the challenge here includes the physical hardships of harsh climate or lack of adequate living facilities, hostile officials, or conflicts with local business practices and values.

6. *Scope and scale of the job.* Managing a large number of subordinates, including subordinates who are geographically separated, and including subordinates who are experts in their own right all provide challenge.

7. *Missing trumps.* The lack of traditionally-required credentials or background characteristics, which requires a manager to establish credibility while learning the new job, also provides challenge.

8. *Starkness of transition.* Finally, challenge is created by the suddenness or the extent of change involved in a transition, sometimes involving personal life changes as job changes occur.

These eight sources of challenge in developmental assignments might be considered traditional elements of challenge for white male managers. They are recognized in many organizations and have been incorporated into the developmental programs and tools used by some. These elements may also figure in the development and success of nontraditional managers, but they may not adequately capture the types and extent of challenge experienced by nontraditional managers whose job situations do not conform to the traditional patterns. The additional or exaggerated challenges that these managers regularly encounter may not be factored into their preparation and assessment which, consequently, may interfere with their progress.

Extra Challenges for Nontraditional Managers

Barriers to advancement create additional challenges for many white women and people of color in management. These barriers include prejudice, isolation, and conflicts between one's career and personal life. It is not difficult to imagine, for example, the increased difficulty of dealing with a boss who not only lacks some skills and has a difficult style, but who is also prejudiced. Similarly, there may be added difficulty in dealing with prejudiced subordinates, peers, and outsiders. The addition of prejudice to these first three characteristics of challenge complicates and deepens the challenge in ways not encountered by many white men. Therefore, the challenge of dealing with prejudiced colleagues may go unnoticed by them.

Perhaps because of prejudice, the standards for performance may be higher for nontraditional managers than for their white male counterparts. In this study and in our earlier research on women in management, we discovered that women and people of color in management are often expected to perform at a higher level than white men who hold or who have held the same job. Doing a job *better* than anyone else has ever done it is likely to add to the challenge experienced by nontraditional managers.

Coping with adverse conditions is another ingredient that may increase the level of challenge for nontraditional managers. In describing the challenge of troubleshooting assignments, for example, white male managers sometimes mentioned the hostility of their co-workers who resented their advice, their attempted interventions, and even their very presence. Also, their limited assignments in foreign countries sometimes entailed coping with capricious or unfriendly government officials. Such hardships are typically confined to certain types of assignments or locations in the reports of these white male managers, but they appear to constitute the daily life of many nontraditional managers, even those in the progressive organizations included in our study.

Our findings indicate there is still a great deal of resentment and hostility from subordinates who dislike reporting to anyone not white and male, and from co-workers who feel threatened working side-by-side with a nontraditional manager. Some colleagues may not be hostile, but merely skeptical. They may not be directly opposed to an integrated workforce, but they suspect that nontraditional managers are simply not up to the task, and they are consequently cautious in the way they relate to, delegate to, and rely on a white woman or a person of color. Like some of those outrightly hostile, these co-workers, consultants, suppliers, and customers may rationalize the presence of nontraditional managers as the outcome of a quota system. A Chinese manager in our study said that her boss had told her to "be as un-Asian as possible" and to have her Asian subordinates "be un-Asian" as well because the department "looks like an Asian connection." She had to be concerned on a daily basis with looking, acting, and *seeming* like an Asian as she performed her job.

The adversity that surrounds nontraditional managers adds to the challenge of the work they are doing. Not everyone is hostile or suspicious of nontraditional managers, and not all white men are immune from being resented, but these responses appear to be considerably more frequent for people of color and white women. For these managers, adverse conditions that are reported as a temporary hardship by many white men are a constant part of their work environment, following them from assignment to assignment, from place to place, throughout their careers.

There is also some evidence from this study and other research that the pressure and visibility associated with their performance may also be greater for nontraditional managers, adding even more challenge to their work. All conscientious managers are likely to feel pressure to perform their job well, but our research indicates that a nontraditional manager is noticed more, watched more, and judged more than a white man, if only because the nontraditional manager stands out in the management ranks of many organizations. Managers in this study and in our earlier study of the glass ceiling for women in management noted that, for many nontraditional managers, the added pressure of working "under a microscope" is frustrating and draining. One Hispanic manager in our study explained, "Those minorities who are going up get excess scrutiny. They are put under a microscope, and there is pressure not to screw up." Being the sole Asian-American marketing manager or the first black executive puts nontraditional managers into a spotlight that relentlessly publicizes their actions. Their observers include not only their bosses and colleagues being curious, if not doubtful, about their competence, but also the other women and ethnically diverse colleagues who desperately want them to succeed so that they, too, may be given a chance to advance someday.

The burden carried by many nontraditional managers to represent their demographic group while performing their job is one that can raise the level of challenge beyond that of white male managers in whatever assignment they have. Because they represent not only their organization but also their ethnic group or gender (and sometimes also the concept of diversity in general), they are constantly called upon to promote the cause. The media want them for stories and profiles. Social scientists want them for research projects. Other men of color or women, with ambitions of their own, want them as role models and regularly call them for advice or favors. Non-profit organizations ask them to speak at conventions. Their bosses sometimes nudge them to serve on committees and task forces as the ranking woman or minority to represent that point of view. Employee groups beckon them to mentor others of the same sex or ethnicity. Top management may want their help to recruit other nontraditional employees. The amount of necessary "volunteerism" within and outside the organization escalates for nontraditional managers, who must also continue to do their jobs in a consistently outstanding fashion to stay in good stead with their bosses.

While some nontraditional managers shun volunteerism, and while some white male managers elect to contribute considerable time to both traditional and nontraditional causes, the reality seems to be that women and people of color are under considerable pressure to choose more and do more. Those who don't support traditional activities run the risk of alienating their white male colleagues. Those who don't support their demographic colleagues risk being ostracized by them as a "queen bee" or the like. Their visibility permits them no refuge from multiple, sometimes conflicting obligations.

Another aspect of challenge for many nontraditional managers is balancing career demands with outside demands. The managers in our study generally agreed that women experience this challenge more than men, because the responsibilities of bearing and raising children, maintaining a household, and managing social relationships are still disproportionately borne by women. Women with the financial means to hire help are typically freed from handling these duties personally, but it does not reduce their degree of responsibility. They still must hire and manage people to perform these jobs, intervene when sickness or problems occur, and account for the results. The continual challenge of juggling home and family demands with job demands creates conflict and stress that women in particular are expected to manage. Some men are also strained in seeking a balance between the two; Hispanic men may be especially vulnerable, as some managers noted, because their culture puts a high value on family life. However, the day-to-day responsibilities of child care or elder care, cooking and cleaning, entertaining, and so forth, are those that further increase the challenge for many women as they pursue their career goals.

Overall, it would not be surprising to find that the level of challenge in a given assignment for nontraditional managers is considerably greater than that experienced by white men. Combining the demands of meeting higher performance standards, regularly confronting adversity such as hostility or harassment, working under a spotlight and contending with the expectations of both nontraditional and traditional groups, and struggling day after day with care-giving and social duties significantly affects the degree of difficulty of a given assignment. Some executives may have concluded that if nontraditional managers have more difficulty performing in an assignment it must be because they are not as capable as their white male counterparts. But this conclusion can be countered with the argument that greater difficulty comes from the extra demands that are both within the assignment and surrounding it. The "same" assignment given to a white male manager and a nontraditional manager is hardly the same at all.

The Danger of Limiting Challenge

Some executives may be tempted to provide some relief by assigning nontraditional managers to less consequential jobs. Yet this is likely to perpetuate a vicious cycle that blocks their advancement. Because of prejudice and other barriers, there is already a tendency to "de-select" women and people of color for strategic, central assignments. Nontraditional managers are already more likely to be put into peripheral or staff positions which are considered to be less important to the organization's performance. Then, when a higher-level opening comes up, they are not likely to get the job because they lack experience in strategic, central posts. The cycle feeds on itself to limit nontraditional managers' advancement potential. These managers will probably be increasingly frustrated that they aren't getting opportunities to prove their worth to the organization in ways that are likely to be recognized and rewarded. And because their credibility as potential executives hinges on a solid track record of important jobs, gaps in their record may cause them to plateau. They may lose opportunities to learn some of the lessons that will help them become effective in higher-level posts. They may feel that the level of challenge is too low rather than too high if they are not experiencing the same elements of challenge that have characterized the careers of managers who preceded them.

Instead of reducing the level of challenge by limiting nontraditional managers to assignments perceived to be less critical (and less demanding), one alternative is to reduce the demands from other sources: use the same performance standards for all managers, traditional and nontraditional; reduce the impact of prejudice; promote a larger cadre of nontraditional managers so that the demands on any of these individuals to represent their sex or ethnic group are lessened; provide benefit packages that allow managers to fulfill outside obligations while pursuing their careers. Alternatives such as these can provide relief from some of the additional elements of challenge without interfering with nontraditional managers' advancement potential. These options not only reduce some of the extraneous challenge that distracts many nontraditional managers from the work at hand, but they also increase the recognition and support needed to keep them going.

Perhaps one of the biggest mistakes made in organizations attempting to increase diversity in management is misusing challenge. Challenge is either heaped onto nontraditional managers until they burn out or, on the other hand, they are protected from overwhelming challenge, which often contributes to their derailment. Relying on challenge alone to develop the leadership potential of nontraditional managers is a dangerous trap. The elements of recognition and support need to be factored in to balance the level of challenge for the leadership development process to be most effective.

Recognition

It is difficult for many white male managers to appreciate the demands faced by people of color and women in most organizations. A policy of equal treatment is often administered from the vantage point of white men. These white men may not recognize the challenge of "fitting in" and countering stereotypes held by co-workers; they may not encounter acts of discrimination and therefore cannot fathom the difficulty of managing the rage caused by it; they may not have been deprived of counsel or colleagueship as they made their way up the ladder. Yet it is important that demands and hardships such as these be recognized in assessing the promise and the performance of nontraditional managers.

Some managers in our study commented that women and people of color seem to be ambivalent about taking key jobs in their organizations. One reason may be that the expected rewards fall far short of the additional demands and sacrifices that will be required. A CEO interviewed for a previous research project told us that women were expected to perform at a level at least as high as men, but that no woman would be promoted into one of the top ten positions in the company no matter how well she performed. Without the rewards to compensate for their investment, many nontraditional managers opt out, adjust their input to match the likely output from their employer, or scale down expectations of themselves to fit their career prospects.

Recognition Comes in Many Different Forms

Some of the most common forms are:

1. *Pay.* Salary and total cash compensation.
2. *Promotion.* Advancement to positions of greater responsibility.
3. *Perquisites.* Company car, club memberships, financial incentives and advice, and so forth.
4. *Participation.* Inclusion in decision-making.
5. *Autonomy.* Freedom to act on one's own without supervision.
6. *Resources.* Staff, budget, and time to do the job.
7. *Respect and credibility.* One's priorities and opinions are considered and valued.
8. *Faith.* The expectation that one's productivity will continue in increasingly responsible positions.

There is still strong reluctance to give nontraditional managers the same authority and rewards that go to their white male counterparts. Unequal pay, for example, is documented even in staff jobs generally believed to be appropriate for women. In the human resources field, a 1990 salary survey reported in *Training* magazine shows that men make 37% more than women in comparable jobs. Only in one of the lower job grades does the average salary for women come close to that for men. In upper management levels, the salary gap may be even greater. A salary study published in 1987 by the U.S. Chamber of Commerce reported that women at the vice president level and higher in corporations make 42% less than men. At one organization in our study, an indicator of success was that female engineers are now making more than 90% as much money as men in the same positions.

People of color and white women always need to be better, to be developed further, in order to be promotable. The tendency in some organizations is to develop nontraditional managers until they are virtually guaranteed success in a position, which sometimes means they must *do* the job before they *get* the job (without the salary increase and privileges). Some managers who have seen the negative impact of promoting a woman or a person of color and watching them flounder in that job are now reluctant to promote another until they are absolutely certain that she or he will succeed. They prefer to give them responsibility for a while before they give them commensurate authority.

The advancement barriers identified in our study create at least some of the discrepancies in recognition. Prejudice, for example, may contribute toward an unwillingness to pay higher salaries or grant perks to nontraditional managers, or to give them freedom to do their job without constant monitoring. Researchers Amado Cabezas and Gary Kawaguchi concluded in 1988 that for Asian-American men and women, "Low returns on their human capital investments rather than deficiencies in their investments accounted for about two-thirds of the income gap relative to U.S.-born white men." Continuing discrimination, they conclude, plays an important part in the lower payoff that Asian-Americans receive for their education and experience in comparison to white men. The lack of career planning and organizational savvy may also be responsible for the loss of promotional opportunities that would better prepare nontraditional managers for senior-level posts. Discomfort may cause traditional executives to exclude people of color and white women from participating in the decision-making process. These and other barriers we discovered limit the recognition available to nontraditional managers.

Recognition plays a significant role in assigning women and people of color to appropriately challenging assignments, and in rewarding their performance in them. One manager in our study mused that white men are "brought along in baby steps" throughout their career, but many nontraditional managers have much more traumatic transitions thrust upon them. Giving women and people of color more credit for their experiences and achievements, even if they have been somewhat different than those of white men, and giving them the resources to make steady, incremental changes in their knowledge and skills, is a difficult task made even more difficult by the need to make up for lost time. It is, however, a necessary component in developing leaders for the future.

Support

In addition to challenge and recognition for their skills and achievements, men of color and women in general also need support systems to help them cope with the additional demands they face. Challenge, even with commensurate rewards, can prove to be an overwhelming burden for managers if there is no relief from some of the demands that conflict with their job responsibilities. Some of the most common forms of support are:

1. *Collegiality.* Friendly association with co-workers.

2. *Acceptance.* Acknowledgment and approval.

3. *Advocacy.* Backing and endorsement.

4. *Permission to fail.* Leeway to make mistakes and learn from them.

5. *Information.* News about the business and the organization.

6. *Feedback.* Data about one's abilities, prospects, and reputation.

7. *Flexibility.* Options to tailor a job to one's own strengths or circumstances.

8. *Stress relief.* Reducing anxiety and tension by accommodating family and other outside demands, and preventing on-the-job hostilities.

The lack of colleagueship and acceptance contribute to the isolation and discouragement felt by many women and people of color in management. Organized employee groups often try to fill that void by helping nontraditional managers feel more comfortable and more confident in their organization, providing camaraderie and encouragement if not training as well. One black manager we interviewed found that his black colleagues helped him reconcile mixed feelings about his work environment:

> There's a schizophrenia about the behavior of blacks in corporations. On the one hand, I want to know why all the decision-makers are white. That's how I feel at home, with my friends. Somehow when I go to work, I don't ask that. The employee group brought the internal me and the external me closer together, more in focus. I'm not as offended, and I don't show the offense at the little subtleties I see. I want to make my point, but I don't want to be branded so my points are discounted.

Advocacy from more senior managers can be difficult to attain for many nontraditional managers who find that traditional managers are simply not comfortable with them or perceive them to be less competent than white men. When they are recommended for a position, they may find that they have no leeway to define or enlarge the job and no possibility of taking actions that are not guaranteed to pay off. Playing it safe may be a condition for continued advocacy, which rules out many opportunities to learn and grow. One executive in our study thought that his company ought to put someone of color or a white woman in charge of a start-up venture, giving the person five years to make it work and, if it does, 15% of the profits. "That's what they do for white males," he said. But many managers avoid the possibility of failure, and the potential rewards and learning that go with it, because failure is still often attributed to a nontraditional manager's ethnicity or sex. One human resource executive described the "undercover racism and sexism" in her company. "If a male makes a mistake," she said, "they attribute it to the individual, not to the sex. But if a black manager makes a mistake, they might say, 'We should try a white manager next time.'"

Information and feedback are also important components of a support system. Networks and mentors, when they are available, perform a valuable service by including women and people of color in the informal information channels and by giving them feedback about their abilities, their performance, their career options, and how they are perceived by others. Developing their organizational savvy is a need felt by a number of nontraditional managers in our study, but the sources of that savvy are often scarce. The white men in higher level positions often don't mingle socially with nontraditional managers, so there are few opportunities to get information through the grapevine. Also, white male executives are sometimes uncomfortable giving constructive criticism on the job to people of color or to women. One human resource manager in our study commented that the lack of feedback available to female managers limits their ability to make the right impression:

Male managers here are hesitant to identify the "soft points" of women. We need a vehicle to give them feedback. Women don't know what they are not doing. They need more awareness of the image they present, when they give the perception of "Are they tough enough?"

Employee groups and networks of nontraditional employees sometimes provide a supportive forum in which criticism is exchanged and valued. Other avenues and sources of information are also needed. A number of nontraditional managers in our study have relied on one or two mentors to give them honest, performance-related feedback as well as information about business plans and problems. For those who don't have regular or structured feedback from a mentor, outside training programs that emphasize assessment and feedback may fill in some gaps.

An important form of support for managers who are increasingly part of a two-career family and who are building leisure and family activities more deliberately into their lives is the leeway to develop their careers in different ways from those used in the past. The relocation requirements for advancement in some organizations, for example, have created serious problems for women and for some men who fear the separation from a spouse, dysfunctional effects on their children, or upheaval of their preferred lifestyle. Some senior managers are beginning to realize that mobility may not be so important for development, compared with other, less expensive alternatives that also broaden the perspective and network of managers. The average cost of relocating a manager is nearly $40,000, according to Kathryn Scovel in *Human Resource Executive* magazine. If the main benefit is a change of scenery, which sometimes happens with unplanned moves, then alternatives make sense.

One large organization in our study had confronted at least one high-potential manager protesting the extensive mobility requirements. The traditional requirement of moving among all seven regions was recently modified; experience in only three of the regions is now needed to qualify for senior management posts. Modifications such as this may help organizations streamline their development practices as much as they help managers who, for personal reasons, do not want to relocate.

A number of the organizations in our study are also doing more to help managers find an acceptable middle ground between career demands and family demands by providing resources for dependent care, maternity leave, and alternative work schedules. Such support makes it possible for women in particular to devote more concentrated time to their work while still fulfilling family obligations.

Finding a Balance

Various types of imbalance are common in the development process, particularly concerning women and people of color. The most typical problem is a surplus of challenge that is not compensated by appropriate levels of recognition or support. When this happens, the drop-out and burn-out rate is likely to escalate. Nontraditional managers who may appear to be incompetent, overwhelmed, or unappreciative may actually be victims of a dysfunctional development strategy. The extraordinary level of challenge often faced by women and people of color, combined with the lack of recognition and support in comparison with that available to white men, helps explain why some nontraditional managers gladly leave their employers.

Other types of imbalance also occur. When the level of recognition exceeds the level of challenge, for example, it is possible that complacency or guilt will result. A fancy executive title and a fat paycheck don't fit well with a job with a vague purpose, little clout and fewer resources. Such a combination may have a debilitating effect not only on the individual's development, but also on how that person's advancement prospects are viewed.

Support systems that exceed challenge or recognition may impair the development process as well. Collegial interaction without much skill-building or productivity gains, for example, might make a company seem more like a social club than a performance-oriented organization. As support systems improve for nontraditional managers, some of their contextual hardships will be reduced, and there will be less need to recognize these kinds of challenges in their performance. Better child care, for instance, helps parents concentrate on their job performance without distraction or guilt; the hardship of conflicting demands is less of a factor to consider in planning or evaluating job performance. It is still appropriate, however, to acknowledge the skills and stamina parents develop through bearing and raising children.

Many organizations rely too heavily on challenge alone to develop promising managers. Some organizations have come to recognize the need to balance all three of these components, but the impact of "hidden" challenges faced primarily by people of color and white women in management is not always considered. As the challenge escalates, the recognition and support systems needed to sustain and replenish new leaders must also increase—even for the most ambitious people.

Many of the organizations we studied, leaders within their industries in terms of developing diversity, are creating a more balanced developmental approach for managers. The guidelines from our research explain in greater detail how a balance can be achieved. Over time, this balance is likely to be a far more effective development strategy for all managers, including the nontraditional managers who represent a growing portion of the talent pool available for leadership positions.

Businesses and other organizations are in great need of leadership. Discussions about transformation, paradigm shifts, and team performance must also address the reality of cultural differences, sexual and racial prejudice, and other factors that affect how we develop and use leadership talent. These difficult issues are all too often omitted in the dialogue of change agents. We must confront these issues squarely in the new era.

Ed Oakley
is co-author of *Enlightened Leadership: Getting to the Heart of Change.* He has significantly impacted the personal and professional lives of thousands of people and the success of scores of organizations. His quest to bring out the best in people began in 1975 when he became a manager at Hewlett Packard. His success in the rapidly changing environment of this leading high tech firm was due to a unique blend of managerial skills and insight into human behavior.

He co-founded Enlightened Leadership International, Inc. in 1987, inspired by the common quest he and his partner Doug Krug shared to bring out the best in people. The company is dedicated to helping people align their hearts, their spirits and their dreams and to take action in a way that creates an organization where there is joy in the work and satisfaction in the accomplishment.

His essay was co-authored with Doug Krug and is based upon their book which is published by Simon & Schuster.

5

An Adventure in Enlightened Leadership

Ed Oakley

Whether adventure means climbing mountains or striving to attain peak performance in an organization, enlightened leaders are dedicated to bringing out the best in others. They prepare team members for shared leadership so that others can play a role when the way becomes too treacherous, too complicated or too much for just one leader to handle.

In business we are literally climbing mountains every day of our lives. But on a recent hike through the rugged Canyonlands of Utah, I knew I wasn't at the office. Fear of failure takes on a whole new meaning when you're confronted with challenges that put your life at risk. This adventure helped me learn a lot about myself. And it helped me learn a lot about leadership.

Back in the safety of my office, I was struck by the significance of what I had experienced, especially as it relates to our company's mission, which is "to bring out the best in organizations by helping to bring out the best in their people." Three points came to mind. First, it is neither fair nor realistic to believe that one person can be prepared to lead in every situation the team faces. Second, leaders emerge naturally as specific situations demand skills and attitudes that are inherent in them, as long as there is encouragement and freedom to do so. And third, we must create an environment that brings out the best in people, thus encouraging them to develop their natural leadership talents.

When focusing on these points, I realized that a team of hikers has many similarities with a team of workers. I'd like to share with you some of the insights I had during our hike in the rugged wilderness of Utah and how they apply to the rugged world of business.

No One Leader Can be Expected to Lead in Every Situation

I was leading the group on a trail that was getting smaller and smaller when suddenly I found us facing a very narrow ledge cut into the canyon, fifty feet above a chasm of rugged rocks. I was paralyzed with fear at the prospect of having to walk that ledge! I certainly would have turned back if that was an option. But it was getting late in the day and we had gone too far to return the way we had come without the provisions and gear it would have taken to spend the night outdoors. At this moment, given this specific situation, I was too afraid to provide any leadership whatsoever.

Just as I experienced a limit to my leadership capabilities on the hike, organizational leaders can find themselves in a situation where their skills and confidence level do not provide for the best leadership. This may be more common now because organizations require levels of expertise beyond anything they have previously known. The good news is that the solutions to virtually any challenge the organization faces can be met with the expertise that already exists within its people. By supporting others in the development of their natural leadership abilities, "the enlightened leader" prepares the organization to meet all of its challenges.

In traditional management, leadership was a matter of positional authority. The person with the highest rank was in charge and every one else was expected to do as he or she dictated. But that view has changed. In the chaotic, dynamic, changing environment we find ourselves in, it just doesn't work. Every one of us has the opportunity and, perhaps, the responsibility to be a leader, regardless of our positional authority. We assume leadership positions every day in our professional and personal lives. The questions to ask are: what kind of leadership are we providing and who is best suited to lead in a particular situation?

An enlightened leader is someone who is so clear that the power and effectiveness of an organization lies within its people that he or she is dedicated to bringing out the very best in them. This means knowing when to lead and when to follow someone you have helped prepare to be a leader. Just as my hiking group enjoyed a rotation of leaders as it climbed through the canyons, today's organizations thrive on shared leadership and collaborative style decision-making.

Leadership Naturally Emerges When Encouraged to Do So

Only one of the people in our group had taken this trail before. So, we initially relied on him to be our guide. It was interesting to see how the groups leadership evolved as the hike progressed and we encountered different situations.

Every person in the group was very aware of and attuned to everyone else, just like the members of a well functioning team are in sync with each other in a business organization. As hikers, we each noticed who performed well in which situations, who needed help where and how endurance fluctuated from person to person. As people gained confidence and felt comfortable with the various phases of the trip—hiking that led to climbing that led to vertical descents and so on—different people opted to lead the group.

When it became apparent that I wasn't going to lead the group across that narrow canyon ledge, it was obviously time for a new leader.

A man who was near the back of the hiking group lowered himself over the trail's edge on our left and managed to work himself to the front of the line. He did this by hugging the cliff and feeling for handholds and footholds. A new leader had emerged!

The man had not demonstrated this kind of skill and confidence earlier in the day and so I had not known that he possessed it. But, throughout the day and through other experiences in his life, he had been preparing himself for a moment such as this. When his particular skills were needed by the team, and he was emotionally ready, he rose naturally to the leadership role to serve us.

There were others in the group who shared my fear about crossing the ledge and we turned to our new leader for help. He rallied our confidence and offered the kind of guidance that enabled each of us to find the courage to traverse the ledge.

Whenever a person chose to lead, as in this case, based on their confidence and desire to be first in the discovery of new territory, the rest of the group naturally recognized its appropriateness and willingly followed. We all benefited from shared leadership because the person who led served as an effective trail blazer—and their enthusiasm for the trail was so infectious that we all had fun!

In a business environment, people experience a similar desire to lead when they are feeling empowered. By inspiring a team to discover its own best answers and entrusting members with the responsibility to consistently work at peak performance, individuals are prepared to lead when the need arises.

Create an Environment that Brings Out the Best in Everyone

During another part of the hike, I was the first person to descend a particularly steep rock chute. Having gotten down with much less trouble than expected, I wanted to tell those who came after me how to do it. The next couple of people responded well enough to my direction, but when a woman who had been struggling with easier situations froze at the top of the chute, I became impatient.

"Come on," I said, "just follow my instructions."

"Wait a minute," the woman replied. "I need to look this over for myself!"

I waited and watched in amazement as the woman took an entirely different route than the one I had prescribed. She easily reached the bottom in less than a minute, beaming with pride and confidence at having navigated her own path.

I thought about this for a few moments, recalling times in the past that I had wanted to do something my way while being forced to do it according to my boss' instructions. These experiences had been very disempowering for me and had limited my energy, minimized my enthusiasm and kept me from doing my best work. So I took this opportunity to refrain from *telling* people how to come down the incline. For those who followed, I performed the role of coach, pointing out some of the options for handholds and footholds that people who had gone before them had discovered. Each climber took a somewhat different route and descended with a sense of personal accomplishment at having mastered this part of the descent themselves.

What a lesson I experienced: helping people find their own way is far more effective than telling people which way to go! This was certainly not the first time I had become aware of the fact that people want to do things their own way. But this real-life situation was such a powerful example of how people want to exercise personal control that it was like waking up to the concept for the first time.

Thinking back on this trip into Utah has helped me to be more centered in the work I do with organizations in the business world. It has renewed my appreciation for the fact that an enlightened leader not only helps to bring out the best in people, he or she must know when to stand aside to allow those people to exercise the skills they have been developing.

People resist being told what to do, but readily commit to their own ideas. Understanding this, enlightened leaders let go of their ego-driven need to have all the answers and allow people to implement *their own* ideas in accordance with a shared vision. To help people access those ideas, utilize "effective questions," that create a nurturing and supportive environment in which team members learn to fulfill their responsibilities with minimal direction.

Enlightened leaders know when to guide and when to let others go their own way.

As the first one down a particular path, an enlightened leader assesses the challenges that his or her team will soon encounter. Based on these experiences, he or she can *coach* those who follow in what they judge to be the most effective route to a given destination. But judgment is very personal. The best route for the leader will not necessarily be the best route for every individual on the team. To be truly effective, the leader acts as a role model but does not insist that the empowered members of the team do things exactly his or her way. That would defeat the value of empowerment.

It is the responsibility of enlightened leaders to create an inspirational environment that is conducive to the development of every person's natural leadership skills, an environment that enables people to find their own best answers. By presenting a larger perspective of a challenge and providing more questions than answers for meeting it, enlightened leaders encourage others to discover the solution that best suits their talents: *to find their own best way down the mountain.*

Climbing Mountains Every Day

The image that my co-author, Doug Krug, and I chose for the dust jacket of our book, *Enlightened Leadership: Getting to the Heart of Change*, is of two mountain climbers silhouetted before a bright sun. The climber at the peak is reaching down to help the person below him. While we do not have any particular fascination with climbing itself, this image is truly an inspirational one for us. There seems to be a spiritual link between people who endeavor to climb a majestic peak and those who endeavor to renew an organization. The practical approaches to personal and professional development that we present, and the forward-focused roles we describe for the leader in all of us, are equally applicable to people in a multi-billion dollar corporation and climbers on a mountain.

In the steep and rocky world of global competition which has become common for many organizations, we can no longer expect just one person to be able to provide the best leadership in every situation. The routes to success are too difficult to find and even more difficult to follow. They take us to unexpected cliffs where a fear of heights can stall a climb, and down into valleys where the endless terrain steals time and energy needed for the achievement of our lofty goal. We need a team of empowered trailblazers so that *someone* is always prepared to carefully guide us over the peaks and quickly through the valleys.

Whether hiking a trail or implementing a quality improvement process, enlightened leadership creates an environment that brings out the natural leadership abilities of everyone. It creates open and trusting relationships. It creates inter-dependence between team members based on people's strengths. It creates supportive relationships to compensate for members' weaknesses. It enables a team to conquer a mountain or master monumental change. Helping every team member access the expertise within them provides the enlightened leader with powerful answers to a question that is common to every person, on or off a mountain: how do we achieve our challenging objectives?

Peter K. Krembs
has been an independent human
resource development specialist
since 1982. He did his graduate
work in communication and industrial psychology at the University of
Minnesota. He was an Organization Development Specialist at Honeywell
and later Vice President and partner at McLagan International, a Twin
Cities-based human resource development consulting firm.

He has specialized in consulting to technical organizations and has
designed and taught special leadership development seminars for technical managers at Bell Labs, Cray Research, Digital Equipment Corporation,
and Hewlett-Packard Company. He has also developed programs for
information systems departments at IDS, GE, and General Mills.

He serves on the faculty of GE's Leadership Development Course for
GE businesses in Europe, Asia, and the United States. Krembs is the author
of The Technical Manager, a video-based training program published by
Addison-Wesley, and co-author of On the Level, a book for managers on
performance feedback skills.

6

Leadership Challenges in Technical Organizations

Peter K. Krembs

The general manager of a four-thousand employee research and development organization examined the results of a feedback survey from his team of direct report managers. The comments indicated that this manager, a PhD chemist with a string of patents to his credit and over 28 years with the company, was too involved in details in the laboratory and was not spending enough time leading the organization.

"I get involved in projects where I have something to add. Wouldn't it be a tragic loss to withhold my expertise? Should I let my experience go to waste?" the chemist lamented.

"It all depends on where and how you want to make a contribution," a friend told him. "The organization needs leadership as well as technical experts."

He shook his head in disappointment. He didn't understand why his management team didn't see things the way he did. Further attempts to help him understand the cost of his lack of availability to address business strategy or to forge a vision for the company were unsuccessful.

This story is all too familiar. A brilliant engineer whose ideas give birth to a new venture is thrust unwillingly into the role of leading other talented people attracted to the growing enterprise. The result is a person who is unaware that his or her heavy involvement in details may be robbing other technical professionals of their opportunity to invent. Ultimately, this often generates organization-wide fear that no one is at the helm of the ship. In large, well established organizations, many of the best and brightest who get promoted because they have strong technical credibility, or because they have the most experience, are frustrated with the transition to a leadership role. They want to retreat to the familiar, concrete, individual specialty work they do so well, and make leading and managing a "lower left hand drawer" responsibility to be attended to only when absolutely necessary.

When there are many layers of management in an organization, a project leader or a first level technical manager might be able to operate more as a technical expert and let a higher level manager integrate and lead the larger group. This is fast becoming a moot strategy, however. Organization restructuring and downsizing is paring away the redundancy of management roles, increasing the vulnerability of an organization to a leadership gap.

The Downside of the Dual Path Approach

The argument is often made that some technical people should be left to do what they do best and shouldn't be pushed into roles with management or leadership responsibility. Many technically-driven organizations have implemented a "dual career path" concept based on this reasoning. The idea is to let technical people follow a succession of increasingly challenging technical assignments, and encourage people who have both the interest and skill in leading people or managing work to pursue a management career track.

While it makes good sense to refrain from pushing people into jobs they are neither prepared for nor want, saying that there is a dual career path in an organization propagates a dangerous myth about the nature of work in an organization. It suggests that the world is made up of two kinds of jobs: technical and managerial. The truth is that effective managers and leaders need to be technically involved enough to be able to integrate work and set credible priorities. They need to have sufficient technical knowledge to know how to ask the right questions and to have the technical people on the work team respect their feedback and judgment. What is equally true is that technical specialists may be able to avoid the title of manager, but they cannot escape the fact that, as they become more experienced and involved in significant projects, leadership and teamwork skills are necessary in order to shape the endeavor and produce results.

Describing work as *either* technical *or* managerial spawns an "us vs. them" mentality. The inevitable outcome of such a split is that people in each of these two categories will see themselves as somehow superior or more important than the people in the other category. This pattern can end up wasting precious time and energy which could be put to much better use.

The direction of organizational change has made the technical vs. management dichotomy anachronistic. The emphasis is shifting from organizing around vertical silos of functional expertise and moving toward much flatter organization structures which focus on lateral work relationships. This means that jobs are not so distinctly separated. It is not possible to sit in a purely technical role while the functional manager provides a buffer or "air cover." Technical specialists must be influential project team members. Managers cannot afford to be too far from the details because of the speed with which the work team configuration needs to change. As organization boundaries become more permeable, so are the boundaries which define a job.

There will always be a few technical "guru" jobs in which the scientist or the inventor will be able to work in a focused and uninterrupted environment. Many of the technical and professional people who were attracted to jobs which provided independence and focus, however, may need to make some significant adjustments in the way they look at their jobs. Working in an organization which plans to operate in a seamless way with people providing leadership based on different areas of expertise at different times means that technical professionals need to be able to balance their energy between technical work and the responsibilities they have to reach out and influence others.

Independence and Focus

Having a technical or professional specialty does not mean that a person is necessarily a loner who dislikes collaborating with others. There are many examples of teamwork and effective leadership practiced by people who consider themselves technical specialists or professionals. At the same time, there are also many people who have pursued their professional development over many years with a strong belief that their value and ability to make a contribution is dependent almost entirely on their unique knowledge and skill in an area of expertise. It is this frame of mind which sets up a need to be recognized for individual rather than group achievements and to be attracted to jobs which provide independent responsibility.

Ed is a man in his early sixties who recently retired from a 39-year career at a large defense contracting firm. A new neighbor asked him what he did when he worked there, and Ed replied that he was an engineer. The neighbor continued the interview and eventually discovered that before Ed retired he was the vice president of a sizable engineering department with several layers of managers reporting to him. It had probably been a good 25 years since Ed had actually done any engineering work by himself, yet he chose to identify himself as an engineer. Perhaps this incident only reflects Ed's need for a convenient label in social situations. On the other hand, it could be an artifact of how he saw himself and what was most important to him about his accomplishments.

The degree to which a technical or professional person is motivated by the need for individual achievement determines the difficulty of the transition to becoming a leader in a seamless organization. David McClelland and his many colleagues have provided a useful framework for understanding individual achievement thinking. Consider the following messages the high achiever might give to him or herself:

Strive to be the very best at what you do.

The desire to stand out as better than others automatically sets up a competitive rather than a collaborative inclination. The high achiever is always wondering if he or she is good enough to be the best, and the only measuring stick available is to compare oneself to others who are considered to be at the top of their areas of specialty. The need to excel, not merely do well, drives the need to constantly compare and determine how to be better.

Always hold yourself accountable to your own
high standards of excellence.

High achievers are typically much harder on themselves than others are when it comes to judging their accomplishments. From the point of view of the achievement-motivated person, you can never be best if you do not hold yourself accountable to higher standards. A student who receives a 95% score on a test may be congratulated for achieving the highest score in the class but might still be disappointed to have missed the 5% and shrug off the compliment. The belief that one's standards have to be higher drives a person to work harder and learn more. It also sets up a foundation for negative judgments of others who, in the view of the high achiever, have settled for mediocrity.

Seek to be individually creative and inventive.

One path to being the best is to do something no one else has done. The insight and unique combination of skill required to create or invent provides an opportunity for individual recognition and proof that a person has excelled far beyond the norm. Doing the creating or inventing alone, however, is an important part of the integrity of the honor. It is this part of the process which can lead to individual ownership and hoarding of ideas. The fear of the individual achiever is that working collaboratively means you can never fully test your own abilities.

What is paradoxical about this is that individual achievement motivation can be the cornerstone of successful breakthroughs, but at the same time become a wedge that frustrates team effort and overall organization success. Our culture has always valued individual excellence, initiative, and the desire to blaze one's own trail. It is important that while we recognize the value of this perspective, it is also the cause of some people having a difficult time working on a team and ultimately leading others. It explains why some people who move into leadership roles become competitors, rather than mentors, of the people who work with them.

A case in point is a management team in a 400-person medical laboratory facility. Each manager has had many years experience in the lab and some are known nationally for their work. Within each technical department, the managers operate as the top technical people who work on the most challenging problems, even though there are competent researchers and highly specialized and experienced lab technicians in every area. The management group reluctantly goes to weekly staff meetings, although several of the managers sit through the meetings in silent protest. Meanwhile, costly mistakes are being made because departments do not inform each other of decisions made within one area which affects another area as the work is passed from one function to another. A hiring freeze in the face of increasing work load caused the director to ask managers to share resources, and the managers tried to develop a plan. The ensuing conflicts resulted in several of the managers not speaking to one another. The work of this organization is directly responsible for saving lives on a daily basis. How could this happen in a professional organization which has such a compelling common vision? Apparently the need to protect one's domain of expertise and retain the right to make autonomous decisions was seen by some as being more important than the overall goals of the lab.

It is important to value individual excellence, high standards, and inventiveness. It is important to appreciate that many people have a strong need for individual achievement. The adjustment which is required has to do with noticing when being best, having high standards, and being inventive needs to shift from being an individual goal and become a team or organization goal. It will take leadership at every level in an organization to help people see that need and to keep people aware of it as they do their work.

The Changing Landscape

The vision of what organizations will be like in the future based on today's trends would have been considered ridiculous only a decade ago. The "virtual" organization, based on the analogy to virtual reality technology, paints a vision in which people no longer draw organization charts. Structure is viewed as illusory. Individuals bring their expertise and experience to a kaleidoscope of changing work teams formed and then dispersed when customer needs are identified and then resolved. There is no distinction between an internal and an external customer, because even that boundary is blurred. People move into leadership roles or share leadership responsibility because it makes sense on the project to be completed, not because they have a title which ordains some permanent right to lead.

Most organizations today still have traditional structures, but the emphasis on flattening organizations and making functional boundaries more porous is definitely the trend. It used to be typical for researchers, design engineers, and manufacturing engineers in a company to work on ideas and turn them into products by sequentially having each group work on "their" part. Communication was most often directed hierarchically, requiring more energy to be focused on going up and down ladders than on the interdependencies among peer experts working on the product.

Today this way of doing business seems absurd. Most large companies have committed to forming cross-functional product teams early in the development cycle, integrating technical design and development experts with those who understand the customer needs and those who know best how to efficiently manufacture the product. This way of working helps a group avoid many of the financial, time and quality costs of addressing requirements late in the product development cycle which could have been factored into the original design.

The ideas for "re-engineering" organizations to work faster and more efficiently are indeed forming wonderful visions. The gap between the concept and the reality, however, sometimes leaves something to be desired. If you happen to be a design engineer who likes being able to develop his or her own best technical ideas, for example, having people from other areas of expertise tell you what they think should be done can appear to the engineer to threaten autonomy and freedom to create. The time required to resolve differences among product team members can be viewed as draining precious energy needed for individual progress on idea generation, technical problem solving or individual task completion. Where is the time to deepen one's expertise if most of the day is spent trying to understand what other's think? From the viewpoint of the technical specialist, the trends in the way organizations work is a vision turned to a nightmare.

Consider Susan, a materials scientist who, after working in a research lab for only two years, came up with a discovery which has great commercial promise. In the old days, the lab manager would have been the liaison to see that the idea was moved into a product development stage. That old structure is gone now, and Susan has been asked to head up a new product development team.

On the one hand, leading the team provides an opportunity to keep an eye on her idea. It gives her the chance to help determine how it is applied in company products. It is also recognition of the importance and quality of her work. Susan becomes ambivalent, however, when she realizes that being a technical expert and leading a product development team are two very different jobs. The role of materials scientist is familiar territory she currently spends fifty to sixty hours a week doing. Being a leader is an unclear responsibility with unpredictable expectations.

She has talked to others who have taken on this kind of responsibility and they describe fragmented days, high stress, and frustration with people pushing for what they want from all directions. The biggest concern of all, however, is the feeling Susan has that she will lose her edge as a scientist as she pulls away from the time she gets to spend in the lab. For her, this is the moment of greatest need for some constructive support and guidance. An *either* technical *or* leadership set of choices is neither helpful nor indicative of what the organization needs. What would help Susan and the organization is a way of seeing how she can balance her expertise with leadership responsibility.

People like Susan, motivated by the need for individual achievement and the desire to pursue technical or professional depth in a special niche of expertise may be disturbed by the changing landscape of organization structure. The people already in leadership roles have a stake in figuring out how to help specialists with important expertise reframe how they see the prospect of acquiring leadership responsibility and prepare for it.

Facing the Challenge

Susan's story has a postscript. She decided to accept the role of product team leader. The experience was not as frustrating as she thought it would be. Yes, there have been some fragmented days, but there have also been days where breakthroughs have resulted from the hard work of the team. Although she had to cut back her time in the lab, she has the option of returning to more focused research once the product team's efforts wind down. The biggest surprise of the experience is that the new perspective she has gained from this experience has given her some new ideas she wants to work on in the lab.

If organizations are going to truly be transformed into much flatter, seamless organizations, then each person who works in such an organization will have to change how he or she thinks about a job. People need to learn how to help each other form and reform their roles as they go about their work.

One of the challenges is to choose not to see individual achievement interest and technical or professional expertise in opposition to what it takes to be an effective leader. Perhaps this picture of the effective technical expert or professional person having both the inner drive to excel and the desire to focus outward to integrate and influence is an image which needs to be planted in school and throughout technical/professional course work in advanced areas of study. How we teach people to see their contributions in the world forms the expectations students have as they leave their formal education and take up responsibilities in their work and personal lives. The shift in the message would be from "be the best that you can be and do what you do better than anyone else" to "be the best you can be and integrate your expertise with others who have different pieces of the larger puzzles we must solve together." It has to be more than what the professor says. This shift in philosophy has to be reflected in how students are presented with problems and how they are evaluated in their response to those problems.

Students leave professional and technical degree programs today having the idea that when they walk into their first job, someone will hand them an already structured problem which has been tailored to their expertise, and that there is an answer they can find on their own that will be the right answer and which will earn them an "A." The reality is quite different. Work problems are totally unstructured. As technically-driven organizations take on increasingly complex problems, they cannot be structured without the integrated contributions of technical design experts, financial analysts, manufacturing expertise, and the point of view of the customer. Furthermore, there are almost always several solutions with pros and cons, none of which is perfect. That means that each person needs to be able to explore each option and debate the implications in order for the optimum solution to be formulated and selected.

If students do not get the message during their formal training, then it is up to organizations to help technical and professional entry level employees see that, along with the expectation that they will use and develop their individual expertise, they will also be expected to influence the integration of effort of people with diversity of expertise and viewpoint. Individual execution is important. But in most organizations that is the only performance expectation of new technical and professional employees. It is still the primary aspect of performance that gets measured and rewarded. Instead of giving the impression that there is only one category of expected performance, that of individual execution of task, entry level employees could be told that there are three areas or categories of expected performance: Individual execution (what you do by yourself), how you structure problems and integrate the contributions of others in the process of achieving results (work management), and how you are able to communicate about the bigger picture and motivate others in relation to the result to be achieved (leadership).

Once the idea that even an entry level technical specialist is responsible for contributing to the leadership of effort in an organization, the second challenge is to provide a meaningful referent for the idea of leadership at that level. When people talk about leadership in an organization, there are two interesting phenomena which contribute to confusion over the concept. First, people usually provide a different slant to the definition of leadership, depending on what they see as the salient value called for in the situation at hand. Second, when they want to illustrate what good leadership looks like, they tend to give an example of what one person does, which leaves the impression that one person leads and others follow.

Defining Leadership

When morale is low, an effective leader is defined as someone who can inspire. When the organization is at cross-roads, a leader is defined as someone who makes tough decisions. When the competition has just come out with your product a year before you have, then the effective leader is the person who inspires risk taking in order to achieve break-neck speed. It seems that the concept of leadership becomes a giant projection screen for people to play out whatever they are most worried about at the moment, and the message is that we need one person to embody this concern to lead us.

This way of talking about leadership is very confusing, making it difficult for the individual to translate the message into something they should consistently strive to do. Furthermore, it plays into the idea that leadership is a separate function someone does to others, rather than supporting the view that leadership is a systems issue which many people have a part in making happen.

An alternative way to talk about leadership is to suggest that there are a couple of things people do whenever they work together which contributes to a team experiencing leadership. One of those things is the ability and willingness of each member of the team to look at the big picture as well as the details. Another thing is the ability and willingness to seek and emphasize the common ground or common stake people have in achieving a result as they go about the challenging process of naming and resolving differences. Rather than one person being responsible for leading others, why not try to have everyone responsible for being both individual contributors as well as contributors to the leadership of the teams they are working in? It is harder to get people to frame leadership in this way because it runs counter to how we talk about the concept of leadership.

The final challenge is to help people learn not just the skills associated with doing work, managing, and leading, but also the "meta-skills" of learning how to balance these areas of focus and shifting gears among these three types of contributions. This requires the ability to step out of one's job and look at what is called for rather than plowing ahead with a single-minded view of the situation. When a person can't help lead a group because he or she is simply too wrapped up in details, the awareness of what is going on helps others explicitly acknowledge what is happening. The person focusing on details can then consciously support and rely on the leadership skills of others in the group to help the team achieve overall results.

As with any discussion of the need for change, the description of what to do about the challenges presented is easier said than done. Rather than getting concerned about specific action steps, perhaps the most powerful thing to do is to start with how these ideas—being a technical expert and contributing to the leadership of a team, or ultimately an organization—are framed together. Instead of mutually exclusive ways of being, the challenge for each of us is to see these types of contributions as integrated. The more inseparably these notions are talked about, the more realistic it will become to think of technical expertise and effective leadership being a natural rather than unusual combination.

Charles F. Kiefer
is founder and chairman of Innovation Associates, Inc., a consulting
and training firm specializing in
enabling organizations to proactively create their futures. He has helped
clients improve their organizational effectiveness with new approaches to
high performance, learning, and creating. His recent clients include
Gillette, Inland Steel, Procter & Gamble, Sematech, and Norwest Bank.

Kiefer co-created the Leadership & Mastery program with Peter
Senge and Robert Fritz, which has become one of the leading senior
executive leadership training programs in the United States. A graduate of
Massachusetts Institute of Technology in physics and management, Kiefer
had held administrative and research positions at MIT and, in addition, he
was on the administrative staff of the United States Senate. He has lectured
widely and has been featured in articles in *Fortune, Industry Week,* and
numerous industry and trade journals.

This essay is an adaptation of an article written for *The Fifth Discipline
Fieldbook*, published earlier this year by Doubleday/Currency.

7

Executive Team Leadership

Charles F. Kiefer

Over the past fifteen years, organizations have become more interested in encouraging high-quality teamwork. Many organizations are making a significant shift at their most senior levels. Despite the focus by the press and Wall Street on the personality of the heroic CEO, these organizations are moving away from the "great individual" model of leadership, and moving towards being led by a *team* of executives instead. This new leadership is sometimes formalized in structures such as "Office of the President" or "Office of the Chief Executive." The "office," in actuality, is a decision-making team of four to nine people. At General Electric, for example, the hub of the company is Jack Welch's "Office of the CEO," consisting of Welch and his three top vice-chairmen. Similar structures have been employed at Electronic Data Systems, Dayton-Hudson, and Polaroid, to name just a few.

Even when an executive team is not formalized in this manner, the individual sitting at the top of the pyramid is rarely the sole leader. Rather, we see a group of people with shared responsibilities and clear accountabilities strategizing together, reaching decisions by consensus, coordinating implementation, and generally performing many, if not all, of the functions previously performed by a Chief Operating Officer. Through this "executive team leadership," these organizations are seeking ways of realizing *all* the talent and intelligence of the most senior people.

There are at least two good reasons why executive team leadership is on the rise. First, the problems our organizations face today are enormously complex and typically have significant political ramifications within the company. The most difficult issues that an executive team faces are often cross-disciplinary or cross-functional. They require a deep expertise in specific areas, complemented by insight into the interrelationships between functions. Issues that confront the "group" or corporate executive team can be even more perplexing. Few, if any, individuals have the intelligence and breadth of experience to deal with this kind of complexity on their own. Yet, it must be dealt with. Consequently, major breakthroughs in team and organizational intelligence are required.

Second, within the past decade there has been a "sea change" in the management of organizations. Managers, reconceiving their own jobs as setting forth broad visions and strategies, now grant subordinates much more power to plan and implement. In such a culture, commands from the top, even from charismatic leaders (who are increasingly difficult to find) may be complied with, but ultimately undermine initiative and commitment. In organizations led by influence, people are convinced and moved when they see a group of people at the top truly sharing a vision and strategy, modeling it in their behavior. When executive commitment and congruency are absent, organizational confidence and commitment are diminished.

Creating a competent, learning-oriented executive team is a new field in management—and a demanding one. It may be a discipline in its own right. Collective leadership is as different from individual leadership as collective learning is from individual learning. Mastering team leadership means mastering a larger and more complex learning agenda, often under more difficult circumstances than any other team in the organization.

The Executive Team Learning Agenda

The executive team must, for example, become good at the core issues that any team needs to master. A short list includes:

gaining alignment around a shared vision, developing the ability to run meetings well, holding unbiased and truthful discussions, setting clear goals, clarifying roles and accountabilities, and capturing and accessing collective knowledge. This generic agenda is challenging. How do you develop the ability to think collectively and raise the Team IQ? There is incredible potential for a team player who can hold markedly different individual points of view and yet talk coherently about them. This potential is acute in the case of executive teams where there is much individual intelligence and experience among the membership. The ability to dialogue openly and truthfully holds wondrous promise. Unfortunately, divergent points of view show up too often, manifesting in tensions and unspoken conflicts. Handling these tensions and conflicts constructively must be mastered or the team's potential is never realized.

The executive team's learning agenda is much broader and includes the development of skills and capabilities that members may not have needed until now in their careers. The agenda is unfamiliar to many managers on the team, since their previous teams required fewer, if any, of these skills. Thus, most executives have had little opportunity to develop them. Nonetheless, each of the elements is significant, and each will require some deliberate work, both among the members of your executive team, and with the people who will eventually become your successors.

Here is the agenda for the executive team:

The Executive Team's Agenda
- Building Shared Vision
- Organizational Assessment
- Strategy Formulation
- Organizational Strategy
- Guiding Organizational Change

Building Shared Vision. While any team must develop its own vision, the executive team must develop shared intent across and within the whole organization. Broad commitment to a new future takes time and generally requires a lot of attention and work. All too often, executive teams return from a three-day "visioning" offsite and proudly disseminate their work to the organization in what resembles a PR campaign. At best, they end up settling for the compliance such a process engenders rather than the true commitment that otherwise might be available. However, to obtain real commitment, a process that is based on involvement and choice is essential; you cannot achieve commitment through a fundamentally coercive process, no matter how well-intentioned. Involvement requires more than one-way communication; choice requires attention to the individual.

Organizational Assessment. Perhaps one of the most difficult tasks for an executive team is to know what is going on within their organization with high accuracy. The information gathering mechanisms we live with today seem to have evolved in ways such that the top of the system has a limited, incomplete, and even biased understanding of reality. You must develop methods that surface and rectify these mechanisms so that, for example, bad news is as likely to come to your attention as good. Face-to-face, two-way communication must be developed deep in the organization, and a norm must be established of responsibly surfacing and naming the truth as completely as possible.

Strategy Formulation. "Strategy as a team learning activity" stands in stark contrast to "strategy developed by experts," even when done collaboratively. The best strategy formulation reconceives the firm and its environment in line with the construction of new mental models, and new organization intelligence. It is often associated with a new organizational "language" that is more consistent with the new strategy. The promise of a learning approach to strategy is a more accurate, more robust view of the future, but it will require that everyone on your team (and many other key individuals) actually think about life differently. A great example of this kind of strategy is the invention of brand management by Procter & Gamble. It completely reconstructed the manner in which consumer non-durable manufacturers did business.

Beyond the formulation of strategy, the bulk of learning may occur in strategy verification—probing and testing the strategy for internal inconsistencies, running pilot experiments in the marketplace, and computer-modeling strategic elements. As new mental models are formed and new language is created to convey those models, the core team and organizational thinking processes evolve and become more robust. Organizational intelligence flourishes. It is here that the emerging field of systemic thinking "struts its stuff." How do the various elements of the strategy actually interrelate? Does the strategy have an inherent integrity and internal consistency? Or do actions taken in favor of some elements have counterproductive and unintended consequences on other elements?

Organizational Strategy

In the course of strategy formulation and verification, the organizational side is often shortchanged. The all too frequent implicit assumption is that once the new strategy is formed, the organization will effortlessly reconfigure itself and succeed. This is never the case. Many brilliant new strategies flounder in implementation because the organization simply configured inaccurately to accomplish that strategy. The obvious "restructuring" that often accompanies a new strategy fails to address the deeper elements that govern strategic success. Often organizational habits and culture are "wrong" for the new strategy. Reward and information systems, recruiting systems, performance standards, and appraisal systems may all have to be radically altered. Thus, the executive team must address and clearly answer the question: What characteristics of an organization will be necessary to accomplish our new business strategy? In short, the team must become competent at organization design beyond moving the boxes around.

Guiding Organization Change

At this point, the executive team is only beginning. You must now master managing organization change—design, structure and implementation. What is an economical and reliable path for the organization to move from where it is to that new state? As mentioned before, this must be accomplished through methods that get the entire organization engaged and committed, both in favor of the shared vision and in a rigorous search for the truth. Often, a significant amount of individual development is required on the part of everyone in the organization. Many people in contemporary organizations are not accustomed to being asked for their genuine commitment. They even may find it threatening. Yet on the other side of this threat, which can and must be vanquished, lies enormous power and individual satisfaction. Aiding others in making that personal transition and guiding that process for the organization as a whole is formidable and rewarding.

Unique Learning Problems of the Executive Team

Your executive team will also have its own unique difficulties in learning. First, for the executive team member, life is more a "zero sum game" than ever before. Earlier in the executive's career, on teams lower in the organization, he or she could get ahead without necessarily "winning" at the expense of another team member. Generally, this is not true for the executive team. One person getting ahead often means another getting left behind, a phenomenon particularly evident around the issue of succession. Lip service to collaboration notwithstanding, this is a very real dynamic on many executive teams.

Second, on the executive team there is generally no appellate court—no tie breaker or higher court of last resort. In most other teams in the organization, if an individual finds himself in conflict with the boss or the team becomes caught in dysfunctional conflict, the team leader's boss can provide a third party perspective. Few boards, if any, do this for the CEO. Or said another way, the person looking over the CEO's shoulder does not function at all like the CEO might when looking over the shoulder of one of his or her vice presidents. The CEO or executive team leader, who should never be impartial, makes the final decision with little recourse for the subordinate, and everyone knows it!

Third, the makeup of the executive team, in-and-of-itself, is a challenge. Typically, executive teams are populated by aggressive "movers" who are used to getting what they want and getting things done. "Group maintenance" skills may be less developed, ironically, than they are elsewhere in the organization. Such skills are typically much less rewarded on executive teams.

Finally, if you are a typical executive team, you operate in an environment that is particularly unforgiving. The organization still longs for heroic leadership, an often deeply ingrained desire that is devilishly hard to be rid of. People are intolerant when executives make mistakes, or when the executives fall short of their efforts to model teamwork, however sincere and well-conceived those efforts may be. Though they are undesired vestiges of an earlier culture, these habits, nevertheless, are still ingrained. When mistakes are made at your level, subordinates can be particularly quick and ruthless in following the all-too-human habit of seeking to place blame.

Taken all together, these circumstances offer a daunting challenge that many teams cannot meet. Sadly, the ultimate shortcoming is often in the team's interpersonal dynamics, which are frequently disastrously bad, and many times mirror those of dysfunctional families. Failing to surmount these difficulties, the team is blocked and its potential unrealized. The resulting blocked condition is generally much worse for the enterprise than if the group were to abandon becoming a "learning team" and instead operate in the former rigid, hierarchical, and non-collaborative style.

Team Learning Agenda

How do you take the first step and design a team learning agenda? Here are some suggestions about how you might proceed:

- Have a heart-to-heart talk within the team about what you sincerely want, both in terms of business results and how you want to work together. Don't settle for stock answers from each other. Talk about what is really important to you.

- Next, have an open and honest discussion about the current reality you now face relative to those aspirations. Don't limit yourself to the problems; be sure to include the good things too! Pay careful attention to what you can and *can't* discuss. Are there "undiscussables?" Can you be fully truthful? If not, can you be truthful about the fact that it is difficult to be truthful? Then, think about a plan to get from where you are to where you want to be.

- Identify those areas in which there is a significant team knowledge or capacity deficit and create methods for learning in these areas. Look at your plan. Anything you don't know for certain how to accomplish is a candidate.

- Determine whether the team has an appetite and commitment for learning. If so, look for ways to reconstruct things that you are already doing to make them learning activities. Try to view problems, mistakes and shortfalls as moments with learning potential.

- Develop some behavioral pledges that you make together to keep yourselves on track.

It is difficult to establish new habits, particularly at the
executive level. As Tod White, the Chairman of Blessing/White,
once said to me about executive development and change: "It's
rare that a person holding four aces asks for a new deal."

At the very least, you should consider assigning a team
member to coach the team in regular reviews to keep yourself
honest on your progress. It may become necessary or desirable to
contract for these kind of services from a skilled outsider,
particularly if you encounter some difficulties in team dynamics.
Given the potential for total organization performance if the
executive team realizes its full potential, this is a justifiable
investment.

Like so many important things in organizational life, executive team learning is one area where another's prescription is of
little value. The executive team that learns together and truly
learns to lead, cannot be cloned or duplicated from some other
organization. Nor can it be adopted from a consultant's textbook.
It must be invented by the team itself.

PART TWO

The Leader's New Responsibility

Leading Change: The Leader as the Chief Transformation Officer
Warren Bennis

Natural Leadership™
Kate Steichen

A Sacred Responsibility
Barbara Shipka

Leading From Within: Taking a Leap of Faith
Tina Rasmussen

Gone are the days when leaders relied upon their titles or positions in the organizations for their "power over" their followers. Tomorrow's leaders are empowered from within themselves and must rely more upon the internal qualities of leadership than the external "cloak of office."

With this inner-directedness comes new responsibility for these leaders. New accountabilities are in store as these men and women step up to their new roles as leaders.

Four authors examine various aspects of this new responsibility. Distinguished author Warren Bennis (*Leaders* and *On Becoming a Leader*) sees the new role of organization leaders as chief transformation officers or "CTOs." Leadership and creativity consultant Kate Steichen demonstrates the importance of understanding our own true nature and the laws that govern it if one is to be authentic.

Organization consultant Barbara Shipka, co-author of *When the Canary Stops Singing: Women's Perspectives on Transforming*

Business, envisions the leader's new responsibility as "sacred"— encompassing a new consciousness. Corporate executive Tina Rasmussen directly addresses the inner-directed quality in her essay about "leading from within." Both Shipka and Rasmussen share stories from their own experience that richen and reinforce their ideas.

The new leader's new responsibility presents a significant challenge to all those who are currently in power—the challenge to be more accepting of uncertainty, to allow for paradox, and to accept true responsibility for the "whole"—the organization, its people, the stakeholders, and the community.

Warren Bennis,
University Professor and Distinguished Professor of Business Administration at the University of
Southern California, serves as the Chairman of the School's Leadership
Institute, founded in 1991. An expert on the process of change in
organizations, Bennis has conducted extensive research on leadership,
especially on the mystique surrounding superleaders and corporate
powers.

The author of 21 books, his most recent ones are *Learning to Lead:
A Workbook On Becoming a Leader* (with Joan Goldsmith), *An Invented
Life: Reflections on Leadership and Change, On Becoming a Leader*, and
Why Leaders Can't Lead. Bennis received the 1987 Dow Jones Award of
the American Assembly of Collegiate Schools of Business for outstanding
contributions to the field of collegiate education in business and management. He formerly served as president of the University of Cincinnati and
currently consults to numerous companies and governments. He received
his PhD from the Massachusetts Institute of Technology.

This essay was previously published in *USC Business* (Winter/
Spring, 1992) and served as the basis for the preface Bennis wrote for
Leaders on Leadership: Interviews with Top Executives.

8

Leading Change:
The Leader as the
Chief Transformation Officer

Warren Bennis

The sudden emergence of the United States as the world's largest debtor, Japan as the globe's richest creditor, and what had been the Soviet Union as its most ardent preacher of pacifism seems, to many Americans, to have turned the world upside down, raising doubts about whether America can—or should—continue to lead. *The Washington Post* cautions American readers to "Kiss Number One Goodbye, Folks."

Compounding the self-doubts experienced by many Americans is the accelerating rate and complexity of change taking place around us. The only truly predictable thing right now is unpredictability. The new chic is chaos chic. Yogi Berra had it right, in his oft-quoted remark, that "the future ain't what it used to be."

The world seems to have been transformed virtually overnight and appears ripe to change again by tomorrow morning.

Inevitably, such global change has had corporate repercussions. Many U.S. companies, for example, feel a sense of helplessness as they lose ground to new global competitors.

A Changing Game

If there is a reason to despair and join the doomsayers in hand-wringing and headshaking, it is because traditional American managers were brought up in a simpler time, when all they had to do was build the best mousetraps and the world beat a path to their doors. "Leadership in a traditional U.S. company," says R.B. Horton, CEO of British Petroleum America, "consisted of creating a management able to cope with competitors who all played with basically the same deck of economic cards." And it was an American game. The competition might have been fierce, but it was knowable. If you played your cards right, you could win.

But that game has changed—dramatically—and strange new rules have appeared. The deck has been shuffled and jokers added. Never before has American business faced so many challenges. Uncertainties and complexities abound.

Constant change disturbs managers. It always has and always will. Machiavelli's observation that "change has no constituency" still rings true. In his book, *Adhocracy: The Power to Change*, Bob Waterman tells us that most of us are like the characters in Ibsen's play *Ghosts*. "We're controlled by ideas and norms that have outlived their usefulness, that are only ghosts but have as much influence on our behavior as they would if they were alive. The ideas of men like Henry Ford, Frederick Taylor and Max Weber—these are the ghosts who haunt our halls of management."

Most of us grew up in organizations that were dominated by the thoughts and actions of the Fords, Taylors, and Webers, the fathers of the classic bureaucratic system. And bureaucracy was a splendid social invention in its time—the 19th Century. In his deathless (and deadly) prose, the German sociologist, Max Weber, first brought to the world's attention that the bureaucratic, machine model was ideal for harnessing the manpower and the resources of the Industrial Revolution. To this day, most organizations retain the macho, control-and-command mentality intrinsic to that increasingly thread-bare model. Indeed, it is possible to capture the mindset created by that obsolete paradigm in three simple words—*control, order, and predict,* or the acronym *COP.*

That mentality was manifested in what was to become a leadership model for a generation of corporate executives—the military. For most of today's senior executives, the military model of management observed while serving in World War II and the Korean conflict served as the guiding principle in how to perform in the corporate arena. It was the army pyramid, the hierarchy, lines of command and division of labor. It was "Rank has its privileges" and "It's lonely at the top."

But we are no longer facing the world of the 1950s, '60s, '70s, or even '80s. The workforce has changed and the world has changed. And while *Business Week* recently wrote about a new breed of "tough" bosses, I see just the opposite corporate leader emerging, one who differs substantially from the traditional dictatorial military commander of the past.

John Sculley, CEO of Apple, told me: "If you look at the post-World-War-II era, when we were at the center of the world's economy during the industrial age, organizations were very hierarchical. That model is no longer appropriate. The new model is global in scale, an interdependent network. So the new leader faces new tests, such as how does he lead people who don't report to him—people in other companies, in Japan or Europe, even competitors? How do you lead in this idea-intensive, interdependent-network environment? It requires a wholly different set of skills, based on ideas, people skills and values. A shift in orientation has occurred in just the last ten years. Traditional leaders are having a hard time explaining what's going on in the world because they're basing their explanations on their experiences with the old paradigm." Sculley also predicted that the World War II fighter pilot (the formative experience of several corporate heads, as well as President Bush) would no longer be our principal paradigm for leaders.

During the last ten years, I interviewed more than a hundred CEOs of leading corporations. While the executives' experiences and personal styles differed, I was struck by several common themes addressing change and how the concept of leadership is being transformed.

If the world were a stable, placid, predictable place, where the rules of five or ten years ago would work today, I suspect all of the CEOs would say, "Terrific. Let's stick with the COP model." But the message that comes through loud and clear in the discussions with the executives is that a new model of leadership is being required.

These CEOs are emblematic of their time, forced to deal not only with the exigencies of their own organizations, but also with a new social reality. These leaders understand that contemporary organizations face increasing and unfamiliar sources of competition as a result of the globalization of markets, capital, labor, and information technology.

The broader factors that underlie all their decisions include the accelerating rate and complexity of change, the emergence of new technologies, dramatic demographic shifts and globalization. For me, all these are reflected in a single incident. Several years ago I invited the Dalai Lama to participate in a gathering of leaders at USC. The living embodiment of thousands of years of Tibetan spiritual wisdom graciously declined—by fax.

New Organizations for the Future

The organizations of the future will be networks, clusters, cross-functional teams, temporary systems, ad hoc task forces, lattices, modules, matrices—almost anything but pyramids. We don't even know yet what to call these new configurations, but we do know that the ones that succeed will be less hierarchical and have more linkages based on common goals rather than on traditional reporting relationships. It also is likely that the successful organizations will embody what Rosabeth Moss Kanter calls the 5-Fs: *fast, focused, flexible, friendly, and fun.*

To be successful, these organizations must have flexible structures that enable them to be highly responsive to customer requirements and adaptive to changes in the competitive environment. These new organizations must be leaner, have fewer layers and be able to engage in transnational and nontraditional alliances and mergers. And they must understand a global array of business practices, customers, and cultures.

The Emergence of Federations

One of the most provocative themes surfacing in some of my interviews, most notably in the remarks of Percy Barnevik, President and CEO of Asea Brown Boveri (ABB), centers around nontraditional alliances. Namely, the idea of a federation is emerging as the structure uniquely suited to balancing the seemingly incompatible drives toward global cooperation and the putting down of deep local roots. This paradox is evident in world politics, where intense ethnic and national identities co-exist with the widespread recognition that new economic and political alliances must be forged outside one's border. The idea of federation is spreading to the political arena as well, with countries forming communities or commonwealths, such as the European Community or the Commonwealth of Independent States.

I'm convinced that federation will be watchword of the 1990s. And I can imagine a time when corporations such as ABB that are simultaneously global and deeply rooted in local cultures serve as models for nations that aspire both to survival in an international economy and to national self-expression.

The danger lies in those organizations hoping to remain constant and maintain the status quo. During a recent conversation with Alvin Toffler, the all-time change guru whose paradigm-shifting book, *Future Shock,* was published in 1970, we tried to name an organization that exists in today's environment that was immune to change and had been stable and prosperous. We couldn't think of one.

Consider this: forty-seven percent of the companies that made up the Fortune 500 in 1979 were not on the list in 1989.

CEO to CTO

The question all the interviewed leaders are addressing— and with apparent success—is: How do you change relatively successful organizations, which, if they continue to act today the way they acted ten or even five years ago, will undo themselves in the future?

It seems to me that the CEOs are telling us that the CEO must become the Chief Transformation Officer, or *CTO.* Each of the interviewed CEOs has discovered that the very culture of his organization must change because, as constituted, that culture is more devoted to perceiving itself than to meeting new challenges.

Yet to transform an organization's culture poses a formidable task. As Robert Haas, Chairman and CEO of Levi Strauss & Co., observes, change isn't easy, even for those committed to it. "It's difficult to unlearn behaviors that made us successful in the past. Speaking rather than listening. Valuing people like yourself over people of different genders or from different cultures. Doing things on your own rather than collaborating. Making the decision yourself instead of asking different people for their perspectives. There's a whole range of behaviors that were highly functional in the old hierarchical organization that are dead wrong in the flatter, more responsive, empowered organizations that we're seeking to become."

Bringing about organizational change in this turbulent environment requires leaders—leaders, not managers. It is an important distinction. Jack Welch, Chairman and CEO of General Electric has predicted (correctly, I believe): "The World of the '90s and beyond will not belong to *managers* or those who make the numbers dance, as we used to say, or to those who are conversant with all the businessese and jargon we use to sound smart. The world will belong to passionate, driven *leaders*— people who not only have an enormous amount of energy, but who can energize those whom they lead."

Management is getting people to do what needs to be done. Leadership is getting people to *want* to do what needs to be done. Managers push. Leaders pull. Managers command. Leaders communicate.

Trilogy for a New Leadership

In addition to the emergence of the CEO as the CTO, the CEOs seem to be telling us that the new paradigm for success consists of three elements: *Align, Create,* and *Empower*—or *ACE.* This trilogy is what effective leadership is all about.

Alignment

Today's leader needs to *align* the resources of the organization, particularly the human ones, creating a sense of shared objectives worthy of people's support and even dedication. Alignment has much to do with spirit and a sense of being part of a team. Great organizations inevitably develop around a shared vision. Theodore Vail had a vision of universal telephone service that would take fifty years to bring about. Henry Ford envisioned common people, not just the wealthy, owning their own automobiles. Steven Jobs, Steven Wozniak, and their Apple co-founders saw the potential of the computer to empower people. A shared vision uplifts people's aspirations. Work becomes part of pursuing a larger purpose embodied in the organization's products and/or services.

Creation

Today's leader must *create* an organizational culture where ideas come through unhampered by people who are fearful. Such leaders are committed to problem-finding, not just problem-solving. They embrace error, even failure, because they know it will teach them more than success. As Norman Lear once said to me, "Wherever I trip is where the treasure lies."

Effective leaders create adaptive, creative, learning organizations. Such organizations have the ability to identify problems, however troublesome, before they become crises. These organizations are able to rally the ideas and information necessary to solve their problems. They are not afraid to test possible solutions, perhaps by means of a pilot program some where in the organization. And, finally, learning organizations provide opportunities to reflect on and evaluate past actions and decisions. This becomes a "learning wheel," to use Charles Handy's apt phrase.

Empowerment

That overused word from the 1960s—*empowerment*—involves the sense people have that they are at the center of things rather than on the periphery. In an effectively led organization everyone feels he or she contributes to its success. Empowered individuals believe that their actions have significance and meaning. Empowered people have discretion, but also obligations. They live in a culture of respect where they actually can do things without getting permission from some organizational parent figure. Empowered organizations are characterized by trust and system-wide communication.

Whatever shape the future ultimately takes, the organizations that will succeed in the white-knuckle decade of the 1990s are those that take seriously—and sustain through action—the belief that their competitive advantage is based on the development and growth of the people in them. And while companies can give such commentary lip service, those characterized by success and dynamic leadership will pay close attention and actually do something by acting on their words.

The men and women who guide those organizations will be a different kind of leader than we've become used to. They will be maestros, not masters. They will be coaches, not commanders.

In the post-bureaucratic world, the laurel will go to the leader who encourages healthy dissent and values those followers brave enough to say no. The successful leader will have, not the loudest voice, but the readiest ear. And his or her real genius may well lie not in personal achievements, but in unleashing other people's talent.

Kate Steichen
is a leadership and creativity consultant to corporations such as 3M,
General Mills, DowBrands, Lintas:
New York, The Clorox Company, and Polaroid Corporation. For the past
decade, she has guided organizational teams and individuals in strategic
visioning, leadership, renewal, community-building, and new product
development. Steichen was vice-president of IdeaScope Associates, a
creative new product development firm, and marketing manager for Parker
Brothers, a subsidiary of General Mills. She has also served as a
psychological and wilderness guide, art school director, graphic designer,
and photographer.

In 1992, Steichen launched the Natural Leadership™ program for
executives. She received her MBA from the Harvard Business School and
her BFA from the University of Illinois in painting and printmaking.

9

Natural Leadership™

Kate Steichen

How do we thrive in this turbulent time of change, when basic economic, social, political, psychological, and physical structures are collapsing around us? New science tells us that change is a healthy, creative dynamic in self-sustaining systems and fields, yet we resist change, especially change that we cannot control. We struggle to learn ... how to be the best leader we can be ... how to be a learning organization ... how to build community in this changing context.

We Need to Remember...

We don't need to struggle. We need to slow down and remember our true nature and remember nature's laws. We once knew, but we have forgotten.

By means of my own direct experience in nature, I have begun to remember nature's laws. These natural laws are the Tao of life, they are about how things work. They represent the natural flow and cycles of life, the benefits of living and working with that flow, and the consequences for interfering with that flow. I haven't invented these laws. These natural laws have been shared with us throughout time by virtually all cultures and religions, and more recently by new science.

For thousands of years, ancient Taoist, Buddhist, and Vedic wisdom has taught of our Oneness. The Upanishads say, "If anyone in the world is hungry, you are hungry. If anyone is suffering, you are suffering." Christianity talks in terms of brotherhood and the consequences of natural law: "We are our brother's keeper." "What ye sow, so shall ye reap." Zen Buddhism teaches that "separateness is an illusion." Recent findings in physics and biology support these same knowings. Bell's Theorem, from quantum physics, indicates that nothing can occur in the universe that does not significantly affect every other thing in the universe. Systems theory views life as dynamically composed of self-organizing systems, with patterns that are sustained in and by their relationships.

But just as new science is beginning to explain these natural laws, many native peoples are breaking their traditional silence to tell us that we have violated natural laws to such an extent that the Earth is in danger. The Kogi tribe of Columbia, for instance, warns us that unless we stop violating natural law, the world we know that currently contains and sustains us is coming to an end. These Wisdom Keepers remind us of the universal natural laws and their consequences, that spring from our interconnectedness to all beings. They suggest that, for instance, when we take from the Earth, we must give something back.

How have we removed ourselves so far from natural laws that we have threatened our very survival on the Earth? We have done so by removing ourselves from the Earth herself. Native peoples know that the most empowering and healing tool that we have available to us is our connection to nature.

"That is why the old Indian sits upon the Earth instead of propping himself up and away from its life-giving forces. For him to sit or lie upon the ground is to be able to think more clearly and feel more keenly."

—Luther Standing Bear,
Lakota Indian chief

Sitting or lying on the Earth supports remembering at the cellular levels of our being, remembering what it means to be a human being on the Earth. We have forgotten what it means to *be*, and we have forgotten what it means to *be human*. Vision and ideas can be inspiring, but they will not manifest, they will not become real, unless they are integrated within our bodies, within our very beings. Our minds can lie to us, but our bodies do not lie. The inner intelligence of our bodies mirrors the wisdom of the universe. Our bodies are a hologram of the universe, in whose cells are recorded the memory of the whole universe and its mechanics of operation. Our physical bodies must be near to the Earth to feel her wisdom, and our minds must be quiet, so that they can integrate with heart and spirit.

> Herbert explained it this way: "We are like long, thin stalks of corn capped with a single gigantic ear. If the 'head' gets too big, the stalk cannot support it. Universities pay attention only to the heads and no attention to the stalks. It is the stalk that carries the spirit to the head."
>
> —Carl A. Hammerschlag, MD
> *The Dancing Healers*

We Are All Natural Leaders...
What it takes to be a natural leader is already within us. We simply need to remember. We need to remember at the cellular levels of our being. We need to remember what our ancestors knew ... remember what it means to be a human being ... to simply be ... remember what it means to lead ... remember what it means to be in relationship, to participate in and influence a system rather than to control it ... remember to consider the overall field, the atmosphere, the feel, before sitting down and solving problems. Natural leaders remember what it means to give up the struggle ... remember what it is to laugh and play and make a difference at the same time ... remember joy and love ... remember who we truly are.

What is the Ecology of Leadership?
Natural Leaders understand that the ecology of leadership means doing what is appropriate using natural laws. Simply ask the Earth what she would do in such and such an instance, and then find the most appropriate means to respond. What kind of

technology would the Earth design for us? What kind of corporation or team would the Earth design for us? The Earth can give us
clues to the ultimate consequences of our actions even if those
consequences are out of our experience realm or will occur in the
distant future.

> Whether they be large corporations, microbes,
> or seemingly inert chemical structures, we are now
> interested in learning about any organization's
> 'self-renewing' properties ... One of the guiding
> principles of scientific inquiry is that at all levels,
> nature seems to resemble itself ... If nature uses
> certain principles to create her infinite diversity, it
> is highly probable that those principles apply to
> human organizations.
> —Margaret J. Wheatley
> *Leadership and the New Science*

Cycles are an inherent part of the ecology of nature. How
might business affect the world if we applied these cyclical
principles to the *ecology of leadership*?

Vision, Action, and Renewal

An ecological model that has grown out of my own direct
experience of life, of work, and of nature celebrates the natural,
cyclical seasons of growth and change. True natural leaders
inherently know and honor this *creative dynamic of vision, action,
and renewal*. All three interconnected and flowing elements in
this ecological model are necessary to sustain a human being or
human organization.

Vision...

Winter flowing into the new life of spring augers vision.
Harrison Owen defines vision as "Spirit bursting out in new and
powerful ways." Inspired vision is filled with new hope, aliveness,
heart, and soul. Organizational vision provides clarity about
purpose and direction, and includes values, norms, and modes of
conduct.

Within the past twenty years or so, vision has more consciously influenced and guided action in business. But while an
appreciation and understanding of vision is growing in the
corporate world, vision is slow to be accepted generally. During

the past election campaign, President Bush remarked disparagingly about "that vision thing." Perhaps this reticence is partly due to our viewing vision in a linear way, as something to strive for in the future, something distant from who and where we are now.

Margaret Wheatley introduces the new science notion of *force fields* and suggests that we understand organizational vision as "a field—a force of unseen connections that influences

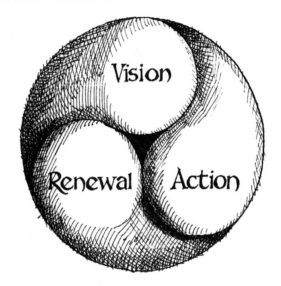

employees' behavior—rather than as an evocative message about some desired future state." An Iroquoian consensus process, as described by Paula Underwood Spencer, creates a similar kind of field: "A circle within which all the People stand."

Organizations have learned that managers do not "buy into" a vision or plan unless they have created that vision together. We need to work with a new vision, to question it, to change or refine it in order to make it our own ... in order to integrate it into our beings, just as we have to till the soil before we can plant seeds in the spring.

Vision cannot be just an idea, it must be authentic to ourselves, to who we are, what we value, and what we do well. A stream's vision, for instance, is its very essence. A stream's vision is to flow. That vision still gives a lot of latitude as to form. For instance, if a boulder blocks its way, the stream simply flows around it. If the stream's banks narrow, the stream simply gains momentum. When the temperature drops, the stream may freeze, but it still has the capacity to flow when the temperature rises again. The stream is so adaptable that it neither wastes energy nor hesitates in the face of necessary change. Natural leaders understand vision as the essence of their organization, and welcome internal as well as environmental or marketplace changes that may require new forms.

> "To live in an evolutionary spirit means to engage with full ambition and without any reserve in the structure of the present, and yet to let go and flow into a new structure when the right time has come"
>
> —Erich Jantsch,
> *The Self-Organizing Universe*

Action...

Summer is a time of warm abundance and action. It is the time to produce and to grow and to have. Action creates results— those we want and those we don't. Inspired action is filled with the spirit of vision, is grounded, and is authentic. Business gives the most rewards for and devotes most of its time to action. We are masters of action throughout the world, though much of that action is not appropriate; it is not in alignment with the laws of nature or with our own beings. Our mechanistic orientation has often rewarded technology for its own sake and ignored whether it was appropriate to the system, culture, or resources to which it was applied. One could argue that we have been better at doing things right than at doing the right thing. A natural leader supports only appropriate action.

Renewal...

Renewal most naturally occurs in late fall and winter, when the leaves are off the trees and life appears still. Renewal is the time to remember our true nature. How do we do that? We remember who we are by becoming silent witnesses, by *being* instead of *acting*. Renewal is the time to be a human *be-ing*. If vision is the inbreath, and action is the outbreath, then renewal is the space between the breaths. Renewal is the time to let go and to make space for a new or refreshed vision to emerge, so that the cycle may begin again.

Renewal is called for when our vision is no longer inspiring or our actions aren't in alignment with our vision. Renewal is the time to assess our work in its own context as well as in the context of our lives and purpose. Renewal asks "What really matters now?" and is the time to tell the truth and to ask questions rather than to give answers. Answers encourage blinders; questions open us up, free and empower us.

Renewal is a time to tell the truth about what is so, and then to face that truth. It is the time to heal our Selves; to remember who we are. And when we remember who we are, we bring our authentic selves forward.

Renewal is a time to surrender what is no longer useful. There is often an aspect of death in renewal, as letting go may require the end of a way of thinking or operating, the end of a product line, closing down a factory, letting go of a dream. The very act of renewal is a surrender of doing. Renewal may or may not be experienced as struggle, depending on how attached we are to that which no longer serves us. Edith Weiner, in *Six Principles for Revitalizing Your Planning,* explains that "The initial key to effective strategic thinking is not learning, but rather forgetting. It requires unlearning and the shedding of old, misguided assumptions."

Once we let go, we often experience a sense of release and new energy. We also experience a sense of spaciousness. The often irresistible temptation is to fill that space immediately, as *not* knowing may be very uncomfortable. This space is best used as a time of questioning and allowing. This space may last a moment, a week, or several months or more in time. This space is the rich, fertile ground out of which true vision emerges.

This space of renewal is also the ground out of which powerful consensus and commitment may emerge. Recently I was engaged in guiding one division of a very large and well-known corporation in agreeing and committing to a marketing strategy which will drive the division worldwide. Once we had completed a thorough strategic visioning process, the executive group met again to decide between several strategies, each of which had its own strong support and rationale. Although we had scheduled a full two-and-a-half days to complete this process, the unusually wise head of the division surprised me and the dozen senior executives present from throughout the continent by stating: "We will take as long as it takes. If we do not reach consensus by the end of our scheduled time, we will reschedule and come together again."

This unusual latitude gave all of us the space for true renewal and clarity to happen. We were given the time to be in the question, no matter how uncomfortable that might have been for some. We devoted over a day to dialoguing in a structured council process, one person speaking at a time, the team learning through listening rather than discussing. We took the time to create the *"circle within which all the People stand."* What needed to naturally emerge did: conflicts, fears, rivalries, and insights. The director of the division remarked to me afterward, "It became painfully obvious which strategy was most appropriate, even to those who initially had the most reluctance. And since that session, I have noticed a new and unusual level of energy and commitment among the entire team!" This division head is a natural leader.

The Gifts of Nature

A senior advertising executive, having completed my five-day Natural Leadership™ program, remarked that she felt "renewed and gained a simplification in how I approach my life ... I will use the approach of 'give it up or just do it' as a way to approach my work [and not sit on the fence]. I learned about how to renew myself which in time I can use to renew others."

Nature Awakens our Memory...

While we can learn from and be guided by the metaphors of nature, deep renewal and true awakening occur most naturally when we are physically present and alone in nature. One client remarked that while her family "loves nature and attempts to be mindful of it ... we have completely forgotten how to immerse ourselves in it. When we go to the shore, climb mountains, etc., it's done as a group ... not alone. We've really forgotten how to be alone 'in a cellular sense'." In nature, we can literally *feel* spirit, we can feel the presence of nonvisible influences that facilitate the processes of creation. Nature not only guides and clarifies our thoughts, nature brings us back to ourselves, to our inner core, in a way that is healing and rejuvenating to the very cells of our being. Nature brings us back to our instinctual, knowing selves.

Nature Guides Our Journeys...

My personal journey awakened the natural leader in my-self, and supported me in my creative and consulting work in using nature as metaphor, guide, and healer. I began remembering my Self a decade ago when I warily departed on a backpacking trip in the Gila wilderness in southern New Mexico. My entire life to that point had centered in major metropolitan cities. I relished the executive's life to which I had grown accustomed. I loved flying about to different cities, being pampered in luxury hotels, and having a staff with whom to share the workload. I smile now at my reluctance to let go of those comforts, at the cost of remembering my humanity.

Several years and several wilderness vacations later, I spent my first week entirely alone on a deserted desert beach. This was not an outward bound journey, in which I scaled cliffs or kayaked down raging spring rivers. I could not roam very far, or else I would intrude upon the territory of another wilderness soloist. And I had been discouraged from bringing along any external distractions, such as a watch, radio, book, or camera.

I was forced to explore inward. At first I experienced boredom. I felt trapped by the prospect of living through a full seven days and nights in an incredibly beautiful but relatively small, very remote area. In time, and I had lots of it, I began to slow down and relax into my surroundings. I was surprised to be able to be alone for such a long time, and never feel lonely. One afternoon I slowly walked along the beach and encountered a huge boulder at the water's edge. I asked the boulder what it was about and it seemed to reply: "I am about taking a stand." And then I noticed how that rock withstood the force of the ocean's waves, the fierce winds, and sand. It supported birds and even the weight of my body without wincing or changing its position. That was true commitment!

As the week progressed, I began to awaken more and more. I noticed, for instance, how a particular cactus stood out more beautifully due to its relation to all the other, different plants around it. I experienced directly the interconnectedness of all of life. I experienced unity, and its mate, diversity. I began to receive many insights about life, about my work, about what truly mattered, and for what I was willing to take a stand. Paradoxically, my body, heart, and soul felt nurtured and healed by this hot, dry, cold, harsh desert as I relaxed more and more deeply into the core of my being.

Nature kept calling me to the point that three years ago, I left the intellectual, psychological, artistic, and corporate buzz of Cambridge, Massachusetts to make my home in a tiny, remote, mountain community in southern Colorado. My only known tether to civilization as I knew it was a telephone, a facsimile machine, and a small, rural airport fifty miles away. I didn't consciously know (or couldn't *remember*) why I needed to move here. I just felt that I needed to learn directly from the land and that I needed to be alone to do so.

My first two years here were full of disappointment, loneliness, and great personal testing. I learned to notice, to wait, and to let go at deeper and deeper levels of my being. I learned to say "no" to opportunities, because, as hard as it was, I knew that I needed to be alone with myself.

In time, more of these moments alone began to fill me with absolute joy and abandon ... of vision and breakthrough, and of deep inner knowing and cellular healing. I awoke many mornings with a smile on my face and a song in my being. I often looked out my bedroom window just at sunrise to see the strong, powerful mountains aglow in a soft, pink-salmon halo.

I needed to remember my roots and I found them here in this rugged, dry, rough, spectacularly beautiful, high mountain desert. My roots are here in what UPS calls an "outlying" area, a community of society's voluntary outcasts: artists, writers, 1960's dropouts, and spiritual monks and hermits. And my roots are here in a place that native shamans have come for centuries to give thanks and to be renewed. Yet my roots are also in the cities and the world of ideas, imagination, and speed. I already knew that world. I needed to remember the natural world.

Nature Brings Forth Natural Leaders...

I am in good company. Throughout time, the way to sustain or create integration, to renew oneself, has been to return to direct contact with nature. Christ, Buddha, Thoreau, Gandhi, Anne Lindberg, Walt Whitman, Rachel Carson, John Muir ... even Teddy Roosevelt, who began life as a sickly New York City boy, returned to nature again and again throughout his illustrious life, and, as President, set aside all the National Forests, where each of us may now return again and again to remember how to bring forth the natural leaders that we are.

Nature is about as far as one can get from the glass and steel world of corporations. Nature provides the perfect opportunity for us to remove ourselves from our ongoing paradigm in order to observe it and possibly change that which informs our lives and our work. It is necessary to slow down and have empty spaces for spirit to reveal itself to us ... to have time to integrate and digest ... to have time to heal ourselves. Nature is the field where healing happens, where body, mind, heart, and spirit are integrated. Nature is the field where natural leaders grow and sustain themselves.

Barbara Shipka's
consulting practice focuses primarily on the arenas of creating a
global orientation, anticipating
increasing interdependence, leveraging growth and transitions, working
with differences and diversity, and developing resilient work roles. Among
her corporate clients are Alliant Techsystems, Cray Research, Honeywell,
IDS Financial Services, Medtronic, The Pillsbury Company, and Wilson
Learning.

She serves on the Board of Directors of The World Business Academy
and initiated the Minnesota Chapter. In addition to the corporate sector,
she has worked with the United Nations, government, the non-profit sector,
and education. She has lived and worked in Lebanon, the Dominican
Republic, Somalia, Ethiopia, the Sudan, Czechoslovakia, and Switzer-
land.

She is a contributing author in the anthology *When the Canary Stops
Singing: Women's Perspectives on Transforming Business* and has been
profiled in *Merchants of Vision* by Jim Leibig and *Who We Could Be At
Work* by Margaret Lulic.

10

A Sacred Responsibility

Barbara Shipka

It was now mid-afternoon, the sun was relentless, and we had spent hours walking in the splendor of the temples of Luxor. We felt hot and tired so we decided to hire a horse-drawn buggy to return to our hotel. The two people I was traveling with were both Lebanese and we all taught together at the same school in Beirut. As we made our way south along the river, the driver and my friends carried on a conversation. Though I usually liked participating with my basic Arabic, on this occasion I spaced out. Later, with much delight, they reported what had transpired.

What they found especially amusing was that the driver wanted to know how wide the Nile was where I came from. They told him that the Nile didn't flow there. He was amazed to hear that and had a hard time believing it. His question was, "But how can people *live* without the Nile?"

Later, as I thought about it, I realized that any direction he went from where he was led him either into lifeless desert or lush, green settlements like his own. His entire world either lived by the Nile or died without it.

Many people from all over the world excitedly visit Luxor. Most visitors encountered by our driver, especially those who looked different from him—as I did—would not speak Arabic and he spoke no other language. Thus, his exposure to the concept of a larger world could easily remain limited. In fact, with so many people visiting Luxor, he could conclude that he lived at the very center of the universe. After all, everyone came to where he was. He isn't alone in holding this view, which has little to do with education or income level. For myself, I notice that even though I have much more experience than he with such things as maps and time zones, distances, and cultures, I also operate as though anywhere I am at any given moment is the center of all that is unless and until I consciously shift my attention to considering a larger reality.

Enlarging the Context

Believing Luxor to be the center of the universe perhaps explains some of the driver's mindset. But what about ours? If, instead, we had been able to consider the intention behind his question—if we had been able to enlarge the context—we might have heard him asking something like, "What is the source-of-water-that-maintains-life where she comes from?" For that is what he was truly asking.

Enlarging the context means increasing the scale within which we live day to day by recognizing that the center of the universe is greater than our individual street addresses and the routes upon which we travel in our daily routines. In *New World New Mind*, Robert Ornstein and Paul Ehrlich write, "... the human mental system is failing to comprehend the modern world." In other words, they are suggesting that the evolution of our minds has not kept pace with what we have created. The way the authors most vividly illustrate the current state of our minds is by saying that we have not evolved beyond seeing danger as a bear at the door of the cave. We still tend to respond or react only to what is most immediate. For example, public interest can easily be maintained for two whales drowning in the Arctic Ocean but we find it much more difficult to sustain our awareness and interest in the plight of life in general.Thus, enlarging our context means making a conscious decision to see more than individual events; to make a daily practice of focusing on the systemic nature of our world and the processes that are evolving within it.

Sifting for Essence

Enlarging the context also means sifting for essence and meaning beneath the veneer of our often hypnotic cultural trance. It means breaking out of a trance more than exchanging one trance for another.

In the last few years, much has been expressed about the "new paradigm" in business. I respect the valiant attempts to articulate emerging values, methods, and scenarios. I say valiant because, by definition, outcomes of transformative change are unknown during emergence. But one phenomenon bothers me. Several writers—including Michael Ray in *New Traditions in Business*, John Renesch in *Creative Work*, Philip Harris in *High Performance Leadership*, and Marilyn Ferguson in *The New Paradigm in Business*—have developed charts that have a left hand column which generally describes the dark, shadow aspects of the old and a right hand column that generally describes the light, visionary aspects of the new. These descriptions can be seductive and misleading. First, they are described in the "old paradigm" form. Secondly, whether consciously or unconsciously, any sensible person I know would want to identify with the right and not the left. As is common in our throwaway culture, there's movement toward throwing away the "old paradigm" for the "new paradigm." Separating the world so literally and linearly is also "old."

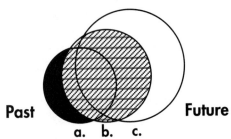

Past   **Future**
a. b. c.

An alternative model to help us visualize the change occurring might be drawn as a series of interlocking circles. First, a crescent moon of the first, smaller circle is being shed (a). Secondly, the next circle is larger because the potential of what is emerging and evolving is greater than has existed until now (b). Another circle grows out of the second (c), and so on. A third, critical aspect is the area of overlap between the circles. This intersect provides grounding spiritually and emotionally in the same way gravity serves us physically.

Instead of trading "old" for "new," we need to sift everywhere for essence—in the ancient and the emerging, facing into the dark and basking in the light, letting what's outside in and what's inside out, simultaneously living in this very moment while considering seven generations to come, knowing that what we do "here" has ripple effects everywhere, playing our individual parts while always being aware of the framework of a larger whole.

Global Goes Beyond Geography

Looking at language can provide important clues to cultural change because language not only expresses our reality but also forms it. We are currently using the word "global" to mean "worldwide" which is parallel to how the buggy driver was using "Nile." Somewhere deep inside of ourselves we know that "global" goes far beyond geography.

Until recently, businesses referred to themselves almost exclusively as "international" or "multinational." The shift to the use of "global," while subtle, is significant because the words have very different meanings and implications. Both "international" and "multinational" are based on our current governmental structure of nation states and refer to relationships based on nations. They both imply that the relationships can be between some nations but not others. "Global," on the other hand, has nothing in particular to do with nations. Other meanings for the word are "universal" and "relating to a whole."

For companies that truly have a vision of being global, the expansion of human minds and hearts is more than geographic expansion. Just as underneath the driver's use of "Nile" was the deeper, more essential notion of water for maintaining life, under our common use of "global" there is also a deeper, more essential notion of wholeness. Therefore, a global business is a business—whether worldwide or not—that has a vision of questing toward wholeness—for itself, for the people within it, for the world at large.

Leadership Goes Beyond Position Power

And what does this mean about leadership and, particularly, business leadership? First, in this context, the definition of leadership extends far beyond position power. In today's world, anyone who has the time, money, and energy to be reading this book must acknowledge her or himself as a potential global leader. Going back to the buggy driver, he may comprehend our interconnected fate at a local or visceral level but he does not have the frame of reference to comprehend the totality of the changes that are occurring on earth. And, relatively speaking, he lives well. The vast majority of our fellow humans can see ahead only a few miles and a few meals—and even that requires good fortune.

Secondly, at this time in human history, business is the most powerful institution on earth and it represents a mushrooming, interconnected infrastructure that blankets the earth and, for the most part, works. Those people with power, authority, and responsibility for making decisions within businesses, by virtue of the powerful position that business inhabits, participate in determining the course of our collective future on a grand scale—whether they acknowledge it or not. Therefore, the more consciously we make choices that serve the whole of our planetary system, the more likely we are to have the luxury of sifting for essence and meaning in any form—whether at an individual or collective level.

The Price of Awareness

Here in the U.S., we have a bittersweet price to pay for being among the wealthiest two percent of human beings on earth and for participating in the powerful arena of business. It's the price of awareness.

I remember a day in Kenya when we stopped our vehicle on the side of the road to take a break—total silence on the savannah except for a whistling wind. In the distance I watched a shepherd with his sheep. I experienced a feeling of romance about his life—so idyllic, such peacefulness. And I realized that I could never get to where he was—because of my frame of reference, my experience. On the other hand, I also remember seeing Ethiopian women leaving the refugee camp in the Sudan very early in the morning to spend the entire day walking miles in an attempt to scrounge enough wood to cook the evening meal—so frantic, such burden. I realized I didn't want to ever get to where they were—that I was, in this case, grateful for my frame of reference, my experience.

A Sacred Responsibility

The price of awareness is enormous but it is not necessarily a sacrifice. It is a sacred responsibility for all of life as we know it.

This is not about ego. It's just what's so. For paying the price, I believe we receive a priceless attending gift. It is the gift of our own individual spiritual healing and evolution; of increased awareness and greater consciousness.

Sacred responsibility goes beyond social responsibility. Individuals and businesses that pick up the mantel of sacred responsibility carry it to a new level of evolution and hold it in a new way. They recognize that the only reason for us to be together in any collective way at all is for the perpetuation of life and the evolution of consciousness. With such a belief, profit remains essential to business viability but its status and importance change. Profit shifts from being an end in and of itself to being a means to an end instead. Keeping a business profitable becomes the means through which a group of human beings may grow, contribute from their deepest sense of purpose in life, and express their creative, generative life force or vitality.

Three Questions

At this point, three questions come to mind. First, why even consider such a radical departure from current conventional wisdom? Secondly, how can one approach this concept of global leadership as a sacred responsibility? And, third, what can we expect as a result?

1. Why Consider Looking at Global Leadership as a Sacred Responsibility?

By virtue of living on earth in these times, we face problems of a nature and magnitude unknown until now. First, the local parts of our global village can no longer live independently of each other. We are inextricably linked together. Focusing on the various symptoms of our worldwide malaise, the veritable societal "squeaky wheels" such as terrorism, poverty, and ethnic or political conflict just seem to be increasing their strength.

Secondly, businesses cannot continue to grow quantitatively. The math of the consumer orientation and our planetary limitations just don't compute except toward implosion or extinction.

Third, a most dangerous obstacle we face is our fear. For, since the fear is uncomfortable, it tends to lead us collectively into denial. The fear and denial seem to come from glimpsing our not knowing what to do or how to control what faces us. It is true that we do not know what to do—we are at our collective level of incompetence. And we do not control what faces us. But then, we never have. The only difference now is that the illusion of control is becoming more and more transparent. Rather than deluding ourselves by thinking that we initiate or control the forces of our world, we must learn to traverse, leverage, and creatively thrive in the context of change.

2. How Can One Approach Global Leadership as a Sacred Responsibility?

The first step is to make the choice. It means answering affirmatively to the questions, "Do I want to commit to expanding the center of my universe, enlarging my context, stepping into my power?" "Am I willing to pay the attending price of awareness?" Once the choice is made to move forward, the possibilities are innumerable. I will suggest three:

- Nurture a Systems Orientation
- Challenge Our Current Assumption About Growth
- Face Into Life-on-earth-at-the-end-of-the-20th Century

Nurture a Systems Orientation

I was recently interviewing people in a large corporation. An aspect of the vision for their division is to distribute power and to create a setting where people can develop more of their potential. To do this, they have chosen to restructure themselves as "self-directed" teams. But people in the organization confuse self-directed with autonomous or on their own when, if fact, inter-dependent goals mean that people are more interrelated and dependent upon each other than ever before. "So big deal!" one leader says. "Let's change the name and get on with it!"

But it's not the name. Even with a name change an under-lying issue remains. The hierarchy remains more or less completely intact in this division. It merely has a veneer of "team" placed on top of it. Changing a structure that has predominated at least since the Roman army is no small, easy, or quickly achieved objective.

We cannot affect our human systems by treating the symptoms—in this case, by overlaying a new form upon an old one. Fundamental change requires that we first collectively change our minds. The change of structures will naturally follow. The altering of basic assumptions can come about through providing frameworks for what's changing in the world, how what's changing affects people and their potential for contribution, what alternative forms we currently know something about, what space there is to create alternatives we haven't yet pioneered. In other words, people must engage in breakthrough experiences about *how* they work together as well as about the work they are doing.

When we sit together and explore the *how* of being together—whether at work or not—we become more and more conscious not only of the specific systems in which we live but also of the nature of systems in general.

Challenge Our Current Assumption About Growth

The traffic is beyond my imagining! My hosts, friends from my days in Africa, tell me stories of daily life in Bangkok. Char talks of taking a book with her whenever she takes a taxi because the traffic can turn a twenty-minute commute into a three-hour ordeal. Terry speaks of disaster waiting to happen what with burgeoning high rise development—fifteen floors and more—and fire equipment that can only reach the fifth floor. As we walk through the streets my complaint is that I can't breathe after a couple of blocks. My lungs literally ache. Even though it's the middle of the day, the sun is red. The air is the worst I've ever experienced—indoors or out. Bangkok is a harbinger of what will be the common urban experience of life on earth—unless some fundamental practices change. But, it doesn't have to be that way.

As I share a meal with a friend and his family in Indonesia, my friend tells me that, recently, the village council—the elders—had seriously considered buying a tractor. On one hand, they discussed, it would be much more efficient than water buffalo and they would then become a modern village. "But on the other hand," it was argued, "we'd have to buy petroleum and some of our people would lose their sources of livelihood." In the end, the elders' decision was to *not* buy a tractor. Their reasoning was that everyone was currently working and eating, living and loving. They had no designs on conquering the next village. Their conclusion was that a tractor had more potential for damaging the fabric of their community than for developing it.

The concept of X% business growth per year, year after year, out into a never-ending future is actually quite bizarre—except we are so used to it that, generally, we don't question it or rethink it. It's fascinating as a collectively held belief because it does not mirror what we know as "health" for living organisms. It does mirror organisms that we cannot control and that have the potential to kill us—like cancer.

It is critical to understand that if businesses wish to continue to have a viable world in which to operate, they must look for alternative ways of growing besides X% additional each year. There are useful clues to consider in the model of growth in natural, healthy life forms where, after a time, the growth that is valued and required is more qualitative than quantitative.

Face Into Life-on-earth-at-the-end-of-the-20th Century

Finally! I'm in India. This is my reward to myself for "hanging in there" through a difficult and interminable year in Somalia. On arriving, I checked into the most elegant and expensive hotel in Delhi—just long enough to have room service, browse in a gift shop, buy English books, watch videos, feel luxurious and leisurely. It was a relief, a way to relax. It felt more like home than any place I'd been in over a year. I understood the rules and was able to get everything I *wanted* in addition to everything I needed. After two days I plunged deeper into India itself.

From the train, I was offered a living tableau of people, villages, and fields on the Indian plain on a hot day in June. Off in the distance I noticed a large cooling tower of the kind that are often seen at nuclear power stations. On a road between the tower and the train, I saw a man leading a cart pulled by oxen. At first, my thought was about how India is a country of such contrasts—ancient oxcart and high-tech cooling tower. Then, that juxtaposition served as the key to unlock a deeper thought.

What came to me was that, with exceptions like the hotel in Delhi and the veneer of cultural specifics like language and customs, Somalia and India are remarkably alike. I began to imagine someone from another planet reporting back to "Mission Control," offering generic and basic observations of human life on earth. Such a being would describe Somalia and India in very similar ways. For example, transportation is primarily self-propelled or by beasts of burden; food is simple, unadorned, routine—and many people do not have enough; most people are born, live, and die without ever having been very far from home.

The report would also point to an anomaly that represents a much smaller area of earth and many times fewer people, but which is enormous in power, if not in numbers. "I've heard this anomaly referred to as the 'industrialized world,'" the report would say "which includes a few isolated enclaves here and there where people also live in the style of the anomaly." Like the hotel in Delhi.

Several years ago, I read an article by Robert W. Fox in *National Geographic* called "The World's Urban Explosion." The statistics of what we can expect in the next couple of decades left me reeling. When I mentioned it to a friend, her response was in the realm of, "Well, don't worry. Someone will figure it out. They always do." On a different occasion another person said, "I can barely handle my own life let alone take on the whole world! I just don't want to hear about it."

Two-thirds of the people in the world live in villages. I have a long standing vision that I think would greatly assist anyone preparing for a leadership role in business. It would be to spend two weeks or so in a village somewhere where the two-thirds live, working with the village people and just hanging out with them on their terms. The underlying assumption is that tremendous benefit with lasting impact occurs through even a very short immersion. I believe that such an experience would change individual "points of view" into much larger "fields of view."

3. What Can One Expect as a Result?

At the individual level, those who embark on this journey will hone natural, intrinsic qualities like inquisitiveness, patience, the ability to observe what's just out of range, cultivating a beginner's mind, humor at oneself, the ability to deeply listen, openness to examining and changing long held beliefs, developing a *field* of view rather than a *point* of view, holding recovery as more important than perfection.... These are the kinds of qualities that are enhanced by viewing global leadership as a sacred responsibility. They live within, but also transcend, all cultures.

At the collective level, the question of what can be expected is not so easy to answer. Transformative changes are already in process. Our current task is one of birthing. Who has known or seen natural birth without pain? Along with the mother, the midwife also expends significant energy in the process. No, it is not an easy task and it will not be completed soon. And yet, by merely viewing leadership globally or holistically and, thus, sacredly, the world is changed. Concrete results in the world at large remain to be seen. In the meantime, the gifts we receive give us opportunity to consciously and deeply engage in the global change process, break out of our cultural trance and limiting beliefs, and create a new level of hope for our common future.

Tina Rasmussen
serves as group facilitator, internal consultant, and coach in her role as corporate Management Development Manager at Nestlé Beverage Company, a subsidiary of the world's largest food company.

Her background includes more than ten years of experience helping executives and managers develop humanistic methods of leading organizations within the high tech, retail trade, financial services, and consumer products industries. She also has been a newspaper reporter and editor of a daily column.

Rasmussen views her role within an organization as a conduit for the expansion of humanistic values. Specific projects she has focused on include diversity, customer satisfaction, and values-based vision and mission linked with strategic planning.

Rasmussen is also a PhD candidate completing her doctoral dissertation on leadership at the Fielding Institute.

11

Leading from Within: Taking a Leap of Faith

Tina Rasmussen

"It sounds great, but it's too soft." "Sure, I want to stick with my principles. But this is *business*. It doesn't fly here." "I have to do it to *them*, before they do it to *me*." "I'm a manager, not a saint." These are commonly heard comments whenever the conversation turns to more humanistic ways of doing business.

In my experience with managers and leaders, I have come to believe that most of them are good people. They believe in moral codes that they try to uphold in their "personal" lives, that is, with their families and friends. Unfortunately, these same leaders often think that the principles they hold dear in their personal lives don't always apply in business. They become split into two beings—adopting one philosophy at work and another at home. This split highlights a critical issue in society: the lack of integration of our core values, which results in fragmentation. Some people believe this trend results from the lack of meaning people find in modern life, especially in their work. Victor Frankl, author of *Man's Search for Meaning*, calls it the "existential vacuum."

Often, people believe the only way to make it in business is to "play the game," to leave their personal values and beliefs at the door when they come to work. They believe that if they were to do the right thing consistently at work, they would "get eaten alive" by the competition, peers, their boss, even the people who report to them. As strong as their intentions might be, people become conditioned to compromising their own values.

Most of us spend nearly half of our waking lives working. We may spend more time at work than we do with our families and friends. Commerce has become the dominant force in industrialized society. It is rapidly superseding government as our primary institution. It has long surpassed the church, which for centuries was the strongest organizational force in society. Even so, it is common to hear people lament the notion that, "On my death bed, I know I won't say 'I wish I had spent more time at work.'" It is a tragedy of the human spirit that people are willing to spend so much of their lives doing something so meaningless.

In response to this, a growing trend in business is toward a more caring—dare we say loving?—type of leadership. As noted in the June 1993 issue of *Training* magazine, "In an environment racked with stress, insecurity, tough decisions and 60-hour weeks, you might expect a resurgence of a management model based on Machiavelli's Prince, Leona Helmsley or some other Theory-X icon. Instead, there's a stirring in the opposite direction: A flood of management books, articles and musings try to make sense of the current chaos by proposing a management model filled with heart—and soul." In addition, a 1990 issue of *Fortune* magazine profiled "the most powerful, encouraging and sometimes disturbing ideas that will influence our lives and our livelihood." One of the encouraging ideas contained in the article was a new altruism and a "spiritualization" of work.

A few authors and practitioners of this new leadership, such as Max DePree and Jim Autry, have documented their approaches and their resulting successes. However, their books are primarily written from the viewpoint of the leader. What is it like to be a follower of one of these new leaders? How does a member of the disenchanted masses feel?

As a management development professional—a middle manager who has worked with leaders for many years—I may have a different perspective than the average employee. I have empathy for leaders because I understand the extreme pressures they face and what a thankless job it can be. However, my perspective may be even more cynical and critical than the average employee, since I have been a personal witness to the negative impact of lackluster leaders who inspire nothing but fear, rebellion, or apathy. In some cases, I have worked with managers who were simply mediocre, not doing any harm but also not doing any good. For these people, I have always had hope, because I believe they truly want to lead in a different way. They just don't know how.

A few years ago, I had the unexpected good fortune to follow a leader who had the courage to believe in a new way. I am about to tell you the story of a different kind of leadership. You will bear witness to how this way of leading can impact an organization over a period of years. After we have reviewed this case study, I will identify the key attribute which distinguishes it from other forms of leadership.

When you are done, you might believe that nice guys *can* finish first. I know I do.

The Case of Santa Barbara Bank & Trust

I started working at Santa Barbara Bank & Trust (SBB&T) on March 4, 1990. I was hired as the Program Development Officer in the Educational Resources Department. My job was to analyze opportunities for the Bank's people to become more competent in meeting the goals of the organization, and then to lead teams which would create tools and processes to accomplish this. My first assignment was to help transform the role of our customer service managers—who oversaw the teller functions in our branches—from a technical, procedural role to a customer service, leadership role.

When I started with the Bank, I knew they were a mid-sized independent institution with about five hundred employees and eleven branches, spanning forty miles across southern Santa Barbara County on California's central coast. I didn't know much else about the company and I knew almost nothing about banking. My expertise was in the fields of adult learning and organizational development.

I began searching for answers to the question: "What is management at Santa Barbara Bank & Trust?" I interviewed all kinds of people, at all levels, in many different areas of the company. I worked with my manager, who practiced a very humanistic style. I researched the company's history and future plans to find out where they had been, and where they wanted to go.

I began discovering things which seemed incredible to me. Because these facts were such an ingrained part of the institution, no one paid them much attention or made them into a "big deal."

Santa Barbara Bank & Trust was founded in 1960 by three well-established local businessmen. They wanted to create a financial institution which would foster economic growth and stability for community residents and businesses. They made the Bank a publicly-owned institution so it would become "the Bank that belonged to Santa Barbara." They even limited the number of shares one investor could buy to insure broad-based community ownership. They established this modest institution with one small office.

Now, more than thirty years later, the Bank has been identified by *Money* magazine as one of the two strongest banks in California, and one the ninety-seven strongest in the United States. Sheshunoff, the leading national bank rating service, has consistently given the Bank the highest ratings of A or A+ for being well-managed.

Although bank stocks generally haven't done well in recent years, Santa Barbara Bank & Trust has shown impressive results. They have increased earnings to their stockholders for the last twenty-seven consecutive years, in an industry where many competitors are closing their doors. Its stock which was originally issued at a value of $1.5 million in 1960 was worth $70 million in 1991.

For many years, the Bank has been the market leader in its area—even with prominent competitors such as Bank of America and Wells Fargo. In 1992, more area residents chose Santa Barbara Bank & Trust as their primary institution than the next two competitors *combined*. From the period of 1987 to 1992, they *doubled* their asset size and market share. During this same period, many other large and small financial institutions in the area were either acquired or seized by the federal government.

The people of Santa Barbara have consistently voted it the best bank in the community. In 1993, after five years as "Best Bank," the newspaper which conducted the poll had to retire it as a "Living Legend" because no other institution was getting a chance. Some years, there wasn't even a runner-up. Based on customer focus groups, a market research firm used one word to describe the Bank's reputation—"noble."

In 1992, the Bank's Chairman of the Board, Don Anderson, was voted Santa Barbara's Man of the Year. This same award had been given previously to one of the founders of the Bank, Rubin Irvin, who greeted customers from his desk in the main lobby until he died in 1989 at the age of 90. "Rube" Irvin also worked with over thirty civic organizations in his lifetime. Of the more than 150 officers, nearly all of them volunteer with at least one non-profit organization.

How has this level of success been achieved? In 1992, Bank President and CEO David Spainhour was asked to address the graduating class of the Pacific Coast Banking School. He was asked to comment on what made SBB&T so successful. He said "I may have a personal vision of what quality customer service should be, but until that becomes a shared vision and others are committed to expanding on it, it won't go very far. So we looked for ways to incorporate reinforcement into our culture to move from personal vision of a few to shared vision by many."

Even within the Bank, we often pondered why the organization was so successful. We didn't consider ourselves to be at the "leading edge" on every new business trend. Some of us came to the conclusion that we were successful because of what we *did*. We did it thoroughly, instead of just *talking* about it. We didn't need to do anything radical, because we had accomplished something few companies do. We had minimized the gap between "*talking* the talk" and "*walking* the talk." As Harvard University Professor Chris Argyris would put it, our espoused theories were fairly close to our theories-in-use.

Bank employees generally believe their presence at work makes a difference, that their contributions matter. An example is the manner in which the planning process occurs. First, managers obtain input up-front from their staff members. Then, representatives from all departments work together to create a cohesive, integrated, bankwide plan. After the plan is finalized, each manager leads a discussion with his or her department, with a senior vice president present to answer questions. The plan is extended to a level of detail in which each employee can determine how his or her own role contributes to the higher purpose. This is then incorporated into each person's job description and performance plan. I remember people leaving those meetings expressing immense pride in contributing to something they thought was worthwhile. Many felt almost overwhelmed at the trouble the company had gone to to make sure everyone had a voice and understood the importance of their role. The first time my peers and I were asked to be active contributors, I remember feeling that it wasn't just a gesture to make us feel good. It was a genuine interest in finding out what we thought was important, and pieces of our ideas could be seen in the final plan.

People at all levels and from many different departments would come together with a common goal or specific mission to produce very creative results. On one project, someone had an idea of a new service that would let us open accounts for new customers without them ever having to go back to their old bank. This would remove the obstacle some people felt of "betraying" their former institution. The person who had the idea wasn't sure how to implement it, so we asked tellers, new accounts people, back-room operations people, and many others from entry level positions to vice presidents. In a very short time, we had a viable new "product" which cost us almost nothing to implement. Within a month, several competitors had tried to copy our method. What they couldn't reproduce was our underlying sense of teamwork, common vision, and empowerment that enabled us to implement it successfully.

Fun is also important at the Bank. One major event each year is the Halloween parade held in front of the main branch. Every department and branch is invited to march around in light-hearted competition for the best costumes and presentation. Some customers enter the contest as well. People from all over town come to watch and each branch is decorated so customers can share in the fun. Most years, a local radio station broadcasts the contest live. It's a great team building activity, a ritual which fosters a sense of community both inside and outside to the Bank. It also lets people know that a balance of fun and work is accepted and valued.

People respect and admire senior management. David Spainhour has been with the Bank since 1966. He isn't a "motivational speaker" in the Lou Holt or Robert Schuller tradition. He couldn't be called a cheerleader. Instead, he is consistent, even-tempered, and caring. He displays a strong character. He wants to know what you think. People are sometimes struck by the fact that, if you meet him in the hallway, he'll ask you questions and then just listen. Sometimes people are uncomfortable and don't know what to say. I always wonder if that happens because its so rare that *anyone* listens these days, let alone the president.

Even though Spainhour is caring, he couldn't be described as soft. He is firm when he needs to be—but not in an autocratic way. This firmness is linked with trust that people want to do their best. Employees respond to this by wanting to live up to his and the Bank's expectations. People are more afraid of letting others down than of being punished.

Yet, despite all this, the Bank isn't perfect. Because people value their relationships with each other, they sometimes fall into a "groupthink" mentality. Because collaboration is valued and everyone's perspective is considered, decisions often take a long time to make. Occasionally, things get bogged down. Some pockets of the organization don't embody the vision as well as others. People get frustrated because they want to stay with the Bank, but can't always find opportunities for advancement.

It's hard to leave the Bank. Some do; many come back. Deciding to leave in 1993 was one of the hardest decisions I ever made. As a result, I now possess a perspective that has allowed me to identify this new way of leading—"leading from within."

Leading From Within—A Different Kind of Leadership
The idea of a more humanistic approach to leadership is nothing new. The movement away from autocratic, "scientific" management methods started many years ago. The human potential movement has had its impact on business as it has on society in general. The result has been the emergence of participative management, empowerment, and so on.

Leading from within extends and builds upon empowerment and participative management. However, it's much deeper, richer, fuller, and more holistic.

Leading from within is different in *philosophy*. It reflects the core of the leader's *being*. In fact, it is a *way* of being. Surely, to lead effectively, one must have a strong set of competencies in key areas. However, techniques alone do not define leading from within. Stephen Covey, author of *Principle Centered Leadership*, makes an interesting observation. He notes that for the first one hundred years, American achievement literature focused on what he calls the "character ethic." This included principles like keeping promises, being honest, and exercising courage. It was the *why* of personal effectiveness. Then, about fifty years ago, it shifted to an emphasis on "the personality ethic." This included techniques like using the right words, projecting a certain image, and adjusting our style. It was the *how* of personal effectiveness. We began to focus so much on the how that we forgot the why. We knew exactly how to get people to do what we wanted them to do, but we stopped caring about whether it was *right* or not. Covey points out that the *how* is very important, and necessary for personal effectiveness. But without the *why*, it is meaningless, unbalanced, and can be misdirected or even unethical.

This is similar to a statement made by British management consultant Charles Handy in a 1992 speech at the University of Southern California Leadership Institute conference, *Reconceptualizing the Corporation: The Role of Leadership*. He said this about modern business: "We may have mistaken a requirement for a purpose. A requirement is to make a profit. But to turn a requirement into a purpose is not right. We have to eat to live, but if you live to eat you become a distorted human being in more ways than one. We have to make a profit to survive, but that's not enough. And I think the major task of leadership is to say, 'What's the purpose beyond the requirement?'"

The distinction between the purpose and the requirements of business is at the heart of leading from within. Leading from within is a natural extension of the leader's personal belief that there is a higher purpose in business beyond making money.

Banking is often viewed as a cold, heartless, even ruthless, industry. The public was barraged with images of crooked bankers being taken to jail during the era of failed savings and loans. Those people probably believed the only way to "make it" in banking was to be cut-throat business people. They might have laughed if someone had suggested that a caring, inspired approach would produce superior results.

Santa Barbara Bank & Trust never invested overseas in junk bonds or overseas. It wasn't consistent with their vision, their higher purpose of being a strong, secure, local bank which existed with and for the community. Chairman Don Anderson led the company to keep its eyes on that simple mission, which was inconsistent with overseas investing.

Because Santa Barbara Bank & Trust's purpose is elevated to a higher plane, it is a warm, comfortable place to be for employees and customers alike. It has *meaning*. The difference between the standard numbers-focused purpose and a higher purpose and vision can be summarized as follows.

Numbers-focused purpose	Higher purpose/vision
• "make a buck" approach	• evokes higher values
• doesn't mean much to employees	• has personal application
• cold and impersonal	• inspirational
• focuses on reports	• focus on bringing out the best in people
• short-term results	• long-term results
• ends when number reached	• continues forever

The key element to leading from within and achieving this higher purpose is simple, although trickier to implement than any list of competencies. Let's consider the core principle of leading from within.

The Leap of Faith

Many leaders have tried to create "Mom and apple pie" vision statements. A large percent end up hanging on the wall, unread. Because of the leader's actions, everyone knows that it's still the bottom line they must concentrate on, even if it means ignoring or contradicting the vision. So how have some been able to "walk the talk," rather than reverting back to old habits when times get tough? How have some been able to rise above, with outcomes of even *greater* profitability? In answering these questions, we come to the key attribute of leading from within. The secret, elusive ingredient is *the willingness to take a leap of faith.*

Leaders must trust their people, their business plans, their intuition, their customers enough to say, "I know what we're doing is right. It provides value to our customers at a fair price.

If we focus on doing the right thing, as effectively and efficiently as we can, we will achieve excellence." Leaders who don't have faith in their company's products and their people's ideas are not willing to take the necessary leap of faith, even though it would lead to long-term profitability by unleashing the organization's human potential.

We never doubt that a garden plant knows how to be a plant. We don't pull it up once a week to see if its roots are growing. If we did, it would never grow. Leaders must have trust that once a meaningful direction is clear and employees are provided with the resources they need, everyone will move to fulfill the vision. Instead of checking up on employees by asking, "Have you done what I told you to do?" people who lead from within ask, "How can I help you be successful?" As former Herman Miller CEO Max DePree writes in his book *Leadership is an Art,* "The first responsibility of the leader is to define reality. The last is to say 'thank you.' In between the two, the leader must become a servant and debtor."

It is in attempting to take this leap of faith that a leader's personal beliefs become important. In studying people who lead from within, one common thread emerges. It is their dedication to personal spiritual beliefs that gives them a foundation of faith and trust in the universe and the ultimate good of humanity. Here, the term "spiritual" does *not* mean religious. It means the animating, life-giving force within a human being; the reality beyond what we can touch and see.

This trust that the good will emerge is reminiscent of a story about the great artist Michaelangelo. When asked how he was able to create a magnificent sculpture out of a lump of marble, he responded that the statue was already contained within the marble. All he did was chip away the excess rock—the parts that were *not* part of the statue.

Similarly, this notion is reflected in the work of noted psychologist Carl Rogers, who believed that it is the nature of human beings to move in a positive direction. According to Rogers, the mechanism for releasing this force of energy is to create relationships and an environment in which the person's natural expression is allowed to emerge.

For people who lead from within, the leap of faith is a natural outgrowth of their innermost, deepest beliefs, whether

The Leap of Faith

In days of old, the steeples rose.
They inspired the awe of those
who travelled in from lands afar
with open arms but weary hearts.

In modern times, the skyscrapers rise
to tower up and pierce the skies.
They are so tall, we feel so small.
And as we enter their great halls
our emptiness is reinforced
by hollow goals and long reports.

Who am I in this grand scheme?
Why should I care, what does it mean?
The inflated titles on business cards
leave me feeling cold and hard.

Our modern spires hold our fate.
We only hope it's not too late
to bring about what once we knew
to be worthwhile, and real, and true.

And when we reach deep down inside
and move beyond our selfish pride,
We realize we can do it, too,
the leap of faith will see us through.

—Tina Rasmussen

these are in the form of Christian religions, Judaism, Eastern religions, New Age practices, meditation, or psychology. These leaders believe that they and their companies are on this earth to provide a service, not just to make a profit, and the way to do this depends on trust in the people and the vision as much as it depends on cold, hard, rational business practices.

Taking this leap of faith isn't easy. One leader told me of an incident in which he had taken the leap, and was now in a position in which the followers—who were also customers—were responsible for setting the fees they would pay the parent company of which he was president. In recalling the moment when he was tempted to revert back, he said he was somehow able to stop and tell himself, "Let it go, remember what it's all about." His commitment to his values and vision was stronger than his fear.

Some people who lead from within have found that the ideology of servant leadership, based on the work of the late Robert K. Greenleaf, fits their values. Many authors attribute the start of this new spirituality in the workplace to Greenleaf, who published his first essay, *The Servant as Leader,* in 1977. Greenleaf's book has quietly crept into the hands of many influential business leaders, and has now been quoted in management books and magazines read by thousands of business people around the world. Many people who practice servant leadership have histories which are as impressive as Dave Spainhour's.

The world may not have huge numbers of people exhibiting this type of leadership. But there are probably a large number who are moving closer to leading from within. If you are reading this book, you may already believe a different way of leading is possible, and even profitable. Perhaps you've had glimmers of it. Maybe you've experimented with it. If so, I hope this essay has given you more concrete evidence that it actually *works,* as well as some ideas on how it takes shape in an organization. Most importantly, we've defined the key ingredient which will let it happen. May you have the courage to *take your own leap of faith.*

PART THREE

Leadership in an Era of Paradox

Servant-Leadership: Toward a New Era of Caring
Larry C. Spears

The Innocent Leader: Accepting Paradox
Elemer Magaziner

Both/And Thinking:
Leading Change in a World of Paradox
Susan M. Campbell

The Koan of Leadership
Robert Rabbin

Learning to live with paradox will be one of the most challenging tasks of the new leaders. In our western world we have become so accustomed to black and white answers —right and wrong, good and bad, plus or minus—that don't contradict each other. We have come to highly value "the answer" and find it difficult or impossible to accept seemingly contradictory solutions or realities.

The challenge of paradox is addressed by four of our authors in this segment, starting with executive director Larry C. Spears who writes about servant-leadership, a concept that may appear contradictory to many traditionalists. Consultant Elemer Magaziner advocates "innocent leaders" whose strengths lie in their ability to let opposites be, without forcing resolution.

Susan M. Campbell, author of five books including the

forthcoming *Survival Strategies for the New Workplace*, pre-scribes "both/and thinking" as a strategy for leading change in this era of paradox. Clarity coach Robert Rabbin stands for increased self-awareness—a key for new thinking for our new leaders.

Each in his or her own way, these authors anticipate a new acceptance, a new challenge—paradox, koan, the seeming con-flict of opposites—for the leaders in this new era. Indeed, this is an exciting time to be alive!

Larry C. Spears
is executive director of the Robert
K. Greenleaf Center for Servant-
Leadership, an international, not-
for-profit membership organization headquartered in Indianapolis. In
addition to his fifteen years of management and leadership experience,
Spears is also a writer, editor, and publications designer. He has been
interviewed by numerous publications, including: *Fortune, The Philadel-
phia Inquirer, Training, The Indianapolis Business Journal, Mother Jones,*
and National Public Radio. Spears is a graduate of DePauw University and
has lectured widely throughout the United States.

Under his leadership, the Greenleaf Center has experienced tremendous growth in its programs and activities since he was named executive
director in 1990. The Center offers a variety of seminars, workshops and
resources on the theme of "the servant-as-leader."

12

Servant-Leadership: Toward a New Era of Caring

Larry C. Spears

"Caring for persons, the more able and the less able serving each other, is the rock upon which a good society is built."

—Robert K. Greenleaf

There is a deep and growing hunger in our society for a world in which people truly care for one another. We long for a world in which people are treated humanely and helped in their personal growth. We long for a world in which our institutions treat workers and customers fairly. We long for a world in which our leaders can be trusted to truly serve the needs of the many, rather than the few.

There is also a growing recognition that we are suffering from a leadership and service crisis in many areas today. In government, business, education, and in other areas of public life, there are concerns that truly caring and effective leadership is becoming harder to find. All too often, it appears to us that people in leadership positions are primarily motivated by desires for power, status or wealth—rather than a desire to serve the needs of others.

As we approach the 21st Century, we are beginning to see that traditional autocratic and hierarchical modes of leadership are slowly yielding to a newer model—one which is based upon teamwork and community. It seeks to involve others in decision making. It is strongly based in ethical and caring behavior; and, it is attempting to enhance the personal growth of workers, while at the same time improving the caring and quality of our many institutions. This emerging approach to leadership and service is called "servant-leadership."

The words servant and leader are usually thought of as being opposites. When two opposites are brought together in a creative and meaningful way, a paradox emerges. And so the words servant and leader have been brought together to create the paradoxical idea of servant-leadership. Consequently, in the past ten years we have seen the emergence of what has become a growing social movement centered around the servant-leader paradox.

Robert K. Greenleaf

"Despite all the buzz about modern leadership techniques, no one knows better than Greenleaf what really matters."
—*Working Woman* magazine

The term "servant-leadership" was first coined in a 1970 essay by Robert K. Greenleaf (1904-1990) entitled, *The Servant as Leader*. Greenleaf, who was born in Terre Haute, Indiana, spent most of his organizational life in the field of management research, development and education at AT&T. Following a forty-year career at the giant communications firm, Greenleaf enjoyed a second career which lasted twenty-five years, during which time he served as an influential consultant to a number of major institutions, including Ohio University, M.I.T., the Ford Foundation, R.K. Mellon Foundation, the Mead Corporation, the American Foundation for Management Research, and Lilly Endowment Inc. In 1964, Greenleaf also founded the Center for Applied Ethics, which was renamed the Robert K. Greenleaf Center in 1985 and is now headquartered in Indianapolis.

As a lifelong student of how things get done in organizations, Greenleaf distilled his observations in a series of essays and books on the theme of "The Servant as Leader." His objective was to stimulate thought and action for building a better, more caring society.

The Servant-as-Leader Idea

The idea of the servant-as-leader came partly out of Greenleaf's half-century of experience in working to shape large institutions. However, the event which crystallized Greenleaf's thinking came in the 1960's when he read Herman Hesse's short novel, *Journey to the East*—an account of a mythical journey by a group of people on a spiritual quest. The central figure of the story is Leo, who accompanies the party as the servant and who sustains them with his caring spirit. All goes well with the journey until one day Leo disappears. The group quickly falls into disarray, and the journey is abandoned. They discover that they cannot make it without the servant, Leo. After many years of searching, the narrator of the story stumbles upon Leo and is taken into the religious order that had sponsored the original journey. There, he discovers that Leo, whom he had first known as a servant, was in fact the head of the order, its guiding spirit—a great and noble leader.

After reading this story, Greenleaf concluded that the central meaning of it was that the great leader is first experienced as a servant to others, and that this simple fact is central to his or her greatness. True leadership emerges from those whose primary motivation is a deep desire to help others.

In 1970, at the age of 66, Greenleaf published *The Servant as Leader*, the first of a dozen essays and books on servant-leadership. Since that time, over a half-million copies of his books and essays have been sold worldwide. Slowly-but-surely, Greenleaf's servant-leadership writings have made a deep, lasting impression on leaders, educators, and many others who are concerned with issues of leadership, management, service and personal growth.

What is Servant-Leadership?

In all of these works, Greenleaf discusses the need for a new kind of leadership model—a model which puts serving others—including employees, customers, and community—as the number one priority. Servant-leadership emphasizes increased service to others, a holistic approach to work, promoting a sense of community, and the sharing of power in decision making.

Who *is* a servant-leader? Greenleaf said that the servant-leader is one who is servant-first. In *The Servant as Leader* he wrote: "It begins with the natural feeling that one wants to serve, to serve first. Then conscious choice brings one to aspire to lead. The difference manifests itself in the care taken by the servant—first to make sure that other people's highest priority needs are being served. The best test is: Do those served grow as persons; do they, while being served, become healthier, wiser, freer, more autonomous, more likely themselves to become servants?"

It is important to stress that servant-leadership is *not* a "quick-fix" approach. Nor is it something which can be quickly instilled within an institution. At its core, servant-leadership is a long-term, transformational approach to life and work—in essence, a way of being—which has the potential for creating positive change throughout our society.

Ten Characteristics of the Servant-Leader

"Servant leadership deals with the reality of power in everyday life—its legitimacy, the ethical restraints upon it and the beneficial results that can be attained through the appropriate use of power."

—*The New York Times*

After some years of carefully considering Greenleaf's original writings, I have identified a set of ten characteristics of the servant-leader which I view as being of critical importance. The following characteristics are ones which appear to me to be central to the development of servant-leaders. They are:

1. *Listening.* Leaders have traditionally been valued for their communication and decision making skills. While these are also important skills for the servant-leader, they need to be reinforced by a deep commitment to listening intently to others. The servant-leader seeks to identify the will of a group, and helps clarify that will. He or she seeks to listen receptively to what is being said (and not said!). Listening also encompasses getting in

touch with one's own inner voice, and seeking to understand what one's body, spirit and mind are communicating. Listening, coupled with regular periods of reflection, is essential to the growth of the servant-leader.

2. *Empathy.* The servant-leader strives to understand and empathize with others. People need to be accepted and recognized for their special and unique spirits. One assumes the good intentions of co-workers and does not reject them as people, even when one is forced to refuse to accept their behavior or performance. The most successful servant-leaders are those who have become skilled empathetic listeners. It is interesting to note that Robert Greenleaf developed a course in "receptive listening" in the 1950's for the Wainwright House in New York. This course continues to be offered to the present day.

3. *Healing.* Learning to heal is a powerful force for transformation and integration. One of the great strengths of servant-leadership is the potential for healing one's self, and others. Many people have broken spirits and have suffered from a variety of emotional hurts. Although this is a part of being human, servant-leaders recognize that they have an opportunity to "help make whole" those with whom they come in contact. In *The Servant as Leader,* Greenleaf writes: "There is something subtle communicated to one who is being served and led if, implicit in the compact between servant-leader and led, is the understanding that the search for wholeness is something they share."

4. *Awareness.* General awareness, and especially self-awareness, strengthens the servant-leader. Making a commitment to foster awareness can be scary—you never know what you may discover! Awareness also aids one in understanding issues involving ethics and values. It lends itself to being able to view most situations from a more integrated, holistic position. As Greenleaf observed: "Awareness is not a giver of solace—it is just the opposite. It is a disturber and an awakener. Able leaders are usually sharply awake and reasonably disturbed. They are not seekers after solace. They have their own inner serenity."

5. *Persuasion.* Another characteristic of servant-leaders is a reliance upon persuasion, rather than using one's positional authority, in making decisions within an organization. The servant-leader seeks to convince others, rather than coerce compliance. This particular element offers one of the clearest distinc-

tions between the traditional authoritarian model and that of servant-leadership. The servant-leader is effective at building consensus within groups. This emphasis on persuasion over coercion probably has its roots within the beliefs of The Religious Society of Friends (Quakers)—the denomination with which Robert Greenleaf himself was most closely allied.

6. *Conceptualization*. Servant-leaders seek to nurture their abilities to "dream great dreams." The ability to look at a problem (or an organization) from a conceptualizing perspective means that one must think beyond day-to-day realities. For many managers this is a characteristic which requires discipline and practice. The traditional manager is consumed by the need to achieve short-term operational goals. The manager who wishes to also be a servant-leader must stretch his or her thinking to encompass broader-based conceptual thinking. Within organizations, conceptualization is, by its very nature, the proper role of boards of trustees or directors. Unfortunately, boards can sometimes become involved in the day-to-day operations (something which should always be discouraged!) and fail to provide the visionary concept for an institution. Trustees need to be mostly conceptual in their orientation; staffs need to be mostly operational in their perspective; and the most effective CEOs and managers probably need to develop both perspectives. Servant-leaders are called to seek a delicate balance between conceptual thinking and a day-to-day focused approach.

7. *Foresight*. Closely related to conceptualization, the ability to foresee the likely outcome of a situation is hard to define, but easy to identify. One knows it when one sees it! Foresight is a characteristic which enables the servant-leader to understand the lessons from the past, the realities of the present, and the likely consequence of a decision for the future. It is also deeply rooted within the intuitive mind. As such, one can conjecture that foresight is the one servant-leader characteristic with which one may be born. All other characteristics are ones which can be consciously developed. There hasn't been a great deal written on foresight. It remains a largely unexplored area in leadership studies, but one most deserving of careful attention.

8. *Stewardship*. Peter Block (author of *Stewardship* and *The Empowered Manager*) has defined stewardship as "holding something in trust for another." Robert Greenleaf's view of all institu-

tions was one in which CEOs, staffs, and trustees all played significant roles in holding their institutions in trust for the greater good of society. Servant-leadership, like stewardship, assumes first-and-foremost a commitment to serving the needs of others. It also emphasizes the use of openness and persuasion, rather than control.

9. *Commitment to the growth of people.* Servant-leaders believe that people have an intrinsic value beyond their tangible contributions as workers. As such, the servant-leader is deeply committed to the growth of each and every individual within his or her institution. The servant-leader recognizes the tremendous responsibility to do everything within his or her power to nurture the personal, professional and spiritual growth of employees. In practice, this can include (but is not limited to) concrete actions such as making available funds for personal and professional development, taking a personal interest in the ideas and suggestions from everyone, encouraging worker involvement in decision-making, and actively assisting laid-off workers to find other employment.

10. *Building community.* The servant-leader senses that much has been lost in recent human history as a result of the shift from local communities to large institutions as the primary shaper of human lives. This awareness causes the servant-leader to seek to identify some means for building community among those who work within a given institution. Servant-leadership suggests that true community can be created among those who work in businesses and other institutions. Greenleaf said: "All that is needed to rebuild community as a viable life form for large numbers of people is for enough servant-leaders to show the way, not by mass movements, but by each servant-leader demonstrating his own unlimited liability for a quite specific community-related group."

These ten characteristics of servant-leadership are by no means exhaustive. However, I believe that the ones I have listed serve to communicate the power and promise which this concept offers to those who are open to its invitation and challenge.

Applications of Servant-Leadership

"Servant leadership has emerged as one of the dominant philosophies being discussed in the world today."

—*Indianapolis Business Journal*

There are a half-dozen major areas in which servant-leadership principles are being applied in significant ways.

1. *Servant-leadership crosses all boundaries and is being applied by a wide variety of people working with for-profit businesses, not-for-profit corporations, churches, universities, and foundations.*

In recent years, a number of institutions have jettisoned their old hierarchical models and replaced them with a servant-leader approach. Servant-leadership advocates a group-oriented approach to analysis and decision making as a means of strengthening institutions and improving society. It also emphasizes the power of persuasion and seeking consensus over the old "top-down" form of leadership. Some people have likened this to turning the hierarchical pyramid upside down. Servant-leadership holds that the primary purpose of a business should be to create a positive impact on its employees and community, rather than using profit as the sole motive.

Many individuals within institutions have adopted servant-leadership as a guiding philosophy. An increasing number of companies have adopted servant-leadership as part of their corporate philosophy or as a foundation for their mission statement. Among these are AT&T Consumer Products Education (Parsippany, NJ), Herman Miller Company (Zeeland, MI), and Schmidt Associates Architects Inc. (Indianapolis, IN). Some institutions have taken this a step further, and have actually reorganized their corporate structures along the "primus inter pares," or first-among-equals model of servant-leadership. Examples of these institutions include Schneider Engineering Company (Indianapolis, IN), Townsend & Bottum Family of Companies (Ann Arbor, MI), and TDIndustries (Dallas, TX).

TDIndustries, one of the earliest practitioners of servant-leadership in the corporate setting, is a Dallas-based heating and plumbing contracting firm which was recently profiled in Robert Levering and Milton Moskowitz's book, *The 100 Best Companies to Work for in America.* The authors discuss the longtime influence that servant-leadership has had upon the company. TDI's founder, Jack Lowe, Sr. stumbled upon *The Servant as Leader* essay in the early 1970's and began to distribute copies of it to his employees. They were invited to read through the essay, and then to gather in small groups to discuss its meaning. The belief that managers should serve their employees became an important value for TDIndustries.

Twenty years later, Jack Lowe, Jr. continues to use servant-leadership as the guiding philosophy for TDI. Levering and Moskowitz note: "Even today, any TDPartner who supervises at least one person must go through training in servant-leadership." In addition, all new employees continue to receive a copy of *The Servant as Leader* essay.

Servant-leadership has influenced many noted writers, thinkers and leaders. Max DePree, Chairman of the Herman Miller Company and author of *Leadership is an Art* and *Leadership Jazz* has said, "The servanthood of leadership needs to be felt, understood, believed, and practiced." And Peter Senge, author of *The Fifth Discipline,* has said that he tells people "not to bother reading any other book about leadership until you first read Robert Greenleaf's book, *Servant-Leadership.* I believe it is the most singular and useful statement on leadership I've come across." In recent years, a growing number of leaders and readers have "rediscovered" Robert Greenleaf's own writings through DePree and Senge's books.

2. *Education and Training of Not-for-Profit Trustees.* A second major application of servant-leadership is it's pivotal role as the theoretical and ethical basis for "trustee education." Greenleaf wrote extensively on servant-leadership as it applies to the roles of Boards of Directors and Trustees within institutions. His essays on these applications are widely distributed among directors of for-profit and nonprofit organizations. In his essay, *Trustees as Servants,* Greenleaf urged trustees to ask themselves two central questions: "Whom do you serve?" and "For what purpose?"

Servant-leadership suggests that boards of trustees need to undergo a radical shift in how they approach their roles. Trustees who seek to act as servant-leaders can help to create institutions of great depth and quality. Over the past decade, two of the largest grant making foundations (Lilly Endowment Inc. and the W.K. Kellogg Foundation) have sought to encourage the development of programs designed to educate and train not-for-profit boards of trustees to function as servant-leaders.

3. *Community Leadership Programs.* The third application of servant-leadership concerns it's deepening role in community leadership organizations across the country. A growing number of community leadership groups are using Greenleaf Center resources as part of their own education and training efforts. Some have been doing so for more than fifteen years now.

The National Association for Community Leadership has adopted servant-leadership as a special focus. Recently, NACL named Robert Greenleaf as the posthumous recipient of its National Community Leadership Award. This award is given annually to honor an individual whose work has made a significant impact on the development of community leadership worldwide.

M. Scott Peck, who has written about the importance of building true community, says the following in *A World Waiting to be Born:* "In his work on servant-leadership, Greenleaf posited that the world will be saved if it can develop just three truly well-managed, large institutions—one in the private sector, one in the public sector, and one in the nonprofit sector. He believed—and I know—that such excellence in management will be achieved through an organizational culture of civility routinely utilizing the mode of community."

4. *Service-Learning Programs.* The fourth application involves servant-leadership and experiential education. During the past twenty years experiential education programs of all sorts have sprung up in virtually every college and university—and, increasingly, in secondary schools too. Experiential education, or "learning by doing," is now a part of most students' educational experience.

Around 1980, a number of educators began to write about the linkage between the servant-leader concept and experiential learning under a new term called "service-learning." It is service-learning which has become a major focus for experiential education programs in the past few years.

The National Society for Experiential Education (NSEE) has adopted service-learning as one of its major program areas.

NSEE has published a massive three-volume work called *Combining Service and Learning*, which brings together many articles and papers about service-learning—several dozen of which discuss servant-leadership as the philosophical basis for experiential learning programs.

5. *Leadership Education.* The fifth application of servant-leadership concerns its use in both formal and informal education and training programs. This is taking place through leadership and management courses in colleges and universities, as well as through corporate training programs. A number of undergraduate and graduate courses on management and leadership incorporate servant-leadership within their course curricula. Several colleges and universities now offer specific courses on servant-leadership. Also, a number of noted leadership authors, including Peter Block, Ken Blanchard, Max DePree, and Peter Senge have all acclaimed the servant-leader concept as an overarching framework which is compatible with, and enhancing of, other leadership and management models such as Total Quality Management, Learning Organizations, and Community-Building.

In the area of corporate education and training programs, dozens of management and leadership consultants now utilize servant-leadership materials as part of their ongoing work with corporations. Some of these companies have included AT&T, the Mead Corporation, and Gulf Oil of Canada. A number of consultants and educators are now touting the benefits to be gained in building a Total Quality Management approach upon a servant-leadership foundation. Through internal training and education, institutions are discovering that servant-leadership can truly improve the way in which business is developed and conducted, while still successfully turning a profit.

6. *Personal Transformation.* The sixth application of servant-leadership involves its use in programs relating to personal growth and transformation. Servant-leadership operates at both the institutional and personal levels. For individuals it offers a means to personal growth—spiritually, professionally, emotionally and intellectually. It has ties to the ideas of M. Scott Peck (*The Road Less Traveled*), Parker Palmer (*The Active Life*), Ann McGee-Cooper (*You Don't Have to Go Home from Work Exhausted!*) and others who have written on expanding human potential. A

particular strength of servant-leadership is that it encourages everyone to actively seek opportunities to both serve and lead others, thereby setting up the potential for raising the quality of life throughout society. A number of individuals are working to integrate the servant-leader concept into various programs involving both men's and women's self-awareness groups and 12-step programs like Alcoholics Anonymous. There is also a fledgling examination underway of the servant-leader as a previously unidentified Jungian archetype. This particular exploration is discussed in a book by Robert Moore and Douglas Gillette, titled, *The King Within.*

Servant-Leadership and Multiculturalism

For some people, the word "servant" prompts an immediate negative connotation, due to the oppression which many workers—particularly women, and people of color—have historically endured. For some, it may take a while to accept the positive usage of this word. However, those who are willing to dig a little deeper come to understand the inherent spiritual nature of what is intended by the pairing of the words servant and leader. The startling paradox of the term "servant-leadership" serves to prompt new insights.

In an article titled, "Pluralistic Reflections on Servant-Leadership," Juana Bordas, of the Center for Creative Leadership, writes, "Many women, minorities and people of color have long traditions of servant-leadership in their cultures. Servant-leadership has very old roots in many of the indigenous cultures that were holistic, cooperative, communal, intuitive and spiritual. These cultures centered on being guardians of the future and respecting the ancestors who walked before."

Women leaders and authors are now writing and speaking about servant-leadership as a 21st Century leadership philosophy which is most appropriate for women to embrace. Patsy Sampson, who is President of Stephens College in Columbia, Missouri, is one such person. In an essay on women and servant-leadership, "The Leader as Servant," she writes: "So-called (service-oriented) feminine characteristics are exactly those which are consonant with the very best qualities of servant-leadership."

Professor Jill Graham, of Loyola University, published an award-winning essay titled, "Servant-Leadership in Organizations: Inspirational and Moral." In this article, she says, "A different starting point in thinking about leadership and leader-follower relationships focuses on the ideal of service. It is the leader who models service by humbly serving the led, rather than expecting to be served by them. Therein is the paradox of servant-leadership."

A Growing Movement

"Servant-leadership works like the consensus-building that the Japanese are famous for. Yes, it takes a while on the front end; everyone's view is solicited, though everyone also understands that his view may not ultimately prevail. But once the consensus is forged, watch out! With everybody on board, your so-called implementation proceeds wham-bam."

—*Fortune* magazine

Interest in the philosophy and practice of servant-leadership is now at an all-time high. Dozens of articles on servant-leadership have appeared in various magazines, journals, and newspapers over the past two years. Another thirty books on leadership have been published which talk about servant-leadership as an important model for now, and in the future.

The Greenleaf Center for Servant-Leadership is an international, not-for-profit educational organization which seeks to encourage the understanding and practice of servant-leadership. The Center's mission is to fundamentally improve the caring and quality of all institutions through a new approach to leadership, structure and decision making.

In recent years, the Greenleaf Center has experienced tremendous growth and expansion. It's growing programs include: the worldwide sales of over sixty books, essays and videotapes on servant-leadership; a membership program; workshops and seminars; the Greenleaf Archives Project; a Reading-and-Dialogue Program; a Speakers Bureau; and, an annual International Conference on Servant-Leadership. A number of notable Greenleaf Center members have spoken at our annual conferences, including most of the authors noted earlier in this chapter. Each has spoken of the tremendous impact which the servant-leader concept has played in the development of his or her own understanding of what it means to be a leader.

Paradox and Pathway

The Greenleaf Center's logo is a variation on the geometrical figure called a "Möbius strip." This figure, pictured below, is a one-sided surface which is constructed from a rectangle by holding one end fixed, rotating the opposite end through 180 degrees, and applying it to the first end—thereby giving the appearance of a two-sided figure. It thus appears to have a front side which merges into a back side, and then back again into the front.

The Möbius strip symbolizes, in visual terms, the servant-leader concept—a merging of servanthood into leadership and back into servanthood again, in a fluid and continuous pattern. It also reflects the Greenleaf Center's own role as an institution seeking to both serve and lead others who are interested in leadership and service issues.

Life is full of curious and meaningful paradoxes. Servant-leadership is one such paradox which has slowly-but-surely gained tens of thousands of adherents over the past quarter century. The seeds which have been planted have begun to sprout in many institutions, as well as in the hearts of many who long to improve the human condition. Servant-leadership is providing a framework from which many thousands of known and unknown individuals are helping to improve the way in which we treat those who do the work within our many institutions. Servant-leadership truly offers hope and guidance for a new era in human development.

Elemer Magaziner
teaches organizations how to use
language to generate a context for
clear thinking. He developed a
technique called project linguistics which has been used by leaders in
corporations, non-profits, and governments during the last fifteen years.
Project linguistics has been used to simplify and clarify project methods,
quality programs, strategic thinking, customer understanding, and culture
change.

He founded Project Linguistics International, a training and consulting
firm which has served clients such as IBM, People's Bank, GE, Pacific Bell,
Hewlett Packard, and Long's Drugs. Project Linguistics International also
offers The Innocent Leadership Program, a workshop for leaders who wish
to move freely among paradigms. Magaziner was born in Budapest, fled
to Mexico, has a liberal arts degree from Reed College, and a masters in
mathematics from the University of Montana. He is currently an international
consultant, seminar leader, writer, and speaker.

13

The Innocent Leader: Accepting Paradox

Elemer Magaziner

"Our love and sacrifice is made manifest more
than in any other way by our not knowing and our
willingness to not know."
—M. Scott Peck, author of
The Road Less Traveled

Leadership, like the other phenomena of our universe that
we endeavor to comprehend, is quite disinterested in what we call
her, what we think she is, or what we believe she must be in the
21st Century. We did not create leadership any more than we can
take credit for the existence of DNA. We have a lot less say in what
she does than we may be ready to admit. Eloquent definitions,
explanations, and predictions may give leaders control over
people, but not over what leadership is.

Leadership is, by nature, an aspect of organization—the
very stuff that gives human institutions and other complex
systems coherence. Organizations exhibit leadership as surely as
stars and planets clothe themselves in a gravity field. Wherever
there is organization, she is present. She does not need a leader
in order to express herself. In fact, the best that leaders can do is
to court her and to align with her wishes. Leaders do not

determine leadership any more than scientists determine nature.

Imagine a seed you have planted in the garden. As it grows, leadership effortlessly directs the growth and emerging structure according to the intent planned within the seed. She is who insures that you get the juicy watermelon you wanted, instead of a turnip or an oak tree. She is who insures that the developing organization incorporates the possibility of future generations. Now imagine the organization of cells that are the body of a graceful figure skater, gliding by on the ice. Leadership choreographs the organization of living elements into graceful dance. She executes just the right combination of managing, monitoring, regulating, controlling, and allowing that makes the flowing performance possible.

Leadership is indifferent to human values, as are other phenomena of our universe, knowing no right or wrong. Both Mahatma Gandhi and Adolf Hitler knew how to tap into her power with exemplary effectiveness. She offers her energy in silent disregard of the value we assign to the outcome.

I was introduced to the awesome energy of leadership before I had any concepts to filter my experience. As a five-year-old child, I watched with fascination as a man extended his arm and fingers towards some power above him. He began crackling with the energy that he had invoked, his gestures and voice building to a crescendo. He exploded in a violent verbal discharge and tens of thousands in his presence echoed the sound, each of them also reaching with outstretched arm to pull in the power. It was exactly like watching a thunderstorm: the palpable energy would build and build until the channel flashed with an explosion of sound, and the echoes could be heard receding into the distance. I had seen the fate of anything that happened to be in the way. This fascinating man had irresistible charisma, a compelling vision for the future of the human race, an ability to inspire tens of thousands with the vision, and to make them want to move towards it. His name was Adolf Hitler.

I began watching other people who could manipulate this immense energy source. They each seemed to have their own special way and their own unique vision, but their influence was clearly visible. Much, much later I learned that these people were called leaders. Leaders seemed to be conduits for the power of a natural principle that was called leadership. I saw them as the lightning channels through which the energy of leadership flows. The energy, like that which is stored in the nucleus of an atom, can be released and then directed to the leader's cause.

When we talk about "leadership in the new era" of the 21st Century, we are predicting only the future of our thoughts about her. Leadership will be no different in the next century than it has been in the last. Our concepts and models of her will surely change, and consequently our relationship to her. But just as the new science that Margaret Wheatley writes about in *Leadership and the New Science* makes no claims about a new 21st Century universe, "new leadership" cannot declare what the nature of leadership shall be. That a group of leadership gurus and visionaries can determine the future nature of organization and leadership is a confusion. It is like astronomers saying that their theories will cause the universe to contract or to expand.

The Innocent Leader

So the premise is this: just as we have learned how important it is to relinquish control over people in organizations, the new era calls for relaxing our mental grip on what is the "best" leadership or the "necessary" structure of organization. Managers, leaders, stewards, or whatever they will be called in the 21st Century, will have stopped insisting on one concept over another. They will not be trying to impose on leadership what they think is "best" any more than they will be imposing on people what they think is "best." They will focus on how they can most effectively relate to what she is. They will not believe in a supremacy of the character ethic over the personality ethic. They will not declare that stewardship must replace leadership. They will see no need to choose service over self-interest, adventure over safety, or partnership over patriarchy. They will be bored with blaming pointy pyramid-like hierarchies and praising flat pancake-like networks. They will not deem issues of task and structure as less key than those of spirit. They will no longer claim that leadership is more spiritual than good management. They will accept that power in organization is by nature both centralized and distributed. They will be interested in how models complement each other and not in how they displace and outdo one another. In short, they will be considerably more relaxed and open about what is "right," "best," or "inevitable" for leadership and organization. They will have lost the zeal for bending the world into alignment with the latest theories. They will be as open about their own thinking as they will be about the objects of their thinking. They will be what I like to call *innocent leaders,* comfortable in the paradox of letting opposites be.

Let's consider some evidence for this premise of innocent leaders. And let's gather this evidence from the same sources which are currently influencing leadership thought. Geoffrey Chew, a physicist as influential as Werner Heisenberg and Niels Bohr, developed the *bootstrap hypothesis,* a theory which unified quantum mechanics and relativity theory. Since quantum and relativity concepts continue to be inspirations for new leadership and organization thinking, the bootstrap hypothesis can provide some valuable insight. According to Chew, all concepts and theories about our world are approximations. Each of them is valid only for a certain limited range of conditions. For each we need to ask: Why does it work? What are its limits? How accurate are its descriptions? Under what conditions does it make sense to apply it?

New science has found that honest answers to these questions all lead to the same conclusion: a lack of any firm, timeless, or absolute foundation. There are no basic building blocks, no fundamental principles, no timeless unchanging formulas. Chew recognized an essential aspect of the way we think about the world, namely that we do not deal with truth, but merely with approximations of limited applicability. His hypothesis and philosophy of tolerance allow the coexistence of any number of models without favoritism. In a British television interview, Chew was asked to predict the greatest breakthrough of science in the future. Instead of describing any new concepts, he answered, "the acceptance of the fact that all of our concepts are approximations." The premise is that this is also the case for the study of leadership. The greatest breakthrough for leaders will not be some new theory or model of leadership and organization, but the acceptance, without favoritism, of any number of them.

If we wish to learn from new science, and the fact that Wheatley's book was selected as the Best Management Book of 1992 by *Industry Week* magazine seems to say that we do, then Geoffrey Chew has something important for us to consider. He might say that management, leadership, stewardship, hierarchy, networks, service, self-interest, profit, control, making a living, short-range thinking, future legacy, personality ethic, character ethic, etc. are all valid and useful. But each by itself is limited because it addresses only some of the reality of people, leadership, and organization. Chew might encourage us to tolerate all of them without favoritism, to use them in combination to obtain a clearer picture of what is real.

Wheatley echoes Chew's philosophy when she writes,

> ... we can move away from our need to think of things as polar opposites. For years I had struggled conceptually with a question I thought was important: In organizations, which is the more important influence on behavior—the system or the individual? The quantum world answered that question for me with an authoritative, 'It depends.' This is not an either/or question. There is no need to decide between the two.

Service or self-interest? It depends. Leadership or stewardship? It depends. Hierarchy or network? It depends. Centralized or shared power? It depends. Is Herman Maynard and Susan Mehrtens' *The Fourth Wave* the destination of business in the 21st Century? It depends—on what business, on what part of the world, on the prevailing culture in the organization, on what is happening elsewhere.

Wheatley describes the inadequacy of looking at the world in machine-like terms where everything is made up of parts and boundaries that separate them. She suggests we relax this compartmentalization, that we stop trying to categorize reality in terms of variables whose values delineate one thing from another. Maynard and Mehrtens agree, arguing the need for seamless boundaries both within and between organizations. Innocent leaders will have seamless boundaries not just for their organizations, but also for their theories. For example, *The Fourth Wave* uses variables to delineate the roles of corporations into the Second Wave, the Third Wave, and the Fourth Wave. The variables used to categorize the reality of corporate roles are: goals, motivation, values, stakeholders, outlook, and domain. For instance, the motivation in the Second Wave is to make money while in the Fourth Wave it is to leave a valuable legacy for the future. The goal in the Third Wave is to create value while in the Fourth Wave to act as global steward; and so on. Innocent leaders will not compartmentalize organizations into such categories. They, like Chew, will appreciate the limited applicability of such a model. They will not attempt to align organization and leadership with one specific set of values for one specific list of variables. They will see such a linear progression of waves not as an accurate description of reality, but as a convenient way to categorize our ideas about reality.

What is Really New?

The French anthropologist Pierre Clastres is more interested in leadership and organization in the past than in the future. He has studied the native peoples of the Americas, Africa, Siberia, and the South Sea Islands. He found that they had been overtaken by what we are now calling the Fourth Wave centuries ago. In *Society Against the State*, he writes,

> The chief must be responsible for maintaining peace and harmony in the group. He must appease quarrels and settle disputes—not by employing a force he does not possess, but by relying solely on the strength of his prestige, his fairness, and his verbal ability... the holders of what elsewhere would be called power are actually without power; where the political is determined as a domain beyond coercion and violence, beyond hierarchical subordination, where no relationship of command-obedience is in force.

The anthropologist Arthur H. Parker also found "21st Century leadership" and organization in the past. The following is an excerpt of his translation of the Iroquois Nation's constitution as quoted in William Fenton's *Parker on the Iroquois*:

> [Chiefs] shall be mentors of the people for all time. The thickness of their skin shall be seven spans, which is to say they shall be proof against anger, offensive actions, and criticism. Their hearts shall be full of peace and good will and their minds filled with a yearning for the welfare of the people of the confederacy. With endless patience they shall carry out their duty and their firmness shall

be tempered by a tenderness for their people. Neither anger nor fury shall find lodgement in their minds and all their words and actions shall be marked by calm deliberation ... [They] must be honest in all things ... self-interest must be cast into oblivion ... [They shall] look and listen for the welfare of the whole people and have always in view not only the present but also the coming [seven] generations, even those whose faces are yet beneath the surface of the ground, the unborn of the future Nation.

In 1754, the founding fathers of the United States invited forty-two members of the Iroquois Grand Council to serve as advisors on confederate structures for the Albany Plan of Union.

The principles heralded in such books as *The Fourth Wave*, Peter Block's *Stewardship*, and Jack Hawley's *Reawakening the Spirit in Work* have already been adopted and successfully used for millennia somewhere on this planet. Leadership and organization are and will be the things that they have always been. The leaders of a new era will realize that leadership is not only indifferent to our values, but also to our notions of time, to these arbitrary boundaries we have placed on experience called centuries and waves. Innocent leaders will probably not write books about leadership in the 22nd Century.

Dr. Clare W. Graves was a psychologist who, in the late 1960s and early 1970s, wrote a script for the plethora of leadership books in the 1990s. He listed not only the concepts and values they would be promoting and borrowing from science and spirituality, but also those they would be rejecting. He saw these books as period pieces, applicable only in cultures with a particular world view at a particular time. This would be the case, Graves contended, because what is seen to be of value by an individual, organization, or society depends on what appear to be the existential problems to be solved. Values are timeless not in that they apply always and everywhere, but only in the sense that they are always available, waiting to become important as the corresponding existential problems arise. Much to my amazement and delight, Dr. Graves even saw that, twenty years later, I would see leadership and organization as natural phenomena to tap into, instead of human constructs to be used as tools or learned as skills. No, he was not a prophet. He just realized that people and cultures adopt exactly the value systems and world views needed to deal with their particular problems. When the problems change, the value systems change.

Grave's value system theory is not well known, but it has been in operation within organizational development circles for about twenty years, finding application in fields such as health, education, politics, and economic development of nations. The theory says that there are patterns of human thought that react to major events such as the Ice Age and the Information Age. These patterns become currents that flow within cultures, determining how we think about business, the family, politics, why we are here, and where we may be in the next century. The theory describes ways of conceptualizing reality that date back thousands of years, and continue to re-emerge.

Grave's value systems theory joins Chew's bootstrap theory in reminding us to relax our mental grip and refrain from favoritism about specific models for leadership and organization.

The Significance of Paradox

Robert A. Johnson, the acclaimed Jungian analyst and author of the best-selling books *He*, *She*, and *We*, tells us that structures at the personal, organizational, and social level will begin to work when we free our thinking from the idea of choosing between seeming opposites, such as service and self-interest. Johnson finds that the human psyche strives for balance, giving both sides of any issue equal opportunity for expression. This happens even when a personal or organizational structure is designed to accommodate only the favored side. The expression of the "undesirable" side is what provides the news media with a reliable supply of scandals, atrocities, injustices, and anti-social incidents. The fabric of the structure is torn because the system, attempting to avoid the discomfiting paradox of honoring both sides, provides no reasonable way to express the forbidden side.

This expression of both sides of issues shows up wherever we care to look, inviting us to appreciate the significance of the paradox. For example, in *Reawakening The Spirit In Work*, Jack Hawley writes about spiritual leadership:

The loving man lives in a loving world, the hostile man lives in a hostile world... Expectations call on the same deep power as belief. What we really expect, we get. Expect the best and chances are you'll get it. Expect the worst: ditto.

In the same book, Hawley claims that organizations contaminate people, that human systems do not support us in living a more pure life, that large organizations are inherently prudent, shrewd, cautious, and cunning, that organizations love to subdue our strength and limit our power: "That's a key element in leadership: being able to hold out against society's [whether it's the company society or the larger society] tendency to eat you up." So a loving man lives in a hostile world, just as a hostile man lives in a loving world. Indeed, all combinations of "loving" and "hostile" are not only possible, but easily coexist in the paradox that reality is.

In *Owning Your Own Shadow*, Johnson writes,

Paradox is the artesian well of meaning we need so badly in our modern world... For some incomprehensible reason we often refuse this paradoxical nature of reality and, in an idiot moment, think we can function outside it. The very moment we do this, we translate paradox into opposition ... We hate paradox because it is so painful getting there, but it is a very direct experience of a reality beyond our usual frame of reference and yields some of the greatest insights ... Every single virtue in this world is made valid by its opposite ... To transfer our energy from opposition to paradox is a very large leap in evolution ... [it] is to allow both sides of an issue equal dignity and worth.

Psychology arrived at the deep significance of paradox through observations of the psyche, and new science arrived at the same place through observations of the physical universe.

I remember being dismayed when I read in Marilyn Ferguson's *The Aquarian Conspiracy*:

While most of our institutions are faltering, a twentieth-century version of the ancient tribe or kinship has appeared: the network, a tool for the

next step in human evolution ... This organic mode
of social organization is more biologically adaptive,
more efficient, and more 'conscious' than the hierarchical structures of modern civilization... Power
is changing hands, from dying hierarchies to living
networks.

I was astonished that she was actually assigning moral
value and vehement comparative judgment to a structural concept.

John Naisbitt seemed to echo this interpretation of the
nature of organization. He writes in *Megatrends*:

Hierarchies remain; our belief in their efficacy
does not. In effect, our belief in the ideal pyramid
structure, which we had talked about redesigning
and improving, came tumbling down, the victim of
its own outdated, top-down power structure. Looking around the world, it was clear to many that the
problems of the day—a sagging economy, political
unrest, and a litany of intractable social problems—were not solvable in a world organized according to the hierarchical principle. The failure of
hierarchies to solve society's problems forced people
to talk to one another—and that was the beginning
of networks.

Let's look at a different side of the organizational structure
story. Ervin Laszlo, a pioneer of systems thinking, writes in *The
Systems View of the World*:

Because the patterns of development in all
realms of nature are analogous, evolution appears
to drive towards the superposition of system upon
system in a continuous hierarchy, traversing the
regions of the suborganic, organic, and
supraorganic. Organization in nature comes to
resemble a complex, multilevel pyramid... Hence
regardless of whether we are talking about physical systems, species of living organisms, or social
systems, we find that those which are likely to be
around are the ones which are hierarchically organized.

All organization, be it in the form of a human body or a corporation, exhibits many structural features simultaneously. We can draw a network diagram to display the interdependencies within any organization. And we can draw a hierarchy diagram to show the integrating relationships among the organization's subsystems and elements. Words like "hierarchy" and "network" are ways of looking at things, and not the things themselves. I read somewhere that a large Japanese corporation used an organizational chart to get organized, then threw it away. The innocent leaders of a new era will echo Wheatley: "... I wonder why we limit ourselves so quickly to one idea or one structure or one perception, or to the idea that 'truth' exists only in objective form."

Being an innocent leader in a new era will be a challenge in paradox. In the uncertainty of a quantum world, when you are in a situation that calls for leading the people around you, how does it feel to speak up as if you know what to do? I invariably feel a pang of discomfort as the words come out. I realize just how close I am to convincing myself of what I'm saying and identifying with it. I think of Peter Block writing in *Executive Excellence*: "To hold something of value in trust calls for placing service ahead of control, to no longer expect leaders to be in charge and out in front. There is pride in leadership—it evokes images of direction." By saying this in *Stewardship*, and declaring his prescription to be our best hope for the future, Block has "paradoxed" himself out in front and set a direction and clear path for others to follow.

Paradox will remind the leaders of the 21st Century to ignore the boundaries of truth and falsehood and to offer the openness of vision. Instead of pitting one concept against another, they will return from the certainty of knowing to the innocence of thinking without boundaries. They will not attempt to force agreement between the nature of leadership and their own designs for a better world. The leaders of a new era will respect the natural indifference of leadership, thereby releasing organizations to respond spontaneously and creatively to the unpredictability of the future.

Susan M. Campbell

is an independent organizational consultant, trainer, and speaker with offices in Belvedere and Rohnert Park, California. A nationally recognized authority on change and conflict management, she consults with Fortune 500 companies as well as smaller organizations from both the public and private sector.

Formerly a faculty member at the University of Massachusetts Applied Behavioral Sciences Graduate Program, she is now on the Adjunct Faculty at Saybrook Institute in San Francisco. She is the author of five books and several audio tape programs on communication, leadership, change, conflict management, group dynamics, and interpersonal relationships.

14

Both/And Thinking: Leading Change in a World of Paradox

Susan M. Campbell

In today's complex organization, everyone's voice needs to be heard. No one group member, not even the company president, can possess all the information necessary to guide the group's actions. To contain disparate perspectives, we must develop the ability to learn from people without necessarily sharing their point of view.

We need the ability to *both* assert our own views *and* respect the views of those who disagree with us. We need to know how to affirm and use our strengths without ignoring our blind spots or limitations. We need *both* the confidence to express our expertise *and* the humility to learn from people who are more knowledgeable. In the new workplace, anyone who works with people will need to know how to provide a container that can hold divergent views and apparent contradictions alongside one another.

Anyone who would lead, facilitate, or attempt to improve any human system (including yourself) must understand that no one and no thing is all one way. No one is always right or always wrong. No one person or group can have all the answers. The good news about this is that we need each other's knowledge and input to help us see the whole picture or put together the puzzle.

The bad news is that we sometimes hate to admit it. Many of us just naturally feel that our way is the right way. The untrained mind has a tendency to go toward certainty, security, and arrogance. This is much easier than embracing uncertainty, the need for others' help, and the feeling of not being in control. We think we need certainty and control for our sense of well-being.

Dealing with different styles and opposing views on a daily basis can feel threatening. But it is only threatening if our security is based on having the right, or the most popular, answer. In the new learning-oriented organization, we cannot afford such myopia. We will quickly learn to value differing perspectives because these add breadth to our knowledge and understanding.

With "Both/And Thinking" people do not have to be similar in styles, or even in values, to work well together. There does need to be respect for each person's view and contribution. But we don't all have to think alike.

Embracing differing perspectives gives us insight into wider markets and a greater variety of potential customers. Differences can be resources instead of nuisances—even as they also make us uncomfortable. Most of us have not learned how to feel at home in a room full of people who are clearly different from ourselves in some obvious way. It is uncomfortable to be in the minority. We have learned to feel safer with people like ourselves. Both/And Thinking helps us feel safe and powerful wherever we go because our intent is to learn from our differences, not to judge or feel judged. We can learn so much from people who are different from ourselves when we make this our intention.

You Need Both/And Thinking

The ability to hold your own position on an issue while at the same time seriously considering alternative views is critical to making sound business decisions. Doing so insures that you won't ignore some potentially important piece of information just because it is uncomfortable to deal with. People who cannot tolerate disagreement, who cannot step outside the conflict long enough to consider all views, are not going to survive in the new workplace. Here is how Jerry and Phil, two business partners in a small computer software company, lost their business due to their inability to utilize Both/And Thinking.

Jerry was known for his hot temper and forceful style. Phil was the more accommodating member of the partnership—easy-going and eager to please. One day Jerry came into the office very excited about an investment opportunity that promised to double the company's net worth over the next year. Phil had serious reservations about the advisability of moving company funds out of the more secure investments they presently held. He held back his objections for fear of creating an uproar. When he had tried to differ with Jerry in the past, he had found himself bombarded with angry accusations and insults. Phil agreed to let Jerry put 90% of the company's assets into the investment.

Two months later the investment went sour, and Phil and Jerry lost their business. Both were operating from an either/or mind set—the idea that if one wins the other loses; or that if my partner disagrees with me, we cannot work together—so someone has to give in immediately. Phil knows now that if he and Jerry had been able to hit the conversation ball back and forth over the net a few times, exchanging ideas about alternatives, they could have developed a viable plan.

The new workplace contains enormous diversity in language, personal styles, values, and cultural expectations. And this diversity is rapidly increasing. If there ever was an era for learning to resolve conflicts and harmonize divergent interests, this is it.

I was recently working with a company where a group of five people from the R&D department were trying to reach consensus about staffing and resource allocation. In attendance were a 25-year-old male Indian Sikh who wore a white turban, a 43-year-old African-American female from Alabama, a 60-year-old white male retired Army Colonel who presented himself as a recovering alcoholic, a 44-year-old Asian male, and a 21-year-old female, recently emigrated from Russia.

All five of these people were well-educated scientists. And all were committed to team and company goals. This was their common ground. They were also individuals with quite different values about how money should be spent and who should be in charge. The tension in the meeting room was palpable. I could sense the mounting frustration and the valiant efforts at self-control. They listened politely to one another, but it was obvious that they were not really paying attention. Each was waiting for a chance to speak—for what that was worth, since no one was listening anyway!

How does work get done in such an environment? Without an atmosphere of mutual respect, people resist one another's inputs, and the system's capacity to learn from its own experience is impaired. Yet competitive, either/or environments are the rule rather than the exception in many organizations. Most of us were taught to think in either/or terms, to divide our world into mutually exclusive categories: this idea is good/that one is bad, she is motivated/he is unmotivated, I'm right/you're wrong, this product is useful/that one is useless. In childhood, the adult view, was right and the childish view, was wrong. In adolescence, belonging to the in-group was good and being in the out-group meant you weren't good enough. In adulthood, we are either successes or failures. It is difficult to conceive that a person could be both right and wrong, both motivated and unmotivated, both successful in some areas and unsuccessful in others. When we pause to think more deeply about how things are, the Both/And view makes a lot of sense. Unfortunately, our thinking is often more automatic than accurate.

Today's complex problems require a Both/And approach. When we fail to see a situation in its totality, we often solve one problem while creating another. Affirmative action hiring is a case in point. Since the 1970s, government agencies and institutions who receive government funding have been required to show proof that they are places of "equal opportunity" employment. Women and minorities have been afforded advantages in hiring that they have not had heretofore. Affirmative action is an important problem and it deserves our attention.

Unfortunately, as this problem is being solved, another is being created. This is the problem of how to prevent resentment and backlash from those who have been denied employment because they are white and male. We need to recognize that every problem has more facets than any group can perceive. That is why we need to consider the problem from the vantage point of both whites and people of color, both males and females, both rich and poor. In the new workplace, we must learn to deal with problems in their full complexity.

Turning Misunderstanding into Learning

Men and women typically get into misunderstandings because of their different culturally conditioned communication styles. Rick and Janelle, while planning their department's upcoming quarterly retreat, have the following conversation: Rick says, "I think we should have it in New Orleans. It's nice there at that time of year." Janelle pauses, then says, "Okay." As we look in on the pair a month later, they are meeting to evaluate the event. Janelle discloses, "I never did think New Orleans was a good idea. I wanted to do it in Virginia Beach." "What?!" exclaims Rick in surprise, "I thought you agreed that it was nice there at this time of year."

As they attempt to unravel their misunderstanding, Janelle learns that Rick proposed New Orleans and then waited for her to object if she didn't agree. That's what he would have done: "Why didn't you speak up if you had a different idea?!" Rick learns that Janelle expected him to ask for her input if he wanted it: "I thought it was a done deal, since you didn't ask for my views. I always invite the other person to tell me what they think after I propose what I want," she explained.

As Rick and Janelle continue their conversation, they realize that their working relationship has been uncomfortable for both of them for quite some time. Janelle has often felt "steamrollered" by Rick; Rick frequently felt criticized because of Janelle's silence. This awareness led them into a conversation where each tried to get the other to behave more like themselves. "Just assert yourself," chided Rick. "Why don't you ask people for their input so they'll feel you're interested?" suggested Janelle.

If we, as observers of this debate, can step back and see these two viewpoints from a Both/And perspective, we see the validity in both views:

It is true, Janelle would do well to develop more assertiveness. It is also true that Rick could profitably learn something from her knack for drawing people out in conversations. If the pair could look at their differences this way, both could come away with important personal learnings.

Both/And Thinking includes the following ideas:

- Each of us holds only a partial view of any situation. We need others' inputs to see the rest of the picture. Both/And Thinking makes organizational learning possible because it promotes the dialogue needed to fill in the gaps in each worker's knowledge.

- Everything and every quality that exists has more than one side to it—an obvious outward manifestation and a subtle, hidden aspect. People, for example, have both their positive, well-developed attributes and their sometimes hidden "flat sides," or less developed aspects. We need one another as mirrors, to reflect to us our flat sides, and as models to help us round them out.

- Because of the at-least-two-sidedness of everyone, we are all ambivalent to a degree. You may both want to succeed at your job and at the same time feel cautious about the added responsibility that comes with success. You may both wish to learn a new skill and fear what you will have to go through during the learning process—like feeling awkward at first. It is best not to over-identify with either side, but instead to realize that you are *both* eager to learn *and* afraid.

- Because of our discomfort with our inner ambivalence, we often project our inner conflicts outward onto our interpersonal relationships. The outer power struggles with others often mirror the inner struggles we are having with ourselves. Thus, if I am in conflict over how to balance work and relaxation in my life, I may find myself in a relationship power struggle where one of us over-works and the other over-plays.

- Both/And Thinking offers a very practical approach for dealing with the people we find most difficult. If I am bugged by my co-worker's self-centeredness, for example, this may reflect an unconscious struggle within myself regarding this unappealing trait. Perhaps I have trouble admitting to any feeling in myself that looks even remotely self-centered. As a result, I tend to let self-centered people walk all over me. This is why I find these people so difficult. But they can be teachers for me as well. In their presence I am pushed to behave more assertively in order to keep myself from being overpowered.

- It is possible to operate both on behalf of the whole (group, company, etc.) and on behalf of yourself at the same time. You can train yourself to see both the parts and the whole at once. A good group facilitator or third party mediator does this. So does any good leader or executive. A leader doesn't feel good about what she has done until everyone on the team feels good. A leader has the capacity to hold in mind "the good of the whole" and behave accordingly.

- It is possible to serve values or ends that might appear to be mutually exclusive or contradictory. For example I can be both demanding and compassionate in my treatment of people. I can listen openly to a viewpoint that I vehemently disagree with and at the same time retain my commitment to my own views or values. This is essential for being a good leader, a good negotiator, a good group facilitator, a good team player, or a good parent.

- Paradox is a fact of life. The harder you try to control the outcome of your efforts, the less in control you feel. The more you try to overcome or escape from some feared outcome, the more this feared thing pursues and haunts you.

Both/And Thinking draws a bigger circle around things that might ordinarily seem contradictory or unrelated. It reveals the subtler relationships and inter-dependencies between things. It enables us to see the order within the chaos, the emerging truth in the confusion, and the meaning in the pain. It helps us reconcile the irreconcilable.

Listed on the next page are three situations as viewed through the Either/Or vs. the Both/And lens.

Either/Or Thinking	Both/And Thinking
That employee is unmotivated. We should fire her.	Most employees have potential for both the wish to excel and the wish to goof off. What conditions foster this person's wish to excel?
Management isn't concerned about employees' needs. It only cares about profits.	It is possible to attend both to individual needs and to company needs. Most companies try to do both, but they may need help from the employees in learning how to best serve individual needs. Creating organizations that support employees is the job of both management and other employees.
If our company grows any bigger, our quality of life will suffer.	Let's search for ways of structuring ourselves that retain the small company responsiveness alongside the efficiency advantages of a larger firm.

Embracing Paradox

Scientists warn us "you can't solve the problem at the level of the problem." Both/And Thinking gets us above the level of the problem so we can see the relationships between things formerly thought to be separate or mutually exclusive. Any time you see the complementarity or connection between things that might ordinarily be seen as separate or opposing, you are engaging in Both/And Thinking. Most of us have had the experience of both caring about a person and being frustrated with him or her at the same time. This is a Both/And moment. Or perhaps you have been in a situation where you could see the potential benefits and the potential problems in a proposal. Life is full of Both/And moments. The essence of the experience is recognizing the underlying unity of opposing forces. When you expand your viewpoint, solutions become apparent that you never would have imagined.

Using Both/And Approaches in Team Building

It is important that all members of a work team appreciate each other's natural strengths and accept each other's limitations. Both/And Thinking gives people permission to be less than perfectly balanced. It validates talking about both what we do well and what we are still learning how to do. When we are candid about disclosing our limitations, the team can design mechanisms to compensate for them. For example, a member of the team may have a tendency to take on too much work and then renege on commitments. While she is learning to manage this problem, the rest of the team can help her (and themselves) by checking in regularly to see if she needs to renegotiate any of the agreements she has made.

In the leadership team of a large metropolitan hospital, the three top administrators—Sheryl, Maureen, and Frank—had three very different patterns of strengths and limitations. Sheryl's style was authoritative. She had a way of inspiring confidence in colleagues and members of the community. That was the good news. The bad news was that she had so much confidence in her own way of doing things that she found herself getting impatient with others. The people working for her often felt either criticized or superfluous. Learning to empower others was a "growing edge" for her.

Maureen's style was more inclusive and collegial. She had a natural, easy way of asking others for their inputs and of allowing others to take the time they needed to get assignments clarified. The bad news for Maureen was that she lacked confidence in her own judgment. Her growing edge was to develop more trust in her own opinions and to risk putting these on the table in team meetings.

Frank was the visionary on the team. He inspired the other two with the big pictures he could paint. On the down side, he was not very comfortable with people. Most of his attention went toward possibilities for improvement and expansion, not toward the day to day operations of the hospital. His growing edge was to learn how to be satisfied with what is, to accept people and the organization, warts and all.

We can see from the descriptions of these three personality styles that conscious team work is important to an organization's success. We probably also know, from being in situations with people like Frank or Maureen or Sheryl, that people with different styles often push our buttons.

In team building, it can be useful to identify the buttons that tend to get triggered in each relationship. The idea here is that we will: (1) each take responsibility for the fact that we do have our buttons or areas of hypersensitivity; and (2) try not to push each other's buttons.

When team members have been through a process in which they disclose buttons and growing edges along with being acknowledged for their strengths, this builds a real feeling of mutual support. Often teams will devise ways to assist each person in achieving his/her own growth goals.

Basic to this work is the philosophy which says: we all have something valuable to contribute as well as something important to learn from our membership in this organization. This is Both/And Thinking in action.

Viewing Everyday Conflicts as Opportunities for Learning

Kurt and Marshall were partners in a small real estate development firm. Kurt complained that he couldn't get his partner, Marshall, to take action on any of the proposals that he made. Marshall complained that Kurt's investment proposals were not well researched. Kurt insisted that this was Marshall's job, not his. "After all, you're the numbers man—I'm just the contractor." And so it went, each one protesting, "I can't do my job until you do yours."

When Kurt and Marshall first decided to go into partnership two years earlier, they assumed that their differences would be an asset. Kurt's talent for finding potential properties would be nicely balanced by Marshall's ability to cautiously evaluate them. But after working together for less than a year, their differences had become intolerable. Marshall was accusing Kurt of "wanting to make an offer on anything with a price tag." Kurt complained that Marshall was "unwilling to even sign a check for the phone bill without researching every item on it."

They were stuck in a "Looker vs. Leaper" power struggle (from the phrase "look before you leap"). Kurt was the risk-taking Leaper, while Marshall was the more cautious Looker. They began exploring their differences by reviewing the history of their working relationship. Doing this reminded them of the feelings they used to have about their differences, of how they originally decided to work together because of their belief that in any real estate deal, *both* caution *and* risk are needed. They traced the history of their partnership from this initial Both/And attraction to its current polarized state.

In looking at why they were initially drawn to the idea of working together, they got into a discussion about what life had taught each of them. They did this by sharing stories from their childhoods. Marshall's childhood had been characterized by upheaval, unpredictability, and insecurity. Kurt's had been calm, predictable, and boring. By now it was becoming obvious to them why they approached the unknown so differently.

Their stories supported the idea that people get into power struggles because *what one person has underlearned,* in the course of his lifetime, *the other has overlearned.* Kurt had underlearned caution, which Marshall had overlearned. Marshall had underlearned risk-taking, which Kurt had overlearned. The polarization reveals what each person needs to learn. And if a dialogue can be created, there may be the opportunity in a relationship to finally learn one's underlearned trait.

As Kurt and Marshall continued to explore their differences with genuine interest, each man saw where he himself was out of balance. Each came to value some of what the other could teach him. And they stopped blaming one another for the stagnation of the business. They correctly diagnosed their problem as each one's inability to trust his own "other side," not the partner. Your other side is the side of yourself you have repressed or denied. You don't know it very well, so it's hard to trust it.

As we saw with Kurt and Marshall, systems tend to polarize, or fall out of balance, at some point during their life cycle. In my book, *Beyond the Power Struggle,* I describe the dynamics of how the power struggle stage often follows an initial period of hope and harmony. This phenomenon is a reflection of the natural process of increasing differentiation and complexity in human systems. If the system can learn to use an awareness of polarity for balancing and integrating the opposing forces within it, it can handle future differentiations without power struggles. If we can learn to view polarization (either/or opposition) as an indication of an underlying polarity (both/and-ness), we can learn from our differences and use them to forge creative solutions. Today's organizations need leaders who believe this is possible.

Summary

Here is how Both/And Thinking can prepare you to manage increasing complexity:

1. The new workplace demands a higher order ability to deal with complexity. To make sound decisions you need the capacity to hold apparently contradictory views in mind long enough to discover the higher order ground that unites them.

2. While international economic barriers are being removed, many cultural barriers remain. As the global business network becomes more integrated, it becomes increasingly important for you to know how to learn from people whose world view is quite different from your own. You need to be comfortable and competent in a very large arena. Both/And Thinking allows you to cooperate and collaborate with people and groups whom you might have avoided previously, thus expanding the size of the world you can operate in.

3. As a Both/And Thinker, you are more apt to spot opportunities for collaborative efforts with other functions, departments or companies. You will be well-poised to forge strategic partnerships and help your organization cut down on the waste caused by interdepartmental isolationism or competition.

4. The successful organization of the future will be structured entirely differently than today's organization. To accomplish this fundamental redesign task, the new leader will need to bring a large number of elements into interplay or dialogue, honoring each part's contribution to the whole.

Robert Rabbin
is a clarity coach for individuals,
companies, and communities. He
founded the Hamsa Institute after
studying meditation for ten years with Swami Muktananda. The Institute's
services include personal leadership coaching, seminars, executive team
development, and retreats.

His purpose is to guide people toward enhanced awareness, the
most potent tool for resolving one's problems and conflicts, and for
discovering and realizing one's highest aspirations. He has worked with
people from all walks of life: corporate executives, entrepreneurs, professionals, ministers, rabbis, and rock musicians.

He has published articles in such magazines as *Creation Spirituality,
The New Leaders, World Business Academy Perspectives,* and *New
Frontier.* Rob has also spoken to a variety of groups in the business,
academic, and spiritual communities, and has been interviewed in
newspapers and on radio. *The Koan of Leadership* was coauthored by
Monika Pichler, president of the Hamsa Institute.

15

The Koan of Leadership

Robert Rabbin

"Attend to self reform and social reform will take care of itself."
—Ramana Maharshi

No one I know has penetrated the koan of leadership. A koan is a riddle, the solution to which can only be found by going completely beyond all conditioning and thought. The solution originates from a place utterly free from image, belief, and concept. The mind that answers a koan is no mind at all; it is empty of all representation. Wrestling with the koan of leadership requires keen reflection and persistent inquiry. We must refine our awareness to have a chance of discovering what might be buried, as a treasure, beneath the layers of conceptual thinking. An *idea* of leadership will always miss the mark; it is too slow and cumbersome; ideas cannot respond quickly enough to reality. This is why leadership is a koan. Any definition or formulation of leadership will miss the mark. Contemplate leadership as a means to become liberated from conditioning and thought. Then you will be qualified to be a leader.

The steady practice of reflection and inquiry develops clarity of mind. Clarity, the state of being free from the impediments of image and idea, allows us to see things simply as they are, not wrapped in our various imaginings. Simple awareness—of ourselves, of others, and of the world around us—is the gift of reflection and inquiry. We cannot be didactic about awareness as we can about leadership. Awareness can't be taught. We have to discover it for ourselves. If we have an interest in awareness, we can only unwrap ourselves from ideas, concepts, opinions, and judgments until awareness itself remains. Awareness itself supplants answers and solutions because it is more real and more useful.

Leaders are people to whom we turn to solve our problems, or to inspire us in some way, so that our lives will be better—freer from suffering, conflict, and difficulty. To solve our problems, we must first understand our problems, clearly and simply, without excess. Lao Tzu wrote that a wise person's greatest achievement is that he finds no problem difficult. I think he means that when we truly *see* the cause of the problem we want to solve, the problem ceases to be a problem. No solution is necessary. What is necessary is simple, spontaneous action that flows from awareness itself. "The most basic precept of all is to be aware of what we do, what we are, each minute," says the Buddhist monk Thich Nhat Hanh. This precept is the key to leadership.

A hundred books about leadership will not make any difference, because leadership is not the problem. Knowledge of leadership theories does not help us to see what is actually happening right now. What is happening right now is too real for any idea to grasp. Awareness, clarity of mind, is the appropriate tool to understand what is happening in reality. Leadership principles must give way to awareness, refined through reflection and inquiry. This is something we must each do for ourselves. We should not depend on others who may have power or authority in organizations or institutions. They cannot help.

Insight *will not* come from specialized knowledge. Solutions *will not* come from experts. Skillful action *will not* come from pretense. Insight *will* come from silence. Solutions *will* come from awareness. Skillful action *will* come, spontaneously, from clarity.

Awareness, especially self-awareness, always makes a big

difference. Self-awareness reveals our true nature to be different from the collage of impressions and beliefs that often fills our minds, creating a huge traffic jam of honking thoughts. Nisargadatta Maharaj, an Indian mystic who died a few years ago, said,

> When more people come to know their real nature, their influence, however subtle, will prevail and the world's emotional atmosphere will sweeten up. When among the leaders appear some great in heart and mind and absolutely free from self-seeking, their impact will be enough to make the crudities and crimes of the present age impossible.

Knowing one's true self is the first task of a leader.

Problems

I was meeting with a client, a corporate president, to prepare for a senior management team retreat on organizational effectiveness. The conversation became quite intimate and he opened up and shared his own vulnerability. He was leaning forward in his chair, shaking with emotion. "When they need help, don't I take care of them? Don't I help them? When they make mistakes, don't I forgive them? But who forgives me? Who helps me? Who will take care of me?" Perhaps he was really asking what many of us ask and spend our lives trying to answer: Who will love me?

He wept. I was silent. I had seen him approach this threshold before, but not cross it. Now that he had, the real issues were clear, and they had nothing to do with the company or his "leadership." The issues were sadness, despair, loneliness, and fear. I suspect that these are often the real concerns everywhere, and that the "problems" we want to fix are actually just symptoms of these more elemental issues.

Later, I remembered a poem by Kabir, a 15th Century Indian mystic:

> We sense that there is some sort of spirit that loves birds and the animals and the ants—perhaps the same one who gave a radiance to you in your mother's womb. Is it logical you would be walking around entirely orphaned now? The truth is, you

turned away yourself, and decided to go into the
dark alone. You've forgotten what you once knew,
and that's why everything you do has some weird
failure in it.

There are "weird failures" all around us, and we all suffer
because of them. We usually externalize these failures and then
try to solve the problems. We give speeches, rattle our sabers,
downsize, cut spending, send food, sell arms. The problems
remain. No one really knows what to do. The more we try to solve
the problems, the more the weird failures seem to proliferate.
Why is this?

Someone once suggested that all of our problems stem from
the fact that we can't sit quietly without anxiety, doing nothing.
An old Zen poem elegantly states, "Sitting quietly, doing nothing,
Spring comes, and the grass grows by itself."

Forgetfulness

A few years ago, I was in retreat with a group of executives.
We were resting beneath ancient redwoods in the Santa Cruz
mountains. A vice-president, in his mid-fifties and a former
Marine Corps pilot, told of how, when he was fifteen, he was
suddenly transported out of his body. He experienced himself as
pure light and was intensely joyful. He felt that he was actually a
part of all living things. He said, struggling for the words and with
soft tears forming in his eyes, that this "light body" was the body
of everything and that love was the universal spirit of life, binding
every living thing together as one.

He said it was the most significant experience of his life,
though he had not spoken of it for over forty years. He sat quietly
for a bit, and then he said that he hadn't known how to fit it into
the rest of his life. So he had gone on without it, heavier and
sadder.

I think this is what Kabir was talking about. There is
something we have all forgotten, and that forgetfulness makes us
heavy and sad. It makes us anxious and fearful and angry. I think
that the weird failures have to do with forgetting who we are, with
turning away from the spirit which gives us radiance. This
alienation causes us to suffer, which appears in the world as
chaos. The chaos in the world, whether it touches us directly or

not, is *our* chaos. We own it. It persists because we do not face ourselves. "Each of us must be the change we want to see in the world," said Gandhi.

Denial

To be in denial means to pretend that what is true is not true. To be in denial means to act in accord with what is not true. When we deny what is true, we think we have nothing to do with our problems, and we cut ourselves off from the consequences of what we do. We will think that things happen *out there,* not *in here.* When we are willing to see what is true, we understand that the problems in the world are a manifestation of our inner turmoil. We quite literally project our inner fears and conflicts and cravings into the world. It seems to me that we ought to first find peace within ourselves. We ought to first become clear and simple inside, and try to come to terms with our inner life. We ought to be honest about our own motives. "Is this problem of violence out there or in here?" asks Krishnamurti. "Do you want to solve the problem in the outside world or are you questioning violence itself as it is in you?" We must each put an end to our own suffering, isolation, and conflict. Then we will know what to do.

Solutions do not exist outside the problem. It's not a matter of imposing a solution on a problem, but rather a matter of seeing that the solution is within the problem itself. This makes clarity essential, because only with clarity can we see the solution within the problem. The poet Rumi wrote, "A true human being is the essence, the original cause. The world and the universe are secondary effects." The condition of the world is a symptom of our own condition. The solution to chaos is in seeing this connection. One must come to see, through honest self-inquiry, how the impulses within oneself manifest in the world. One must come to see how the problems we seek to correct in the world originate within our own consciousness.

Shortly after the Exxon tanker Valdes changed the ecology of the Alaskan coastline, the *San Francisco Chronicle* quoted Exxon Chairman Lawrence Rawl as saying, "It's not really clear to me why everyone is angry."

Joy

Wynton Marsalis said about Louis Armstrong, "He is the greatest figure in the history of American jazz because he brought so much joy, happiness, and love to people. There was no barrier between his horn and his soul." Do we, as leaders trying to end conflict and suffering, know the power of joy, the joy of removing the barrier between our horn and our soul? Does our soul break out in what we do, in our work, in our relationships, or are we burdened with sadness because what is beautiful within us finds no expression?

If we want to do something good for ourselves, for our families, companies, and communities, we should remove the barriers within us that prevent the music of our soul from flowing out into the world. As long as we do not know what we are, fundamentally, the music of our soul will be muted and we will continue to create chaos in the world.

I remember George Bush, when he was President, saying that we were going to go to Iraq "to kick some ass." One might guess that this made him happy and proud, and that his victory made him joyful. I am not talking about that kind of joy.

Winning

Our leaders often have to prove that they are not wimps, that they are strong and brave. In looking at the world, one would think that systematic killing is the most dramatic way to prove oneself. However, a great warrior named Morihei Ueshiba, the founder of Aikido, taught his students, "The secret of Aikido is to harmonize ourselves with the movement of the universe and to bring ourselves into accord with the universe itself."

Ueshiba was invincible. No one could touch him, let alone defeat him. Still, he realized that no matter how great one became in martial skill, there was a greater power. Ueshiba, one of the finest martial artists of the 20th Century, came to know that:

> Winning means winning over the mind of dis-
> cord in yourself. How can you straighten your
> warped mind, purify your heart, and be harmo-
> nized with the activities of all things in nature? You
> should first make God's heart yours: It is the great

Love omnipresent in all quarters and in all times of the universe. There is no discord in love. There is no enemy of love.

Reality

Do we know what reality is, or do we, like our ancestors in Plato's allegory, sit chained in caves and mistake reality for shadows dancing on the dim walls?

In our bodies are 100 trillion cells. Imprinted within its DNA, each cell is inscribed with the knowledge of what it is to do—each cell is encoded with enough knowledge to fill 1,000 volumes. How is it, then, that we do not know what to do? How is it that we are so often confused, anxious, frightened, and violent? Our alienation from inner radiance causes this. This alienation is called ego, a habitual mental tendency to identify with limiting patterns of being.

Jean Klein, a European teacher of non-dualism, suggests, "When the ego is abandoned, there is only silent awareness, total presence. This silent presence frees us from the patterns fabricated by the ego, thus opening out before us a whole new world of energies." I think we know intuitively that the world beyond the ego and our conditioned, patterned responses to life is the world of reality. If we can find our way there, we will surely make good decisions.

Disruptions

Our conditioned, patterned way of living in isolation from the true self may be disrupted by the unexpected. An accident, a sudden reversal of fortune, the death of a loved one, or a confrontation with our own mortality can open a window to another world of significance. Another way in which disruption may appear in our lives is through grace, an encounter with someone who has been overwhelmed by reality and who naturally projects that inner state out into the world, where it is experienced by others.

I experienced one of these disruptions a few years ago at the Mt. Madonna Center in Watsonville, California. It is a retreat facility founded by Baba Hari Dass, an Indian yogi who has not spoken a word since 1952. I was co-facilitating a planning session for a management team of a computer chip manufacturing company. I had arranged a private meeting with our group and Baba Hari Dass, who communicates succinctly and humorously by writing on a chalkboard. We visited with him for about thirty minutes, asking a variety of questions, including several about spirituality in business. When our time was over, I went to thank him. Something came from his eyes that I had experienced coming from the eyes of my teacher, Swami Muktananda, many years earlier. It was a kind of light that could penetrate very deeply into one's being. One is touched at the core: it is the touch of reality, or grace, and one awakens to another world of significance.

As I walked outside with our group I suddenly felt very strange, light-headed, and off balance. I told my associate to continue on without me, that I would catch up in a minute. I wandered into a grove of trees, found a boulder, and sat down. Something pierced my heart. I bent over and started crying. It's very hard to say what occurred to me then. It is probably difficult for all of us to speak of these moments—so full of silence and beauty and awakening.

When I stopped crying, I sat still for a long time. Everything about me seemed newly alive, radiant, as though I was seeing these common things for the first time: flowers, trees, rocks, dirt. It seemed that everything was breathing! I felt light and spacious, extending beyond the familiar boundary of my body. I became aware of an orderly connection between things, much as when you finally piece a puzzle together you see how each piece fits into the other to form the whole. I was relieved of a burden I didn't know I was carrying. I was embraced by a profound peace.

When these disruptions of our conditioned, patterned way of living occur, it's as though we see another dimension of life about which we were ignorant. The mask of appearances falls away, and we see something profound about life. We experience something of the timeless, the real, that which gives radiance to us in the womb. It's beyond words, and the mind hardly grasps it. In these moments, the fortifications against the soul dissolve, and a new perspective appears.

We see that if we want things too much, we can do ourselves and others much harm. We know how angry we can get when we don't get what we want. It's easy to start pushing and tearing at things to fulfill our ambitions. We can't think straight; we can't see clearly what's really going on.

We know it is not right to profit from someone's suffering or misfortune. We should not create and promote images of fear and abuse. There is enough terror in the world already, created by ignorance and hatred. Why would we want to create more? We can easily justify doing so, and the rewards may be great. We can't let ourselves off the hook so easily. We can't say, "I'm just giving people what they want." If we see only profitability, we are likely to become tense and greedy. We are likely to continue along the path of alienation.

Sometimes we can do things that no one will know about. That doesn't mean we should do them. It's one thing to take a cookie from the cookie jar when we're kids. It is quite another matter to steal someone's money or pour toxic waste into their drinking water, or to kill and bury hundreds of people under the secret cloak of national interests. We should not do everything we can do just because we won't get caught or because we are able to obscure our true motives and accountability.

When we are quiet and open, we can hear the conversations of animals and birds, even plants, stones, and soil. Everything is alive, everything endures hardships and joys, and everything feels pain, to some degree or another. When we are touched by grace, we know that kindness is natural. Our conditioned, patterned way of living is often a barrier to our natural kindness. We do not have the right to needlessly inflict pain on others. Whenever any suffering is an outcome of our actions, we must find another way.

Leaders who want to solve problems and end suffering ought to remain friendly with epiphanies when they happen, by accident, crisis, or grace. These are not apparitions or hallucinations, though they may seem fantastic. It's just the world as it is, seen simply with awareness uncluttered by conditioning. For example, we may know someone who has died, only to return to life after experiencing that great mystery. We ought to be open to what these people have to say. We should not be constricted by ignorance, because we might be able to learn something valuable about life, about reality.

Each one of our thoughts and actions is a pebble that we throw into a pond. Sooner or later the ripples will come back to us. We are all affected by what each of us does. We will not be able to remain isolated from the ripples of our thoughts and our actions. If we want to know whether our actions are straight or crooked, we have but to consider that their ripples will wash over the person we most love.

Being

Our state of being is the real source of our ability to influence things. Anxiety, tension, and grasping all distort reality. When reality is distorted, we can't see what's really happening and we won't know what to do. As we become cleansed of pretense, we become simple, quiet, and clear. In this state we will be less likely to project our "problems" into the world. We will not need leaders to straighten us out or to fix our lives. Inasmuch as we have led ourselves into peace, we may remind others: Without peace, how can we bring love into the world? Without love, how can we know reality? If we don't know what's real, how can we lead?

It seems magical when the sun of reality breaks through the clouds of confusion. It can happen in a moment, when thinking and worrying collapse into emptiness. This is why we like to stare at the ocean, or stand in a stream, or lose ourselves in the endless sky. When we do that, we become empty, and the magic of reality becomes clear. Tom Robbins wrote, "Disbelief in magic can force a poor soul into believing in government and business."

There is a power that is greater than any one of us, and greater than all of us. That power is not different from us, nor are we different from it. It's just that that power is greater than we are. It's the power spoken about by the warrior Ueshiba.

Someone once took a Zen Buddhist monk to hear the Boston Symphony perform Beethoven's Fifth Symphony. The monk's comment was, "Not enough silence!" If we are interested in leadership, which means understanding the true cause of suffering and conflict, then we should become friends with silence. Silence opens a window to reality, and reality opens the door to good decisions.

Silence helps us to see the seductive power of our own justifications—the way we become sure and proud of our ideas and positions, our views and our solutions. "Silence is permanent and benefits the whole of humanity," taught Ramana Maharshi. "Silence is unceasing eloquence. It is the best language." Silence is like a vast sea, glass smooth, utterly still.

Max Picard, a Swiss philosopher, wrote, "Silence has greatness simply because it is. It *is*, and that is its greatness, its pure existence." Silence is the communion we call love.

About twenty years ago, I took up the practice of not speaking as a way to encourage inner silence. At first it was very hard, because the talking continued automatically in my head. The words crowded into my mouth; I just wouldn't let them out. After a week or so, I began to notice the thinking and talking. It was as if another person was inside of me. That person just noticed what was otherwise an automatic process of thinking and talking. After another week or so, that person grew large and encompassing. He was just there, watching and noticing silently.

After another week or so, I could hear the awareness breathing, purring like a cat. My thinking slowed down, and the crowd of words in my mouth thinned out. I began to feel extremely relaxed, still, and quiet—just like a cat sleeping in the sun. My senses became very acute. I could hear a leaf as it fell in the air. I could feel people approaching before I could see them. I could sense what was about to happen. I could notice the thoughts and impulses arise within me while considering their qualities. I didn't have to act each one out, automatically. Yogi Berra once said, "It's amazing what you can observe just by watching."

After another week, I couldn't find "me" anywhere. I just sort of disappeared. I had crept into everything, and so "I" became "all." I began to see a soft light surrounding whatever I looked at. Everything seemed linked by this etheric light. The purring breath that I had noticed before was now everywhere. I was mostly aware of the soft light, the purring breath, and an unbreakable stillness.

My teacher at that time had told me to meditate on the mantra *hamsa*. He said that hamsa is the vibration of that consciousness which pulsates in every atom of this universe. He said that, by paying attention to the point between the incoming and outgoing breath, or to the space between two thoughts, one could experience the truth of hamsa. He taught that hamsa was the pure vibration of life itself, unconditioned by form or thought, and that it pervaded everything. In my experiment with silence, I must have stumbled into hamsa.

At the end of two months, I became ill with the flu. I started thinking and talking again. Now, twenty years later, I often get distracted with worrying about one thing or another. I spend a lot of time trying to solve problems and make my life better. But something of that encounter with silence, with hamsa, remains because, every so often, when I least expect it, that purring cat will jump from everywhere to remind me of reality.

I once flew on the Concord from London to New York. One can see not just the green, tan, and brown squares fitting together in a coherent whole, but also the curve of the earth. The perspective from that altitude is astonishing. We will want to get an equivalent perspective from an inner altitude in order to be effective leaders. Nisargadatta Maharaj once said to a gathering of people in the living room of his small home in Bombay, "A quiet mind is all you need. All else will happen rightly. Self-awareness effects changes in the mind. In the light of calm and steady self-awareness, inner energies wake up and work miracles."

PART FOUR

New Thinking for New Leaders

Leadership and the New Science
Margaret J. Wheatley

Catching the Wave: Changing Minds in a Changing World
John D. Adams

For Radical Change: The Buck Stops Here
Martha Spice

Leadership: The Values Game
Carol McCall

While the preceding segment addressed an important aspect of thinking differently—accepting paradox—this portion of our book directly focuses on the need to literally "change our minds." Underlying assumptions and core beliefs must change to accomplish this task—something that was itself unthinkable just a decade or so ago.

Changing our minds can be quite threatening to the ego, especially after investing so much time and energy in learning what beliefs would best serve us in "getting by" in the world. We learned how the physical world behaved and adapted as best we could under whatever circumstances we found ourselves. Now, we are being told, everything must change.

Margaret J. Wheatley, bestselling author of *Leadership and the New Science*, describes how quantum theory and other discoveries in the physical sciences over the past several decades are outpacing the mechanistic mode for our present thinking. Consultant John D. Adams, editor of *Transforming Work* and

Transforming Leadership, suggests means for changing habitual patterns of thinking.

Martha Spice explores the "new frontier"—the inner journey of deep accountability and personal responsibility for the new leader. Leadership development trainer Carol McCall addresses the issue of key values for the productive and service-oriented leaders of the future.

While all of our authors agree that new thinking is essential for the leaders of tomorrow, these four are calling specifically for changes that effect a transformation of the personhood of the new leader.

Margaret J. Wheatley
is president of The Berkana Institute, and was formerly associate
professor of management at the
Marriott School of Management, Brigham Young University,   and a
principal of the consulting firm of Kellner-Rogers and Wheatley, Inc (KRW).
KRW is actively engaged with clients in experimenting with organizational
redesigns that support the speed, flexibility, resiliency, and autonomy
required in today's environment.

Her most recent book, published in 1992, *Leadership and the New
Science: Learning About Organization from an Orderly Universe*, was
named "Best Management Book of 1992" in *Industry Week*. Dr. Wheatley
received her doctorate from Harvard University's program in Administration, Planning and Social Policy. She holds an MA in Communications and
Systems Thinking from New York University, and has also been a research
associate at Yale University. Her essay is excerpted from her book of the
same name, and is published with permission of the publisher, Berrett-
Koehler Publishers, San Francisco.

16

Leadership and the New Science

Margaret J. Wheatley

I am not alone in wondering why organizations aren't working well. Many of us are troubled by questions that haunt our work. Why do so many organizations feel dead? Why do projects take so long, develop ever-greater complexity, yet so often fail to achieve any truly significant results. Why does progress, when it appears, so often come from unexpected places, or as a result of surprises or serendipitous events that our planning had not considered? Why does change itself, that event we're all supposed to be "managing," keep drowning us, relentlessly reducing any sense of mastery we might possess? And why have our expectations for success diminished to the point that, often, the best we hope for is staying power and patience to endure the disruptive forces that appear unpredictably in the organizations where we work?

These questions had been growing within me for several years, gnawing away at my work and diminishing my sense of competency. The busier I became with work and the more projects I took on, the greater my questions grew. Until I began a journey.

Like most important journeys, mine began in a mundane place—a Boeing 757, flying soundlessly above America. High in the air as a weekly commuter between Boston and Salt Lake City, with long stretches of reading time broken only by occasional offers of soda and peanuts, I opened my first book on the new science—Fritjof Capra's *The Turning Point,* which described the new world view emerging from quantum physics. This provided my first glimpse of a new way of perceiving the world, one that comprehended its processes of change and patterns of connections.

I don't think it accidental that I was introduced to a new way of seeing at 37,000 feet. The altitude only reinforced the message that what was needed was a larger perspective, one that took in more of the whole of things. From that first book, I took off, seeking out as many new science books as I could find in biology, evolution, chaos theory, and quantum physics. Discoveries and theories of new science called me away from the details of my own field of management inquiry and up to a vision of the inherent orderliness of the universe, of creative processes and dynamic, continuous change that still maintained order. This was a world where order and change, autonomy and control were not the great opposites that we had thought them to be. It was a world where change and constant creation signaled new ways of maintaining order and structure.

I don't believe I could have grasped these ideas if I had stayed on the ground.

During the past fifteen to twenty years, books that translate new science findings for lay readers have proliferated, some more reputable and scientific than others. Of the many I read, some were too challenging, some were too bizarre, but others contained images and information that were breathtaking. I became aware that I was wandering in a realm that created new visions of freedom and possibility, giving me new ways to think about my work. I couldn't always draw immediate corollaries between science and my dilemmas, but I noticed myself developing a new serenity in response to the questions that surrounded me. I was reading of chaos that contained order; of information as the primal, creative force; of systems that, by design, fell apart so they could renew themselves; and of invisible forces that structured space and held complex things together. These were compelling, evocative ideas, and they gave me hope, even if they did not reveal immediate solutions.

Somewhere—I knew then and believe even more firmly now—there is a simpler way to lead organizations, one that requires less effort and produces less stress than the current practices. For me, this new knowledge is only beginning to crystallize into applications, but I no longer believe that organizations are inherently unmanageable in our world of constant flux and unpredictability. Rather, I believe our present ways of understanding organizations are skewed, and that the longer we remain entrenched in our ways, the farther we move from those wonderful breakthroughs in understanding that the world of science calls "elegant." The layers of complexity, the sense of things being beyond our control and out of control, are but signals of our failure to understand a deeper reality of organizational life, and of life in general.

We are all searching for this simplicity. In many different disciplines, we live today with questions for which our expertise provides no answers. At the turn of the century, physicists faced the same unnerving confusion. There is a frequently told story about Niels Bohr and Werner Heisenberg, two founders of quantum theory. This version is from *The Turning Point:*

> In the twentieth century, physicists faced, for the first time, a serious challenge to their ability to understand the universe. Every time they asked nature a question in an atomic experiment, nature answered with a paradox, and the more they tried to clarify the situation, the sharper the paradoxes became. In their struggle to grasp this new reality, scientists became painfully aware that their basic concepts, their language, and their whole way of thinking were inadequate to describe atomic phenomena. Their problem was not only intellectual but involved an intense emotional and existential experience, as vividly described by Werner Heisenberg: "I remember discussions with Bohr which went through many hours till late at night and ended almost in despair; and when at the end of the discussion I went alone for a walk in the neighboring park I repeated to myself again and again the question: Can nature possibly be so

absurd as it seemed to us in these atomic experiments?"

It took these physicists a long time to accept the fact that the paradoxes they encountered are an essential aspect of atomic physics....Once this was perceived, the physicists began to learn to ask the right questions and to avoid contradictions...and finally they found the precise and consistent mathematical formulation of [quantum] theory.

...Even after the mathematical formulation of quantum theory was completed, its conceptual framework was by no means easy to accept. Its effect on the physicists' view of reality was truly shattering. The new physics necessitated profound changes in concepts of space, time, matter, object, and cause and effect; and because these concepts are so fundamental to our way of experiencing the world, their transformation came as a great shock. To quote Heisenberg again: "The violent reaction to the recent development of modern physics can only be understood when one realizes that here the foundations of physics have started moving; and that this motion has caused the feeling that the ground would be cut from science."

For the past several years, I have found myself often relating this story to groups of managers involved in organizational change. The story speaks with a chilling authority. Each of us recognizes the feelings this tale describes, of being mired in the habit of solutions that once worked yet that are now totally inappropriate, of having rug after rug pulled from beneath us, whether by a corporate merger, reorganizations, downsizing, or a level of personal disorientation. But the story also gives great hope as a parable teaching us to embrace our despair as a step on the road to wisdom, encouraging us to sit in the unfamiliar seat of not knowing and open ourselves to radically new ideas. If we bear the confusion, then one day, the story promises, we will begin to see a whole new landscape, one of bright illumination that will dispel the oppressive shadows of our current ignorance. I still tell Heisenberg's story. It never fails to speak to me from this deep place of reassurance.

I believe that we have only just begun the process of discovering and inventing the new organizational forms that will inhabit the 21st Century. To be responsible inventors and discoverers, though, we need the courage to let go of the old world, to relinquish most of what we have cherished, to abandon our interpretations about what does and doesn't work. As Einstein is often quoted as saying: No problem can be solved from the same consciousness that created it. We must learn to see the world anew.

There are many places to search for new answers in a time of paradigm shifts. For me, it was appropriate that my inquiry led back to the natural sciences, reconnecting me to an earlier vision of myself. At fourteen, I aspired to be a space biologist and carried thick astronomy texts on the New York subway to weekly classes at the Hayden Planetarium. These texts were far too dense for me to understand, but I carried them anyway because they looked so impressive. My abilities in biology were better founded, and I began college with full intent to major in biology, but my initial encounters with advanced chemistry ended that career, and I turned to the greater ambiguity of the social sciences. Like many social scientists, I am, at heart, a lapsed scientist, still hoping that the world will yield up its secrets to me in predictable formulations.

But my focus on science is more than a personal interest. Each of us lives and works in organizations designed from Newtonian images of the universe. We manage by separating things into parts, we believe that influence occurs as a direct result of force exerted from one person to another, we engage in complex planning for a world that we keep expecting to be predictable, and we search continually for better methods of objectively perceiving the world. These assumptions come to us from 17th-Century physics, from Newtonian mechanics. They are the base from which we design and manage organizations, and from which we do research in all of the social sciences. Intentionally or not, we work from a world view that has been derived from the natural sciences.

But the science has changed. If we are to continue to draw

from the sciences to create and manage organizations, to design research, and to formulate hypotheses about organizational design, planning, economics, human nature, and change processes (the list can be much longer), then we need to at least ground our work in the science of our times. We need to stop seeking after the universe of the 17th Century and begin to explore what has become known to us in the 20th Century. We need to expand our search for the principles of the organization to include what is presently known about the universe.

The search for the lessons of new science is still in progress, really in its infancy, but I have the pleasure of sensing those first glimmers of a new way of thinking about the world and its organizations. The light may be dim, but its potency grows as the door cracks wider and wider. Here there are scientists who write about natural phenomena with a poetry and lucidity that speak to dilemmas we find in organizations. Here there are new images and metaphors for thinking about our own organizational experiences. This is a world of wonder and not knowing, where scientists are as awestruck by what they see as were the early explorers who marveled at new continents. In this realm, there is a new kind of freedom, where it is more rewarding to explore than to reach conclusions, more satisfying to wonder than to know, and more exciting to search than to stay put.

I no longer believe that organizations can be changed by imposing a model developed elsewhere. So little transfers to, or even inspires, those trying to work at change in their own organizations. The new physics cogently explains that there is no objective reality out there waiting to reveal its secrets. There are no recipes or formulae, no checklists or advice that describe "reality." There is only what we create through our engagement with others and with events. Nothing really transfers: everything is always new and different and unique to each of us.

It is not important that we agree on one sure-fire application. That is not the nature of the universe in which we live. We inhabit a world that is always subjective and shaped by our interactions with it. Our world is impossible to pin down, constantly changing, and infinitely more interesting than we ever imagined.

I have chosen to think about the meta-issues that concern those of us who work in large organizations: What are the sources of order? How do we create organizational coherence, where activities correspond to purpose? How do we create structures that move with change, that are flexible and adaptive, even boundaryless, that enable rather than constrain? How do we simplify things without losing both control and differentiation? How do we resolve personal needs for freedom and autonomy with organizational needs for prediction and control?

The new science research comes from the disciplines of physics, biology, and chemistry, and from theories of evolution and chaos that span several disciplines. Scientists in many different disciplines are questioning whether we can adequately explain how the world works by using the machine imagery created in the 17th Century, most notably by Sir Isaac Newton. In the machine model, one must understand parts. Things can be taken apart, dissected literally or representationally (as we have done with business functions and academic disciplines), and then put back together without any significant loss. The assumption is that, by comprehending the workings of each piece, the whole can be understood. The Newtonian model of the world is characterized by materialism and reductionism—a focus on things rather than relationships and a search, in physics, for the basic building blocks of matter.

In new science, the underlying currents are a movement toward holism, toward understanding the system as a system and giving primary value to the relationships that exist among seemingly discrete parts. Donella Meadows, a systems thinker, quotes an ancient Sufi teaching that captures this shift in focus: "You think because you understand *one* you must understand *two*, because one and one makes two. But you must also understand *and*." When we view systems from this perspective, we enter an entirely new landscape of connections, of phenomena that cannot be reduced to simple cause and effect, and of the constant flux of dynamic processes.

Explorations into the subatomic world began early in this century, creating the dissonance described in Heisenberg's story. In physics, therefore, the search for radically new models now has a long and somewhat strange tradition. The strangeness lies in the pattern of discovery that characterized many of the major discoveries in quantum mechanics. "A lucky guess based on shaky arguments and absurd ad hoc assumptions gives a formula that turns out to be right, though at first no one can see why on earth it should be." I delight in that statement of scientific process. It gives me hope for an approach to discovery that can influence the methodical, incremental, linear work that leads to the plodding character of most social science research.

The quantum mechanical view of reality strikes against most of our notions of reality. Even to scientists, it is admittedly bizarre. But it is a world where *relationship* is the key determiner of what is observed and of how particles manifest themselves. Particles come into being and are observed only in relationship to something else. They do not exist as independent "things." Quantum physics paints a strange yet enticing view of a world that, as Heisenberg characterized it, "appears as a complicated tissue of events, in which connections of different kinds alternate or overlap or combine and thereby determine the texture of the whole." These unseen *connections* between what were previously thought to be separate entities are the fundamental elements of all creation.

In other disciplines, especially biology, the use of nonmechanistic models is much more recent. At the outer edges of accepted practice (although gaining slowly in credibility) are theories like the Gaia hypothesis, which sees the earth as a living organism actively engaged in creating the conditions which support life, or Rupert Sheldrake's morphogenic fields, which describe species memory as contained in invisible structures that help shape behavior. Some of what we know how to do, Sheldrake argues, comes not from our own acquired learning, but from knowledge that has been accumulated in the human species field, to which we have access. Whole populations of a species can shift their behavior because the content of their field has changed, not because they individually have taken the time to learn the new behavior.

So many fundamental reformulations of prevailing theories in evolution, animal behavior, ecology, and neurobiology are underway that, in 1982, Ernst Mayr, a noted chronicler of biological thought, stated: "It is now clear that a new philosophy of biology is needed."

In chemistry, Ilya Prigogine won the Nobel Prize in 1977 for his work demonstrating the capacity of certain chemical systems (dissipative structures) to regenerate to higher levels of self-organization in response to environmental demands. In the older, mechanistic models of natural phenomena, fluctuations and disturbances had always been viewed as signs of trouble. Disruptions would only more quickly bring on the decay that was the inevitable future of all systems. But the dissipative structures that Prigogine studied demonstrated the capacity of living systems to respond to disorder (nonequilibrium) with renewed life. Disorder can play a critical role in giving birth to new, higher forms of order. As we leave behind our machine models and look more deeply into the dynamics of living systems, we begin to glimpse an entirely new way of understanding fluctuations, disorder, and change.

New understandings of change and disorder are also emerging from chaos theory. Work in this field, which keeps expanding to take in more areas of inquiry, has led to a new description of the relationship between order and chaos. These two forces are now understood as mirror images, one containing the other, a continual process where a system can leap into chaos and unpredictability, yet within that state be held within parameters that are well-ordered and predictable.

New science is also making us more aware that our yearning for simplicity is one we share with natural systems. In many systems, scientists now understand that order and conformity and shape are created not by complex controls, but by the presence of a few guiding formulae or principles. The survival and growth of systems that range in size from large ecosystems down to tiny leaves are made possible by the combination of key patterns or principles that express the system's overall identity and great levels of autonomy for individual system members.

The world described by new science is changing our beliefs and perceptions in many areas, not just in the natural sciences. I see new science ideas beginning to percolate in my own field of management theory. One way to see their effect is to look at the problems that plague us most in organizations these days or, more accurately, what we *define* as the problems. Leadership, an amorphous phenomenon that has intrigued us since people began studying organizations, is being examined now for its relational aspects. More and more studies focus on followership, empowerment, and leader accessibility. And ethical and moral questions are no longer fuzzy religious concepts but key elements in our relationships with staff, suppliers, and stakeholders. If the physics of our universe is revealing the primacy of relationships, is it any wonder that we are beginning to reconfigure our ideas about management in relational terms?

In motivation theory, our attention is shifting from the enticement of external rewards to the intrinsic motivators that spring from the work itself. We are refocusing on the deep longings we have for community, meaning, dignity, and love in our organizational lives. We are beginning to look at the strong emotions that are part of being human, rather than segmenting ourselves (love is for home, discipline is for work) or believing that we can confine workers into narrow roles, as though they were cogs in the machinery of production. As we let go of the machine models of work, we begin to step back and see ourselves in new ways, to appreciate our wholeness, and to design organizations that honor and make use of the totality of who we are.

The impact of vision, values, and culture occupies a great deal of organizational attention. We see their effects on organizational vitality, even if we can't quite define why they are such potent forces. We now sense that some of the best ways to create continuity of behavior are through the use of forces that we can't really see. Many scientists now work with the concept of fields—invisible forces that structure space or behavior. I have come to understand organizational vision as a field—a force of unseen connections that influences employees' behavior—rather than as an evocative message about some desired future state. Because of field theory, I believe I can better explain why vision is so necessary, and this leads me to new activities to strengthen its influence.

Our concept of organizations is moving away from the mechanistic creations that flourished in the age of bureaucracy. We have begun to speak in earnest of more fluid, organic structures, even of boundaryless organizations. We are beginning to recognize organizations as systems, construing them as "learning organizations" and crediting them with some type of self-renewing capacity. These are our first, tentative forays into a new appreciation for organizations. My own experience suggests that we can forego the despair created by such common organizational events as change, chaos, information overload, and cyclical behaviors if we recognize that organizations are conscious entities, possessing many of the properties of living systems.

Some believe that there is a danger in playing with science and abstracting its metaphors because, after a certain amount of stretch, the metaphors lose their relationship to the tight scientific theories that gave rise to them. But others would argue that all of science is metaphor—a hopeful description of how to think of a reality we can never fully know. I share the sentiments of physicist Frank Oppenheimer who says: "If one has a new way of thinking, why not apply it wherever one's thought leads to? It is certainly entertaining to let oneself do so, but it is also often very illuminating and capable of leading to new and deep insights."

John D. Adams

has over twenty-five years experience in organization development
and change management for North
American and European companies. His recent clients include Sun
Microsystems, Motorola, Weyerhauser, The World Bank, British Airways,
and Cessna Aircraft Company.

He is engaged in research to discover the essential qualities
necessary for successfully making enduring changes in both individual
habit patterns and corporate cultures. He has been a visiting Professor at
The University of Leeds, England, and frequently has served as an adjunct
faculty member at The American University, Bowling Green (Ohio) State
University, The John F. Kennedy University (California), The California
Institute of Integral Studies, and The Saybrook Institute.

He is author of the long-popular *Understanding and Managing
Stress* series and co-author of *Transition* and *Life Changes*. John has served
as the editor of numerous collections of readings including *New Technologies in Organization Development, Organization Development in Health
Care organizations, Transforming Work,* and *Transforming Leadership.*

17

Catching the Wave: Changing Minds in a Changing World

John D. Adams

"If I continue to believe as I have always believed,
I will continue to act as I have always acted.
If I continue to act as I have always acted,
I will continue to get what I have always gotten."
—From a speech by Marilyn Ferguson,
August, 1984 (Original source unknown.)

The above statement is quite simple, and to most people, quite obvious. It is also quite powerful, in that it suggests to us that if we want to get different results from life, such as greater fulfillment from our work, we must learn to behave consistently differently from the way we have been behaving up to this moment. Further, if we are going to behave more successfully it suggests that we ultimately have to support that change in behavior with new ways of thinking.

My own work over the past three decades has frequently been focused on supporting people who have wanted to make changes in their lifestyles to prevent illness and promote health. I have repeatedly been struck by the inherent truth of the above statement. I have observed many of these people make strong commitments to change, such as to eat less fat in order to lose weight, only to learn later that they had reverted to their former "less healthy" behaviors. Others who have made similar commitments have been successful in making desired change, and I have been curious as to what was different between those who have been successful and those who have not.

The most challenging question that those of us who work with individuals claiming they want to make personal habit changes is: "How can we help people make changes that 'stay changed?'"

There is a parallel challenge in "making changes that stay changed" in organizational improvement efforts. Teams and organizations face the same challenges in accomplishing enduring changes that individuals do. Action plans created during team retreats are seldom implemented back on the job; organization-wide commitments to develop more positive communications habits are rarely realized; expensive and widely publicized system-wide improvement programs become "flavor of the month." Desired changes in the "corporate culture" seem to be very fragile, with reversion to the original culture being the result all too frequently.

How do we help systems make changes that last?

This chapter explores this question by examining some of the cognitive (or consciousness) aspects of our experience. My goal is to demonstrate that these usually overlooked cognitive aspects exert a very major influence on our abilities, both individually and in organizations, to make changes.

Human beings are the only animal on earth which has the capacity to think about *how* we think. Unfortunately, however, most of our waking experience is spent in what I refer to as the "autopilot state," in which we do *not* consciously think about *how* we are thinking. According to *Meeting the Shadow*, Ronald Laing, the late Scottish psychiatrist, made this point very eloquently over twenty-five years ago:

> The range of what we think and do is limited by what we fail to notice. And because we fail to notice that we fail to notice, there is little we can do to change, until we notice how failing to notice shapes our thoughts and deeds.

Default Settings and the Autopilot

In computer terminology, the term "default" means the automatic settings contained in a software program. For example, most word processing programs in the U.S. are designed to automatically set the top, bottom, and side margins on a piece of paper at one inch. Individually, one's mindset can be considered to be made up of a large number of default settings—our beliefs, assumptions, and values are automatic and predictable. As a result, our habitual ways of responding to situations also fall into consistent, though unconscious, default patterns.

The statement at the beginning of this chapter describes one of the key characteristics of the default settings of the "autopilot" and its natural tendency to be self-fulfilling and self-reinforcing. This tendency can also be described by the following diagram.

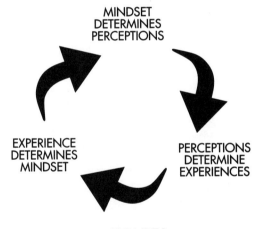

MINDSET
DETERMINES
PERCEPTIONS

PERCEPTIONS
DETERMINE
EXPERIENCES

EXPERIENCE
DETERMINES
MINDSET

FIGURE 1
The Relationship among Perceptions,
Experiences and Mindset

Default Settings

Our perceptions determine what we actually experience in a situation because they make us receptive to some stimuli and "blind" to others. Those of us who expect to find problems in a given situation are usually able to find them; while those of us who expect to find opportunities in the same situation will also be successful. Our experiences determine our mindsets. Beliefs and attitudes are formed as a result of the repetitive, thematic messages we receive from authority figures during our first 10-15 years, as well as those we develop for ourselves by means of repetitive "self talk." It appears that our subconscious can only say "yes" to any suggestion made to it; and with the accumulation of "yeses," a given message solidifies into a belief.

Our mindsets determine what we perceive in a situation. Those of us who have an optimistic, positive, self-directed outlook generally expect to find opportunities, while those of us with a pessimistic, negative, disempowered outlook generally expect to find obstacles or difficulties.

The result then is that perceptions, experiences, and mindsets affect one another in a cyclical way. Our mindsets become self-fulfilling, self-reinforcing, and self limiting. In order to be fully successful in accomplishing an enduring change in behavior—that is, in establishing a new habit and extinguishing an old one—we must break into this cycle and create new mental models (beliefs, assumptions, values) that support the establishment of the desired new habit.

The self-reinforcing nature of the cycle suggests another quality of the autopilot mindset. When we are operating "in autopilot"—that is, when we are not thinking about how we are thinking—the subconscious operates in ways to protect the status quo default settings. It is impossible to support commitments to change habitual behavior with altered mental models unless we shift from autopilot to choice, and consciously alter some of the default settings.

Most frequently, when we are not getting the results we want, we try even harder with the same behaviors that have not been working—a reflection of our autopilot tendencies to be self-protective. In order to consistently behave in new, more appropriate ways, it is ultimately necessary to alter how we are thinking about the situation, through questioning our beliefs and testing our assumptions. Few of us have received any education in how to do this. It's as if our subconscious is continuously whispering "don't rock the boat" in our ears.

The organizational parallel is reflected in the fact that the culture of the organization also operates to protect the status quo whenever changes are attempted. Over the years, innumerable organizations have attempted to improve their effectiveness by implementing system wide programs such as sensitivity training, team building, management by objectives, job enrichment, quality of work life, quality circles, and total quality. Unfortunately, more often than not these programs have not accomplished their objectives.

One of the reasons for this is that the default settings most of us have adopted reflect aspects which are contradictory to the basic aspects required to fully adopt programs such as these. Most particularly, most people have learned to adopt a rather *short term focus* (time dimension)—the 10:00 o'clock deadline virtually always takes precedence over the strategic plan.

Second, most of us have learned to adopt a rather *local focus* (space dimension)—my/our needs take priority over your/ the organization's (or society's, or the planet's) needs. One department's efforts to win a larger budget, at the expense of another department and perhaps at the expense of the company's overall performance is one common example of this kind of thinking.

Third, most of us have learned to adopt a *reactive/responsive focus* (attitudinal dimension)—in which following the rules and correcting deviations take precedence over creating and working towards the realization of a strong, compelling vision.

And fourth, most of us have adopted the attitude that "If it ain't broke, don't fix it!" (strategy dimension)—*fixing symptoms* as they arise and otherwise not thinking much about how to anticipate and prevent problems and to *build capacity* in the system. As an example, the government is likely to focus on protecting present worker's jobs at the expense of longer term damage to the global environment.

From Autopilot to Choice: Building Versatility

When we look into the fundamental nature of the historical series of organizational effectiveness programs, it becomes obvious that everyone of them is based on mindsets that are different from those which prevail. If we look at each of the following four focuses as the left end of a continuum, we will notice that the success of almost every organizational improvement requires a focus at the opposite end of these dimensions.

SHORT TERM OPERATIONAL	—————— TIME DIMENSION ——————	LONG TERM STRATEGIC
LOCAL REDUCTIONIST	—————— SPACE DIMENSION ——————	GLOBAL SYSTEMIC
REACTIVE RESPONSIVE	—————— ATTITUDINAL DIMENSION ——————	CREATIVE INITIATING
NO STRATEGY TREAT SYMPTOMS	——— PREVENTION STRATEGY DIMENSION ———	OPTIMAL VITALITY BUILD CAPACITY

FIGURE 2
Four Key Dimensions of Mindset

It is NOT my intention to suggest that we should learn to move our mindsets to the opposite ends of these dimensions, and abandon the short-term/local–reactive/symptom-treating mindsets. Such a move wouldn't help us at all—we'd soon be lost in an idealistic vision of the global future and be totally ineffective in the local present!

What is needed is an increase in *versatility*, which may be defined as appropriate flexibility. Put another way, we need to learn to expand our range of comfort along each of these dimensions (and probably others as well!) in order to operate effectively in today's increasingly turbulent and unpredictable world. Peter Vaill uses a metaphor suggesting that we have moved into a period of "permanent white water" all across American and European society. My own experiences support Vaill's metaphor, in that every organization I have been involved with in recent years is facing major changes and uncertainties.

If we are to be successful at "surfing on the waves of change," we must learn to change our minds! We must be able to operate with ease along the entire length of these dimensions. If a critical mass of people in an organization learn to operate in this way, organizational improvement programs are almost guaranteed to succeed. If no attention is given to altering our default settings, these programs will almost always fail.

The Search for the Quick Fix

It is especially important that the top team develop this versatility. If they continue to lead the organization from a short-term/local/reactive/symptom-fixing autopilot mindset, they will run out of patience long before the effectiveness of the program is demonstrated. The change effort will stop when it runs into the "brick wall" of the traditional structures and "ways of doing things." It also is completely natural, whenever the pressure builds up in a situation, such as is widely true in today's turbulent environment, for our mindsets to collapse to the extreme left end of each of the four dimensions.

John D. Rockefeller has accurately, I think, described how the organizational systems we have created operate to protect the status quo.

An organization is a system, with a logic of its own, and all the weight of tradition and inertia. The deck is stacked in favor of the tried and proven ways of doing things and against the taking of risks and striking out in new directions.

When the environment presents conflicting demands to a business, all too often management's response is "who's mad at us today?" rather than recognizing the need for an overall strategy. Doing *more* of what one is already doing is rather limited in today's climate. At some point, our managements' teams absolutely must adopt fundamentally new ways of thinking which can support new ways of working. Another characteristic of how the autopilot mindset works is that it always attempts to influence others to share the same default settings, thus further reinforcing the status quo.

Changing the Default Settings

If we wish to foster versatility in consciousness along the four dimensions introduced earlier (short term - long term/local-global/reactive-cocreative/symptom fixing - building capacity), it is necessary to create mechanisms which raise questions that can only be answered by moving to the other end of a dimension.

For example, to move to more long-term thinking, one must regularly be asked questions like "What do you predict will happen if this trend continues?" To move to global thinking, mechanisms are needed to regularly ask questions like "What does the larger picture look like?" To move to more creative thinking, frequent responses to questions such as "How would you use a magic wand?" or "What would be a more innovative way to approach the situation?" And finally, to move to a capacity building strategy, there must be a regular focus on developmental opportunities.

When faced with a challenge, some people are more inclined to avoid looking at the new habits of thinking or behavior, preferring to dwell on the old ways of thinking and acting, which are familiar and comfortable even though one may be aware that they are not effective. Obviously, when this happens, the resistance will overcome the original felt need to make a change.

In the same changing situation, others are more inclined to attend to only the new habits of thinking or behaving, and overlook any needs to break the old habits or, in some cases, even to take time to grieve the loss of the comfortable old ways of operating. When this happens, the default settings may continue to operate and defeat the desire to change.

The overlap of the declining old mental model or behavior and the emerging new mental model or behavior is often a period of discomfort. Unless the person making the change is deeply committed to completing the change, regression is a likely outcome.

Another diagram, portrayed in Figure 3, describes what often happens when one sets out to learn a new habit.

When one becomes aware that he or she is not getting the results he or she wants, and concludes that a change in either thinking or behavior or both is needed, one moves from Cell I to Cell II—from being unconscious about being unskilled in some way to becoming conscious about that shortcoming. As the person learns the needed new skill or mental model, they find that they are able to practice it whenever they are conscious of using the new skill.

As an example, let us suppose that a person we'll call Robin feels frustrated on the job because of being unable to influence the boss to delegate work differently. With this realization, Robin enrolls in an influence skills workshop and learns both behavioral skills and mindset techniques that can help to influence the boss successfully. Robin leaves the workshop in Cell III.

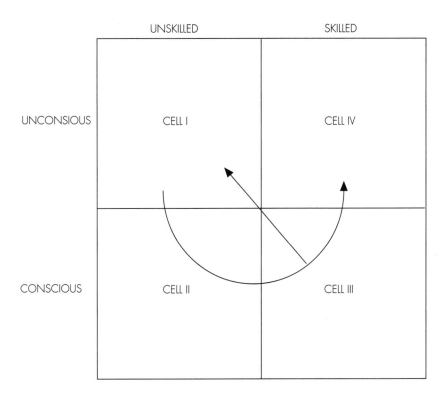

FIGURE 3
Steps in Learning a New Habit

Upon returning to work, Robin finds that the new techniques work very well and prepares carefully before entering the boss's office (maintaining Cell III). Before long, the boss appears at Robin's desk with an urgent demand, and she forgets to use the new techniques and fails to be influential. Robin vows to never let this happen again. The next morning, the boss is again waiting at Robin's desk with another "fire drill" and with fire in his eyes. Before Robin can call the new techniques to mind, the battle is already lost. With a few more instances like this, Robin concludes that there is no way to influence the boss and decides that the workshop was a waste of time. Many will find this situation to be very familiar. If we do not find ways to keep ourselves in Cell III for an extended period of time, our own and other people's autopilots will pull us back to Cell I before the new habit can sink in (moving us to Cell IV).

Most seminars and workshops leave the participants in Cell III. Most organizational effectiveness programs leave the employees in Cell III. The assumption, really a pipe dream, is that movement to Cell IV will be forthcoming if everyone will just act rationally. Much more often than not, however, within a short period of time, most participants have reverted to Cell I and the experience of the workshop has faded into the dim and distant past.

Case Examples

The same thing happens in organizational improvement efforts. Let's look at a case study in changing just one element of an organization's culture to elucidate how this process works at the level of the collective. Several years ago, I was involved for a long time with an R&D organization in the aerospace industry in an organization development effort. In the course of our work together, we conducted a survey which led to the conclusion that the worst norm (cultural habit) this group had was "Around here, you only get feedback when you screw up."

As we discussed what should be done about this and other findings of the survey, the members of this group readily agreed that they were being overly cautious in their approaches to the research activities, because they wanted to avoid the usual stream of critical comments. Obviously, research activities don't always lead to success, and criticism abounded when someone got negative results from the computer or from a wind tunnel test.

They agreed unanimously that they had to give more positive feedback, both to stimulate a more aggressive approach to research and to develop a more fulfilling workplace. However, when I returned a few weeks later to follow up, no one was yet giving any positive feedback to others!

During our exploration of the reasons why they had failed to follow through on their commitments, one group leader stated that he felt that if people thought they were doing a good job, they might become complacent. This created an outcry from the aerospace engineers and scientists in the group. The group leader said he'd give it another try, and acknowledged that his assumption was probably faulty.

One of the senior engineers in another group announced that he had worked long and hard on a critical project, and was able to complete a critical phase of the work just in time for a budget meeting, at which money was approved to continue the project. Following the meeting, the engineer's boss had been lavish with his praise. The engineer reported that during the following weekend, he had thought about the positive feedback, and had concluded that his boss would now just give him more "impossible assignments," so he had discounted the feedback, and admitted that he was trying to stay out of the boss's sight!

Thus we see that both the "senders" and the "receivers" had found ways to rationalize not changing their cultural habit of only giving negative feedback. Once again, the autopilot had protected the status quo.

The group reiterated the importance of making this change to more positive performance feedback. In the process of exploring how to get this desirable new habit "installed" in everyone's minds, they suggested two mechanisms for generating repetitions of the new behavior (and thereby keep themselves in Cell III, in Figure 3).

Since everyone in the group had to attend one or more meetings most days, they suggested that every meeting begin with a review of how their performance feedback goals were being met. Later on, many people admitted that they would consciously stop by someone's work station and make a positive compliment, so that they could give a good account of themselves at the opening of these meetings. These repetitions, even if they were not particularly heartfelt on occasion, eventually paid off.

The other suggestion was from the leadership team of the group. They rightly, I think, concluded that it would be important to the success of their commitment to give more positive feedback throughout their department, to "walk the talk" consistently. To develop more comfort with being positive, they suggested that they go around the table at the beginning of their weekly staff meetings, with each person giving someone in the room an honest compliment. Each week, they pushed each other to dig deeper with their compliments. Eventually, the top team became comfortable with saying positive things to each other, and they were seen with increasing frequency walking the halls making genuinely positive statements.

After several weeks, the performance feedback norm changed throughout the group, and remained changed on a "permanent" basis.

The primary learning from this experience was that, both on the individual and on the organizational levels, the autopilot operates to protect the status quo, and that establishing a new habit is probably more difficult than was the establishment of the original habit it is to replace. One primary reason for this is that we often think it will be easy to make the change, when in fact there are all kinds of subtle pressures to regress and not change after all.

One need only consider how many times a baby falls down before it learns to walk comfortably—probably hundreds of times. Yet the baby doesn't give up. When we choose to adopt a new pattern of thinking or behaving, we need to be just as dedicated as the baby.

Changes That Stayed Changed

The R&D case study illustrates the principles of establishing a new habit successfully. First of all, there absolutely must be a critical mass of people who hold a *"passionate"* or *"heartfelt"* commitment to making the change. Nearly all changes take longer than originally anticipated to get firmly into place, and there are almost always snags and unforeseen circumstances to contend with. Most of the staff in this department felt that it was absolutely essential that they make this change, and were willing to do whatever it took, and spend whatever time was necessary, to be successful. They were not about to give up because of the early setbacks!

Second, it also is essential that there be lots and lots of *repetitions* of the new pattern. How many is unknown, but usually, there is a need for far more repetitions than are undertaken.

In order to guarantee a sufficient number of repetitions, *mechanisms* or *structures*, such as the meeting agenda in the above case example, are generally an absolute necessity. *There simply has to be a way of requiring and supporting regular daily practice of the desired new behavior.* If structural mechanisms which require repetitions are not created, most people and organizational groups will regress to their former ways of operating.

Rewards for the new way of operating (and withdrawal of rewards for the old way of operating!) also seem to be essential. What this means in organizational improvement activities is that the performance review and reward systems must be changed if the culture needed to support the organizational improvement can be expected to change. In the case of personal change, it is important that the person pause to celebrate his or her successes before moving on to the next personal development project.

The aerospace group did not have a significant amount of budget for making cash rewards, but they were able to create a number of meaningful, less tangible rewards to further reinforce and support the change towards more positive feedback.

It also seems to be very important that the intended change be explicitly aligned with the *values and purpose* of the person or group undergoing the desired change. The aerospace group valued good science and good development. Their purpose was to advance the state of the art in their particular technology area. They could easily see how a more positive environment would allow them to pursue their science and push the state of the art more effectively than did their present critical environment.

The final lesson from this case is that changing the auto-pilot takes place best if only *one change project at a time* is undertaken. If wholesale change is attempted, the autopilot's abilities to protect the status quo will win out most of the time. I find that I am frequently advising my clients to "go slow to go fast."

In summary, I am proposing that the following characteristics must be present if we are to make changes that stay changed. This list may not include all of the needed qualities, but if there are a few more, I am convinced that the items listed are among the essential qualities:

1. Passionate or heartfelt commitment;
2. Structures or mechanisms which require *and support* repetitions (or practice);
3. Rewards for the desired new behavior and withdrawal of rewards for the old behavior;
4. Alignment with closely held values and purpose; and
5. Making changes in a one step at a time fashion.

Martha Spice
is a leader coach and principal in
Growth Dynamics, Inc. with her
partner and husband Alan Gilburg.
They provide support, through consultation, coaching, and team building
to those leaders at all levels who are serious about building healthy, high
performing organizations.

She has created Breakthrough Thinking programs which address the
personal change process for the healthy high performer and which
empower individuals to break through self-imposed limitations to the
exercise of expanded personal leadership. She has led seventeen groups
of committed individuals through the firm's One Year Program demonstrating the close relationship of personal growth to business success. She
speaks regularly on topics of personal mastery and managing change.

Gilburg, a pioneer in the development of leadership programs
grounded in value science and personality type, co-authored this essay.
Together, Spice and Gilburg direct The Leadership Laboratory, a program
of practice, reflection, and development for senior executive candidates.

18

For Radical Change: The Buck Stops Here

Martha Spice

A few years ago, my partner Alan met with a plant manager of a large factory who was committed to installing quality initiatives. His value diagnostic assessment showed him to be excessively focused on getting tasks completed while paying little attention to long-term quality system issues. Upon seeing his report, the plant manager immediately remarked, "It looks like I am the problem here. If this plant is going to improve, I have to change."

More recently, a leader of a seventeen-person video production unit came to me and said, "My team is griping, back biting, gossiping, and generally having difficulty working together. I have tried everything to change the situation. Tell me what I need to do to change the way I lead."

These rare individuals immediately grasped their very personal role as pivotal transformational officers in their organizations. They looked inside themselves for answers and were willing to address their own changing first. They stand in marked contrast to the more usual example of pointing the finger of blame or of directing others to change. This extraordinary practice turns out to be radically appropriate for the current chaos in modern business. Everything that might produce better results faster must be explored.

I am increasingly inspired by leaders at all levels who are finding the courage to plant their feet and take responsibility for what is happening in their organizations by beginning with themselves. They are also finding that this stance—and the accompanying small shifts in thinking and behavior—produce both immediate and far reaching changes which ripple through-out the organization. In our practice, we are beginning to call this active shift, with gratitude to President Truman, "buck stops here leadership."

For those who truly see that things must change and are visionary and courageous enough to consider a new way to direct their own energies, we offer our experience that *buck stops here* thinking is the fastest way to get results. Here's why, and here's how.

Organizations Need Radical Change

"The evil in the world is committed by the people who are absolutely certain they know what they are doing."
—M. Scott Peck

Few would argue that there is a need for radical change. Most of our institutions are in some state of dysfunction. Most Americans are dissatisfied with the institutions which dominate our society: education, politics, health care, government, big corporations, families, neighborhoods, cities, the economy. More-over, our environment is becoming more fragile by the day and our infrastructure decays as we speak. The list is long and filled with seemingly intractable problems. We are definitely in a dilemma about the leadership we require as illustrated by large number of CEOs who have been asked to resign recently.

While this situation has evolved, we haven't been sitting idly by, simply watching Rome burn. Using solid, practical American know-how we have experimented with a variety of solutions, such as MBO, Time Management, participatory man-agement, visioning, employee empowerment, TQM, re-engineer-ing, work redesign, bone-deep cost cutting, and down-sizing. These are but a few of the ways leaders have been working at fixing our failing institutions.

These fixes, however, have not been drastic, nor deep enough. They primarily assume that the answers lie in some new technique, or a manipulation of the organization chart. We concur with organizational consultant Marvin Weisbord in his book, *Discovering Common Ground,* that "making a difference is partly concept, partly method, partly window of opportunity, hardly ever a technique and entirely a matter of will." The members of each institution/organization must care enough to change the habits and patterns of behavior—their own—which now constitute the "dis-ease" in the organization.

This is no easy matter. Hundreds of thousands of people in 12-step programs attest to the difficulty of such change. Changing one's diet, smoking, drinking, exercise regime often takes constant, directed, intense reinforcement with new habits. Further, this change process must be buttressed by the individual's clear intention to live according to a deeper connection with what they really want, knowing both the benefits of changing and the consequences of maintaining the status quo. In most cases, the individual in the process of making the change benefits most often from the support of others who back the fundamental intention to change and hold the individual's feet to his/her own fire.

Organizations and institutions, however, are far more complex than individuals. Hence, change efforts need to be targeted toward creating the habits and patterns that will carry the new sets of desired results. My firm conviction that the fastest, most efficient and effective way to institute change is for the leaders themselves to model the new habits and patterns they want others to adopt. The *buck stops here* stance suggests an invitation to look afresh at the power of one's action, one's thinking and one's impact—the real impact.

A Call to Deep Responsibility

"I must first be the change I want to see in my world."
                                                —Mohandas K. Gandhi

What leaders at all levels do, or don't do, matters! Their behavior is scrutinized by everyone in the organization. A raised eyebrow, a sideways glance, an intonation, all are minutely analyzed for meaning in order to figure out "what's OK and not

OK around here." Deeply accepting that "what I do matters" and then acting on that acceptance is the essence of the *buck stops here* stance.

Here's a simple example of the power of executive action. In a two-day training program I noticed that every participant was in his/her seat prior to the announced starting time, so that we were able to maintain an exact schedule, even after lunches and breaks. This was apparently a norm in this regional agency whose 35 senior members had gathered from five cities. We commented to the Regional Director that we had rarely seen such attention to promptness. He said that he had set the standard when he arrived as director three years prior. Without fanfare he simply started all his meetings on time. Sometimes they were short meetings. If people came as much as 5–10 minutes late, they could easily have missed the entire meeting.

Contrast this with a recent request to conduct a Time Management course for every member of a large association. The Executive Director decided that everyone needed it. Probing for reasons was not welcomed. Devising ways to get at the source of the problem was not an option. The unmistakable message sent to the employees is that *they* needed to be fixed—by executive decree.

In the first example, the Regional Director, within a month after his arrival, had set the norm for managing meetings and time with barely a word spoken and no outlay for training programs. He used the tremendous leverage of example. He "walked his own talk," thereby promoting a radical change in norms in his entire organization. I am sure that both leaders shared good intentions. One was successful in acting them out himself. The other, having attempted to "fix" others may still be mystified that people aren't behaving as he would like.

Taking the *buck stops here* stance means accepting the idea that "I am responsible for the fact that people are not behaving the way I would like." It calls for serious personal scrutiny. It calls for ferreting out the gaps between my intentions and my behavior and owning up to the mixed messages I may be giving. It calls for reminding myself that while I typically measure others by their behavior, I nevertheless measure myself by my intentions. Any discrepancy means trouble for me, as leader, when my every move is being analyzed.

Personal scrutiny takes courage and commitment. The very act of self-scrutiny sends an important message, "I intend to be in the continuous improvement and learning business." Today, everyone is expected to be a "leader." With matrix management, project teams and tasks forces one after another, anyone may expect to find themselves as the designated leader. However, it is the CEOs and vice-presidents who have the most leverage for "modeling" change. More than anyone, those at the top must personally create the healthy environments which guarantee them as employers of choice for today's discriminating knowledge workers.

One "employer of choice" who captured my enthusiasm is the owner of a $10 million firm. He talked with great seriousness about wanting to triple his company's sales and create a healthier work environment with clearer expectations and higher standards for professionalism and service. As he took a critical look at himself, he recognized that he was retaining a group manager who represented an entirely opposite set of operating values. This was sending a serious mixed message to the others who worked for him. His willingness to look at his own behavior in the situation enabled him to act with integrity and get more of the results he really wanted.

In another example, the leader of a thirty-person government regulatory team was willing to own up to her team members about the ways she had dishonored some of them, had acted in a brusque manner as if she didn't care about them, and had retreated behind her office door, making herself inaccessible. In a *buck stops here* speech, she gave permission to openly discuss what had been previously seen as "undiscussible." She told them she wanted to be accessible, support them wholeheartedly, and move forward with their help. This sincerity, combined with her own respected competence, transformed the team's willingness to cooperate in meeting the challenging tasks at hand. One year later, the team is still flourishing.

Buck Stops Here Thinking

"The real voyage of discovery lies not in finding new landscapes, but in having new eyes."
—Marcel Proust

By observing those who use the leverage of their own changing to create results, I have noticed that three deceptively simple questions help leaders make a difference.

1. What do you really want for your organization?
2. Are you willing to have it?
3. Are you willing to create new practices?
   Make new choices?

The video unit leader took her changing very seriously. "Are you willing to have the kind of productive and creative, empowered team you say you want?" She responded, "Of course." She soon realized that, if she was part of the system and the system wasn't working, she had to take responsibility for her role in the way this system operated. She had to look at the fact that a part of her was not "willing" to have what she said she wanted. When she got down to it, and really looked at what she was doing, she had to admit she was micro-managing, solving their problems for them, not setting clear directions, nor clarifying roles. She concluded, "My behaviors have created the problems I now face and I now see what I have to do differently."

The plant manager found it easy to articulate the positive results he wanted. He also acknowledged the parts of himself that were not on the program, as illustrated by his own undermining behavior. He noticed how his constant "fire fighting" with daily problems made it near to impossible for his staff to install quality-oriented process improvements. In his *buck stops here* speech, he pledged to his staff that he would back off his pressure for immediate results and asked for their help to keep him on track. He chose to receive weekly feedback from them on how he was doing and, in the process, inspired his workers with the power of making continuous personal improvements. Along the way, the plant achieved all the bottom-line improvements ahead of schedule; they did it with a renewed spirit of calm, cooperation, and excitement.

Owning up to one's collusion, albeit unintended, with unwanted results is a matter of character. It represents the truth of the matter—at least the part of the truth which is usually undiscussible. We say: "Awareness is the price of admission to the change game." The awareness of these two leaders led immediately to their own changing and to the results they wanted. The real bottom line lesson is: "I don't have to push others to change. When I concentrate on modeling what I want, the others will take their cues from my example and do their own changing."

The Buck Stops Here: Developing the Stance

"The radical change is the change AT the top,
not the change ORDERED by the top."
—Martha Spice

Our organizations and institutions need good leaders in every leadership slot. We can no longer be casual about developing them. The competitive global market place continues to make demands on organizations and institutions to be innovative, quality conscious, customer focused, socially responsible, and internally flexible and strong.

Our firm conducts a senior leader candidate development program. In it, we ask, "What are the qualities and characteristics of the leaders who bring out the best in you?" Never have we come across anyone who had no idea at all what such characteristics and qualities might look like. Quite the contrary, people do have clear pictures of their best leaders. Although the lists are long, we mention those character traits with which elicit broad agreement. Leadership that brings out the best in others consists of: not protecting an image, lack of ego, delegating and sharing power, risk taking, admitting one's own ignorance, inspiring by example, accepting disagreement, trusting and respecting others.

On the other side, a consensus is clear about the kind of leaders who crush spirit. Those who attract the most scorn berate associates in public, have no goals beyond being the "boss," talk more than they listen, are secretive and perfectionistic, look constantly to feathering their own nests, and do not communicate freely and openly.

Our senior level colleagues told us: "We know what kind of leader we want and what we don't want. We've known it for many years. We haven't seen anything different in the way our predecessors have conducted themselves after 'developing themselves.' There has been only lip service to this list. What does it really take to change?"

This is more than a rhetorical question. It demands an answer. It is a common human trait to judge others by their behavior, and to judge ourselves by our intentions. And, since our intentions are generally quite honorable, nothing much changes—that is, until we are willing to welcome and take in feedback on the effects of our behavior on others.

What does it take for leaders to see the gaps between behavior and intention and then operate from an aligned, intentional, and behavioral clarity that dramatizes their commitment to change? The leader candidate group slowly realized, it was up to them to stop complaining and waiting for others above them and around them to change. It was an issue of character, commitment, and responsibility, and they better get on with it. They had to determine what they cared about, seek honest feedback and do something with it. Starting now!

Behind Every Organizational Change Lies the Need for Personal Growth

"Example is not the main thing in influencing others; it is the only thing."
—Albert Schweitzer

Character, commitment, and responsibility require discipline. Here's an example of one way to work with discipline—from the inside out:

Deeply Probe for Your True INTENTION

- What do you personally care to achieve in your life? What is your passion?
- What do you deeply care that your organization achieve?
- How do you personally care to be (as a leader, parent, spouse, citizen)?

All successful enterprises are fueled by the creative human spirits of individuals each acting in alignment with their own highest values. Change is blocked by keeping up a front, performing as we "should," denying that we've been seduced away from our preferences by the trappings of power and "success." What really matters to you? This may be a time to ponder basic questions.

How will it look when it's achieved? *Seven Habits of Highly Successful People* author, Steven Covey, calls it keeping the end clearly in mind. Others add: If you haven't defined for yourself what it looks like, how will you know when you see it? How will you know what to plan for?

Bob Jones, a pseudonym for a senior executive in a small corporation, was committed to establishing more honest and creative teamwork in his Engineering Unit of 100 people. As he pictured the details of what he wanted, he saw team leaders offering appreciation, asking for input, reflecting after each meeting to capture the improvement opportunities. He saw team members learning from their mistakes, offering their expertise in a constructive way, everyone learning from each other.

Follow Bob through these steps as he lives out his serious commitment to a healthy, high performing unit starting with himself.

Build AWARENESS of Your Own Impact on Those Around You

What is the truth of what is happening now relative to your intention? In his article, "The Work of Leadership," in the *Harvard Business Review*, General William Pagonis writes how he prided himself on his listening ability—until a regular feedback mechanism that he had instituted reported that he was not perceived as a good listener. Seeking more details, he was told that his habit of sifting through mail while listening gave his staff the impression he wasn't really paying attention to them.

A commitment to building awareness takes courage. Blind spots abound. One senior leader of our acquaintance who cares deeply about the performance of his mid-size organization asks for risk taking, initiative, and creativity from his workforce. However his brusque manner of dealing with new ideas that do not conform with his own, leaves his associates fearful and unwilling to risk speaking out. His practice is not discussible. He has no idea about the impact of his behavior. Therefore, he unwittingly continues to sabotage himself, promoting exactly the opposite of what he really wants.

Jones, on the other hand, was so committed to improving the teamwork in his unit that he sought feedback about his own performance. He learned that he, himself, wasn't seen as part of the team. People did not feel his interest in them. People saw him as never giving recognition for jobs well done. Aware of the power of a modeling presence, he chose to behave differently and delighted subordinates with his "new" level of expressed interest and attention.

Live Out Your Intention in PRACTICE

Clearly awareness is not enough. It is only a first step. It is neutral. It creates space for something new. Awareness of current practice allows potential for a variety of adjustments—adjustments toward more clearly fulfilling one's intention. One must pose the question: What do I need to do differently to send a more consistent message of what I really want? How can I better walk my talk?

General Pagonis had a simple answer. He immediately started listening—without sorting mail.

Bob Jones took on these four disciplines and surprised himself with the power of attention.

Focus: I sit for 5 minutes a day thinking about my intention to have teams working together well. I continue to talk to myself about all the factors that are important to me.

Observation: I observe myself as I give or avoid giving recognition so I can learn more about my habits and patterns.

Action: I specifically use my own team meetings to model: a) recognition of contribution, and b) total participation in assessing what's working and not working, setting the meeting model I want them to emulate.

Feedback: I ask one person a week to describe the leadership traits under which he/she most flourishes.

PERSIST Bravely

It takes true courage to start with oneself first, do what's right, keep it going, go after the feedback on how it's working, and open the doors so that more and more things become discussible. It is particularly risky because so many leaders look at this approach with great skepticism. "How can I maintain my authority to lead when I open myself up to feedback or do my continuous improvement in public?"

It is surprising to discover that vulnerability, the act of taking deep responsibility, and doing one's best while owning up to mistakes, can actually augment one's credibility. Do workers want their leaders to be superhuman? Possibly. However, they'd probably prefer them to be self-correcting.

I spent three hours with the leader of a 700-person unit whose group was engaged in its own version of a TQM change effort. Together we focused on her leadership role and practice. I can only attest to her courage in the process of a deep and honest exploration, summarized here.

Q. What do you want from your people in this effort?
A. "An empowered workforce."

Q. What part of you may be unwilling to have this?
A. "The part of me that wants to stay in control, that wants them to do things my way."

Q. How can you make a new choice and align behind your own worthy intentions?
A. "I can 'fess up' and invite them to be full partners with me in planning our work."

As a result of our exploration, within 24 hours she had publicly acknowledged the ways she was only partially delegating tasks, such that her people were prohibited from really taking the responsibility. She asked for her group's support to make some changes in the way she herself did business. She gave what we now call, the *buck stops here* speech. She no longer blamed others for their lack of empowerment. She took 100% responsibility for the current situation in her organization. She apologized for not modeling from the top what she wanted to occur throughout her organization.

With this act alone, she sliced through the cynicism and inaugurated a new day. She modeled giving more than lip service to the task of making changes. She had made the undiscussible discussible. To her surprise and delight, two of her subordinates were inspired to stand up and publicly acknowledge the ways they, too, had been hindering the progress of the organization by not fully trusting their associates, micro-managing, and withholding information.

In the short term, she was wildly successful and gained immediate credibility and support. I am sad to report that because neither she nor her senior team members realized the *maintenance requirements* of such an important breakthrough, the gains dissolved in time. Along the way, we learned to more fully develop the system of the "buck stops here" practice we now recommend.

The Time is Now

"The world will not evolve past the current state
of crises by using the same thinking that created
the situation."
—Albert Einstein

By offering the challenge for radical change in this chapter, it is not our intent to diminish the efforts of those who are doing their best in a time when the rules are changing and the pressures unprecedented. The demands are such that we must look at every possibility for nourishing spirit in our organizations to solve complex problems and heal our organizational turmoil.

This is a time of paradox:

• In order truly to learn, we have to admit not knowing;

• If we are to empower, we have to give up control; and

• If we are to lead, we have to command, first of all, ourselves—to walk the talk.

To give up needing to control, to admit to being wrong or inexpert, or to move out of our comfort zones are courageous acts. According to Chris Argyris, Harvard professor and author of *Knowledge for Action*, we are automatically skilled incompetents in that we know exactly how to cover our tracks, look good in front of others, tout our expertise, avoid embarrassment, and somehow gain the upper hand. These defensive routines are deeply embedded in most organizational cultures. However, they are skills that no longer serve us.

On the eve of the release of Vice-President Al Gore's "National Performance Review," an attempt at "reinventing government," I overheard a conversation between two "been around a long time" bureaucrats. One said: "I don't expect much, but there are always *some* good ideas that will actually work." The other disagreed: "I have no hope at all. I bet that none of the recommendations will address the need to *reinvent the leaders!*"

As we each find our places along the hope-cynicism continuum at a time when life seems to have no simple answers, cynicism may win out. That would be sad, for without hope for the future, where is the energy to move forward? A clear and radical signal inspiring hope would be the willingness of leaders at all levels to start with themselves. Dr. W. Edwards Deming has taught us that the leader's job is to work *on* the system rather than *in* the system. We dare not forget our need to work on our own individual, personal, internal system, our own habits and patterns that drive our behaviors, sometimes independently of our espoused intentions.

Taking responsibility for one's internal system of thinking and acting and its impact on organizational life is a courageous act. It has been such a privilege to have had a ringside seat as so many people change their lives and their organizations by being willing to see themselves differently. In so doing they have managed to change the tune and thus the dance of all those around them.

The all-too-familiar alternative continues to seduce us to blame others, point the finger, disregard our own gut messages about our roles, pass the buck, and make excuses. This is the easy and well traveled road which insures the permanence of the status quo and perpetuates a model that continues to leave all of us more demoralized.

The unexplored territory of the inner journey toward deep accountability and responsibility is "the new frontier" for our time and it represents a powerful untapped resource. It may be *the* important vehicle for the radical changes we both desire and require in our businesses and organizations. If readers agree, perhaps we should work with it quietly. Too many important, powerful concepts (excellence, participation, quality, empowerment) have lost their meaning and potential for impact when turned into three-day programs, motivational slogans, or the fad of the month. We cringe to think about what would happen to the *buck stops here* speech if it were taught in management school. *Buck stops here* leadership is first an individual, deeply transformational process. It means looking within in addition to looking without. It is an opportunity to look carefully at one's fundamental intentions and to begin to measure behaviors and their impact against those intentions—and then do something about it.

> "Let him who would move the world, first move
> himself."
> —Socrates

Carol McCall
is co-founder of The World Institute
for Life Planning Group and the co-
creator of the Design Your Future
Workshop. She has dedicated her professional life to the development,
training and coaching of individuals in the areas of personal growth and
communication.

She has over twenty-five years experience as an educator, therapist,
manager, and entrepreneur. She is a graduate of Northwestern University
and is a pioneer in the field of life planning—a structure through which
people are listened to, coached and supported to success. She has taken
advance degree work at University of Chicago, Stanford University,
University of California at Berkeley, and San Jose State University.

19

Leadership:
The Values Game

Carol McCall

When I began to write this article, I recognized a gnawing sensation that I will call "fear." What was this "fear" about, I wondered? Here I was writing an article for inclusion in an anthology with people like Warren Bennis, the "Leadership Guru," and I had the thought, "What could I say that hasn't been already said by him?" Well, wait a minute! I have always had something to say about a subject that is near and dear to my heart—leadership and values. I have dedicated the past thirty years of my life to the development of human beings—in one capacity or another—mother, teacher, consultant, therapist (including work with the criminally insane). This experience should give me some credibility to writing about leadership.

However, what I returned to were my values, communication, and contribution. The leadership program that I co-founded with a partner, Mike Smith, speaks to exactly what was going on with me. The name of this program is Leadership, Productivity and Service: Freedom Course. By returning to my values, I was able to speak from contribution, not from the disempowering thought: "What will someone think about what I'm saying?" How simple—to "bypass" all the nonsense chatter and get to the point.

Our program development is based on several premises. I will highlight a few in this article.

We define "values" as the heart of what is most important to each of us—a place to empower and return ourselves in order to go beyond our self-imposed limitations.

Premise: Leaders Take Risks—Value: Risk

The paradigm of leadership that we are creating in our year-long program is one in which the leader is a coach. As a coach, one is expected to "walk-the-talk," not just give lip service to platitudes, but possess the courage to risk, tell the truth in the moment, and have inspiring conversations that take people through a powerful process that activates them to breakthrough results. What are the inspiring conversations that activate people to breakthrough results? These conversations are based on thought-provoking questions that the person being coached must search for, think about, ponder, and arrive at several possible solutions/conclusions that might otherwise have been missed.

We've discovered that people get stymied by "giving the answer." It's all too easy for the leader/coach to "give the answer." In the coaching that we promote, there is no "the answer." There are answers, and we look with the person to ascertain which ones will work the best in the current situation. It's a risk for most of us to "let go" and allow others to think for themselves. I say that one of the most challenging areas of development for leaders is to recognize when they are no longer "needed." We promote the idea that a leader's job is to duplicate oneself—leaders developing leaders who develop leaders. A frequently asked question is: "What about the followers?" The response is, we're all followers in some area. You may be a leader in developing a successful franchise business and a respected peer in the franchise industry, but in the auto industry, you're most likely a follower. We've observed there is no dearth of followers in any walk of life.

One of the principles we present, to empower leaders to take personal risks, is the "research" principle. What makes this principle palatable is that, when one is in "research," there are no "wrong" answers, actions or results. There's only what's discovered as useful or not useful during the "research." What has become clear as we work with leaders to take risks is that the job is not to reduce the risk but to empower the leaders in the face of the risk. Placing risk under the design called "research" provides freedom for many who dare to do what so many are unwilling to do—risk.

When a leader/coach takes personal risks, the coach is able to make unreasonable demands on those being coached. The coach risks stretching, and stretches others. What is possible is encountering the penetrating power of our word—the ability to do what we say we will or won't do. When that encounter happens, the "axis of risk" happens simultaneously. This axis is what I perceive to be the median of growth.

For most leaders, saying "no" is a great risk; particularly at those times when they would have thoughtlessly said "yes." All too often we say "yes" to avoid the risk of looking bad, not being "nice," not being liked, or protecting whatever we think there is to protect. What we fail to see is that by saying "yes" when we mean "no," we lie. We've placed our credibility in jeopardy and disempowered all parties involved. We've disempowered the person we've just lied to by interacting with them as if they are too fragile to hear the truth. "No" is a powerful word. Have you noticed most two-year-olds "rule" the world with it. Used with timing and as completion, "no" has the possibility of altering one's life.

We regularly invite the leaders to have something "at risk" when they are establishing their goals. People who have something to "play for" use coaching to support themselves. One of our leader's goals was to double the net income of his practice, without layoffs, in ninety days. He put his monthly salary at risk if he did not increase net income by 25% in the first quarter. He was involved in every call; getting coached two to three times extra each week. He came in at 100%. Risk provides breakthroughs, shifts our perspectives and leads to potent action.

Premise: Leaders Listen—Value: Listening

Most of us think we listen. Well, we do. We listen to ourselves. We listen as in "hurry up and finish what you're saying, so I can speak 'cause I already know what you're about to say and I can say it better anyway." Or we listen, "Yeah, yeah, yeah, what do you have to say that's of value to me?" How about the listening, "Yeah, right! Prove it!"? A speaker has about as much opportunity to be heard in a roaring crowd of football fans as he/she would standing in front of someone listening to the prior conversations. Whatever we're listening to, it's rarely to the speaker. Listening allows the speaker to recognize and experience being fully heard. It requires us to set aside our preoccupations and bring full attention to what's being said "now."

Listening is a gift. It is the nucleus of communication. The value—listening—requires us to give up the "right" to interpret what's being said and remain present to what is being spoken. Listening requires us to hear the speaker's commitments, concerns and possibilities.

"What do you mean, hear the speaker's commitment? How do you listen to someone's commitments? Sometimes people just aren't committed!" This is a frequently heard response. Our premise is that everyone is committed. The person may not have the *same* commitment as the one you do, but that doesn't mean there is *no* commitment. As a leader whose purpose is to empower the speaker, listen to the commitment that's there. People are committed to something. It may be a commitment to not making commitments—that's a commitment. Listen to people's concerns: jobs, family, children, travel, education, dreams. A frequently voiced concern is: "When I enroll in this leadership program, what happens to my freedom, time, family, and friends?" The concern is usually one of over-extension and the possible exclusion of loved ones. This concern gets addressed by having the person schedule in their "commitment management system" as a daily habit—time for spouse, friends, family, and self. Listening for people's concerns, commitments, and possibilities honors rather than manipulates.

What's become increasingly clear about the value—listening—is that it cannot be done thoughtlessly. The listener must be present. The moment it becomes a technique, the speaker recognizes the absence of affinity. Listening as a value provides affinity. The speaker is heard outside the boundaries of our individual judgments, evaluations and opinions. Empathic, agenda-less listening allows for how others perceive and interpret their world. To listen to "another's listening" allows them to be heard at a depth that, perhaps, they've never known and provides us with the opportunity to be heard by others with the same profundity, thereby establishing for the speaker and listener a sense of wholeness, well being, and affinity.

Value: Integrity

Telling the truth in our society is no easy feat! We live in an era where half-truths, "white-lies," lying (as long as you don't get caught), and "diplomacy" are all part of our style of communication. The paradigm that we're creating in our leadership course is: one—tell the truth in the moment. What's really the thought you're having right now? This is not intended to be brutal or thoughtless. There is a concern for how the communication is delivered. It is not a dump-session. Secondly—give up certain "rights." There are rights we have entitled ourselves to.

Example 1. "I won't call you on yours and you don't call me on mine." *Example 2.* "It's OK not to keep my word/follow-through. No one will notice, besides no one else can be counted on either." *Example 3.* "OK! I'll play 50%/50% as long as you play 50%/50%. What's wrong with this picture? Well, it's not honoring the value integrity. The instant we don't tell the truth in the moment, we have eroded our self-credibility. Those annoying self-doubts begin to creep in and we wonder how, if we don't keep our word in the "small" things, we will ever keep it in the things that really count? Playing 50%/50% is not the paradigm of empowerment for cultivating leadership in oneself or in others.

The paradigm we're creating is one of playing 100%/0 on your part and 100%/0 on mine. I'm 100% responsible for my speaking, my clarity, and being heard. In this equation, you're 0% responsible for my speaking, clarity, and being heard. For the value integrity to be reciprocally honored, the listener needs to be 100% responsible for his/her own speaking, clarity and being heard. As the receiver, I am 0% responsible for the speaking, clarity, and being heard by you. I do not "check out" as I listen.

There is a principle to which we ascribe called the 2°—Two Degrees. We use the nautical compass as an analogy. There is a point on the compass called "true north." When we're off-course by 2°, then life might begin to look like a series of lies, upsets, explanations, being righteous in our opinions, dominating others, unsuccessful relationships, financial worries, and chronic illness. By jogging 2° to the left, we're back on course. How does one "jog" 2° to the left? Tell the truth in the moment. "Do the right thing." This "truing" of ourselves gets us back on course, allows for completion of what was started, and makes possible the beginning of complete health. While these statements may seem simplistic and obvious to the casual observer, as far as I can tell it is the most difficult state for the most articulate, skilled leader to achieve and sustain. It requires the "willingness" to be comfortable with the discomfort of confronting the status quo; the "courage" to create powerful partnerships sustained through consistent authentic discourse, clarity of purpose and the tenacity to complete.

Value: Accountability

Accountability requires us to amplify self-responsibility with a never-ending format of rigor. Most of us consider accountability as a "bad" word—a word to be avoided—much like responsibility. How most of us hear accountability is as a "should." We reject the word "should" and regard it as one of the most insidious words in the English language. We prefer to fill our statements with "will," "won't," "no," "yes," "choice" and words that evoke freedom of expression and choice of actions. We promote accountability through teamwork. Accountability requires us to develop a team of interactive partners who assist us in constantly realizing our goals—a team that constantly assists us in realizing our goals also expedites our results.

The American culture is a "fast-paced, want-it-now" culture. An aspect of this "demand" culture/velocity, gets addressed through team coaching. Team coaching is successfully implemented during a daily telephone conference call in which each team member is held accountable for the results they say they will produce that day. The team comes to the conference call, each member with a result he or she will accomplish that day; they get coached in ways to achieve their respective goals and return the next day for check-in and feedback on what happened the prior day. Through this team coaching approach, our partnerships become simultaneously self-reliant and interdependent. In the conventional flow of life, most leaders unwisely choose to "go-it-alone"—the "John or Jayne Wayne" syndrome. Collaboration with others is crucial to accountability.

Accountability—living our life purpose and honoring our values—demands that we become aware of the web of interpretations that has formed our personal reality and participation in life. Becoming aware of this schematic—our paradigm—opens up a myriad of possibilities to which we were previously blind. When blind, we are unable to be accountable. When we see what we did not even know was there to be seen, we will act in our own best interest, the interests of others and embrace accountability.

Value: Service

"To truly rule is to serve," says an old Chinese adage. Although the idea of service is frequently associated with subservience, the most powerful posture of leadership is to empower the values of others through service. When I first began working in the arena of values and life purpose, I discovered that my life purpose is "to serve those who serve." Upon the discovery of this simplistic purpose, I was both relieved and perturbed. Being an African-American female, "service" had a slightly different ring to me than I suspected it might have to others who were not of my ethnicity. In the moment of this discovery of my life purpose, a paraphrase from the Bible came to me: "The truth shall set you free." What they forgot to tell me was that, in so doing, it would also tick me off.

What I have since come to discover is that service is the ultimate partnership with people. It occurs when we authentically claim and champion someone else's excellence, success, and fulfillment. Service is having the commitment to, and the appreciation for, what it takes to perform beyond our self-imposed limitations. People are grand; they are also deeply inauthentic. Service provides one with the opportunity to champion and claim the greatness of another, while making room for their embedded inauthenticity. Service is a state of being. It is both an art and an honor to catalyze achievements greater than our individual selves through service. Service is making a pledge and having an unswerving dedication to someone's dream or mission, and not relinquishing that pledge until that dream/ mission is actualized. For example, my vision for the year 2020 is to have 20 million leader/coaches empowering people's life purposes and supporting a culture that lives and produces from its values. Service enables people to look together, free from criticism or accusations, into what will be included here or there to produce the desired result. Service is tenaciously "partnering" another through the challenges of difficult decisions, confrontive episodes, and the abrupt surcease of communication. Service is powerful leadership and coaching in the face of no agreement.

Value: Vitality

We are currently witnessing a transition from the prevailing culture that defines leadership as one that is based on personal characteristics such as age, race, sex, background, eighteen- to twenty-hour work days, one-sided interests, and priority given to special interest groups. In the upcoming millennium, leadership will not be based solely on a set of attributes, nor information acquisition, but on the well-rounded diversity, lightness and flexibility that a leader intertwines to form a braid of meaning into life. The quintessence and paradox of being a leader lies in our vitality. One of the agents that robs leaders of their vitality is "what they're hiding." In our monthly four-day leadership sessions, we cover, in detail, the premise that leaders contribute what they're hiding.

Most of us interact with each other as if only one side of our personality existed. What we've observed is that a leader's "persona" is "to know what he/she is doing all the time." Most leaders have no idea what they're doing and their greatest fear is that someone will discover this truth. I am not implying that leaders don't have information on a given subject matter. For the most part, leaders are "over-informed." What's being addressed here is the pretense of knowing exactly how they're going to respond in a given situation, with an exact answer to every possible question. Hiding or pretending places an enormous toll on one's vitality. Most leaders do not have a safe environment in which to observe and receive feedback. By the end of the four days we've developed a humor and lightness so that we don't take ourselves quite so seriously.

Vitality is a fulcrum for acquiring new avenues to a lifestyle that allows one to live a life of no regrets.

This leadership—the "values game"—is not a task to be accomplished in a weekend, or even over a period of months. It is a life-long endeavor and one well worth the investment for those who choose to "play." To paraphrase what one of our most proactive leaders said, "This...is for people to gain personal freedom—dissolve fears, inhibitions, anger, limitations, inadequacies—all those human things that keep us from being all that we can be. This...allows people to remove the ceiling from their lives, enabling them to make a quantum leap in their personal power and professional effectiveness."

PART FIVE

Implementing New Leadership

Attributes of Leadership
Max DePree

Winning Trust
Perry Pascarella

A Conversation with Norman Lear
Stewart Emery

Where does the "rubber meet the road," as an old expression goes? Where does all this philosophy and new thinking get us when we go back into the office, the boardroom, or the shop floor?

How do we begin to implement, to execute, this new behavior? How are these new values expressed in the day-to-day affairs of the enterprise?

Three of our authors provide some wisdom in this final portion of this collection. Executive Max DePree, author of *Leadership is an Art* and *Leadership Jazz*, identifies a dozen attributes he believes are valuable for the new leaders. Publishing executive Perry Pascarella, author of *The Purpose-Driven Organization*, focuses on the leader's need to earn trust from his or her colleagues and coworkers.

Finally, Stewart Emery interviews TV genius Norman Lear on the subject of leadership. Emery, himself a bestselling author, extracts from Lear a call to action—for business leaders to declare publicly what they know privately—that business is values-driven and spirit-directed.

Each of these three authors plus the subject of Emery's

interview, Norman Lear, has experience at putting his values to work. Each of these four men have taken public stands and "walked their talk" as they managed their companies, led their teams, and implemented values that they personally held near-and-dear. This final segment of our collection will inspire you to consider how you will implement *your* values—to declare publicly what you know needs to happen in the workplace.

Max DePree
is Chairman of the Board of Directors for Herman Miller, Inc., an
international company engaged
in the design, manufacture, and sale of office furniture systems and related
products for the health-care industry. he began his career with Herman
Miller, Inc. in 1947 and worked in nearly all areas of management,
including a period of eighteen months in Europe directing the international
operations. During the last eight years he served as chief executive officer.

He is a member of the Board of Trustees of Fuller Theological
Seminary in Pasadena, California, of Hoye College in Holland, Michigan,
and on the advisory boards of The Leadership Institute at the University of
Southern California and of the Peter F. Drucker Foundation for Nonprofit
Management. DePree is a member of the *Fortune* magazine National
Business Hall of Fame and is the author of two books, *Leadership is an Art*
and *Leadership Jazz*. This essay is excerpted from his book *Leadership Jazz*
and is used by permission of the publisher.

20

Attributes of Leadership: A Checklist

Max DePree

I arrived at the local tennis club just after a group of high school students had vacated the locker room. Like chickens, they had not bothered to pick up after themselves. Without thinking too much about it, I gathered up all their towels and put them in a hamper. A friend of mine quietly watched me do this and then asked me a question that I've pondered many times over the years. "Do you pick up towels because you're the president of a company, or are you the president because you pick up towels?"

Leadership is a serious meddling in the lives of others. Besides picking up towels, what other traits or attributes quality us to accept the job of leadership?

Some of my friends call me a man of many lists. Here is a list that may help you coalesce your thinking about the good work of leadership. In spite of my admiration for lists, to catalog the attributes of a leader is like fighting the Hydra. Like Hercules, I confront two more heads every time I write one off. In examining one aspect of leadership, I soon discover that I think of something else equally important. Just another proof that leadership is something we never completely understand.

Other people have made lists about leadership. A good one is "The Tasks of Leadership," a chapter in John Gardner's book

264 LEADERSHIP IN A NEW ERA

On Leadership. I find that a list brings a sort of discipline to my thinking, and I look at a good list as a musical score. Before it really comes to life, it must be interpreted and performed. How that is accomplished or how you use a list is more up to you than to me.

Above all, leadership is a position of servanthood. Leadership is also a posture of debt; it is a forfeiture of rights. You see! One quality of leadership always implies another. Where does one stop? Here is my list. See what you think.

Integrity. Integrity is the linchpin of leadership. Where integrity is at stake, the leader works publicly. Behavior is the only score that's kept. Lose integrity, and a leader will suddenly find herself in a directionless organization going nowhere.

Vulnerability. Vulnerability is the opposite of self-expression. Vulnerable leaders trust in the abilities of other people; vulnerable leaders allow the people who follow them to do their best. An invulnerable leader can be only as good as her own performance. What a terrifying thought! One caveat: Remember that there is no such thing as safe vulnerability.

Discernment. You cannot buy discernment: you can find it. Discernment lies somewhere between, wisdom and judgment. Leaders are required to see many things—pain, beauty, anxiety, loneliness, and heartbreak. Two elements to keep your eye on: the detection of nuance and the perception of changing realities. What kind of antennae do you have?

Awareness of the human spirit. In a special way, all the qualities of a good leader stem from this one. Without understanding the cares, yearnings, and struggles of the human spirit, how could anyone presume to lead a group of people across the street? In modern organizational jargon, person skills always precede professional skills.

Courage in relationships. Followers expect a leader to face up to tough decisions. When conflict must be resolved, when justice must be defined and carried out, when promises need to be kept, when the organization needs to hear who counts—these are the times when leaders act with ruthless honesty and live up to their covenant with the people they lead.

Sense of humor. Sometimes the best humor is deadly

serious. I've often wondered why. Part of the reason must be that a compassionate sense of humor requires a broad perspective on the human condition, an accounting for many points of view. Surely true leaders have it. You'll find a sense of humor essential to living with ambiguity.

Intellectual energy and curiosity. When you are fortunate enough to lead a group of people, opportunities arise constantly to learn from those people. The very complexity of life today has turned decision making 'into a process of learning and discovery requiring great intellectual vigor of leaders. We cannot make good decisions unless we accept the responsibility for learning frantically the things that produce them. If you are intent on learning frantically, you actively seek out what followers can teach. And when you seek out the competence of your followers, you begin to enable them to fulfill their potential. When followers are allowed to do their best, they make leadership infinitely easier, and you're free to learn even more. A wonderful cycle, don't you think?

Respect for the future, regard for the present, understanding of the past. Leaders move constantly back and forth between the present and the future. Our perception of each becomes clear and valid if we understand the past. The future requires our humility in the face of all we cannot control. The present requires attention to all the people to whom we are accountable. The past gives us the opportunity to build on the work of our elders.

Predictability. To their followers, leaders owe predictability as a human being. This differs from predictability in strategic planning or decision making, something leaders also should pursue. Leaders must be calculable forces in organizations; they are not free to follow a whim. For example, since leaders are especially responsible for the vision and values of an organization, I would grieve over an unpredictable tender of a group's birthright and future. Something to keep in mind here: Tending vision is as difficult as conceiving one.

Breadth. A vision of what an organization can become has room for all contributions from all quarters. To borrow from Walt Whitman, leaders are people large enough to contain multitudes.

266   LEADERSHIP IN A NEW ERA

Comfort with ambiguity. "Leader" is not always a position. Whatever one's position, the amount of ambiguity involved is directly proportional to the amount of leadership required. Healthy organizations exhibit a degree of chaos. A leader will make some sense of it. The more comfortable you can make yourself with ambiguity, the better leader you will be. Organizations always delegate the job of dealing constructively with ambiguity to their leaders.

Presence. I think that the ability to stop is an important trait of leaders. Many large manufacturing plants have a fleet of bicycles that allow people to save time on trips to various areas of the facility. Such is the case at Herman Miller, but we have placed a restriction on the use of our bicycles. No supervisor may ride one. The reason is simple: You cant have a conversation or ask a question from a bicycle. You can't tap a person going by on a bicycle on the shoulder and say, "Could I talk to you a minute?" Leaders stop—to ask and answer questions, to be patient, to listen to problems, to seek the nuance, to follow up a lead. Leaders quietly and openly wait for the information, good and bad, that enables them to lead.

I hope this list has both pricked your thinking about leadership and opened you to the potential of leaders. Perhaps one need remember no more than what a friend of mine once said to me. "Leaders stand alone, take the heat, bear the pain, tell the truth." I am constantly excited by what there is to learn!

Perry Pascarella
is vice president of Penton Publishing Inc., the publisher of thirty-five
magazines and periodicals, and
former editor-in-chief of its flagship magazine, *Industry Week*. He has
written four books, including *The New Achievers* and *The Purpose-Driven
Organization*.

He was an early crusader for humanistic and participative management and for corporate social responsibility. In 1992, he received the
American Business Press' Crain Award, given annually to the individual
"who has made outstanding career contributions to the development of
editorial excellence in the business press."

He has adapted his essay from an article that appeared in the
February 1, 1993 issue of *Industry Week* magazine.

21

Winning Trust

Perry Pascarella

How far will people follow your leadership? Many factors determine the answer to that question, but one thing is for sure: They will follow you no farther than they trust you.

Many experts have created lists of the characteristics of leaders. "Trust" always makes the list even though few of us understand where it comes from. Is it given, or do you have to earn it?

People don't *give* you their trust. They *invest* it in you because they want to draw strength from your character—honesty, integrity, and so on. But, no matter how great your character, you may fail to win trust unless you reveal that character through your actions.

You tell the truth as you see it. You try to serve the best interests of your organization in all your decision making. Yet, your subordinates, peers, or senior managers may still not trust you. Certainly, matters of character come into play in determining whether a would-be leader is trusted, but even the highest integrity and best intentions won't protect you from getting into situations in which you find that people don't line up behind you. Why?

For one thing, policies and practices of the company have a lot to do with the trust climate in which you operate. How well it treats employees and retirees, how much effort it puts into educating and equipping employees, how fairly it pays and promotes them—all these things help determine how much trust people have in "the company" and in individual leaders within it.

In addition, even with all the best human resource policies, an organization may still wind up with a poor trust climate if strategies aren't clear and tactics aren't in synch. Trust gaps can exist, not only from one level of the hierarchy to another, but among fellow workers within any level—even at the top. They are caused more often by poor communications than by poor character.

The degree of difficulty in winning trust rises exponentially in organizations that are attempting to generate employee involvement and empowerment. Their intended structure and management style depend on trust more than do the tactics of traditional organizations. But, as change explodes, people are especially vulnerable to feelings of insecurity. Any shortcoming in trust can trigger uncertainty and fear, blocking the flexibility needed for keeping up with changes in technology and markets. Messages about participation and teamwork only heighten perceptions of hypocrisy if you're seen as not "walking the talk."

On the other hand, you as an individual can be a big influence on the trust level through your actions regardless of your company's policies and practices . People will put up with a "bad company" if they trust their boss or if they enjoy exciting team-relationships with their peers.

The telling factor is the cumulative effect of one-on-one, day-to-day relationships. Trust is won or lost by how well you know yourself, how open you are to letting others see who you are, and how well you demonstrate your willingness to know who they are. All of these things depend on you. None of them depend on the company.

Success depends on more than having the right character. It depends, too, on what you do and don't do. It's easy to *look* wrong or unintentionally *do* wrong to others. Here are some suggestions for avoiding the sins of omission and commission to which even saints can fall victim:

1. ***Demonstrate that you are working for others' interests, as well as your own.*** Don't deny that you want something

from the organization—the opportunity to exercise your talents, financial reward, recognition, whatever makes going to work important to you. You may be altruistic and willing to subordinate your wants to the group's, but any self-respecting person does have personal wants. People expect you to have them. They are on the watch to learn how much your wants harmonize with theirs.

Peers, subordinates, and bosses will look at you in terms of whether your track record indicates that you aim for the corporate good or for protecting your personal turf. They will observe whether you build and enable others to excel or treat them as competitors.

If you're not demonstrating respect for others, you have to expect them to conclude, "If you don't respect me, then I can't trust you to look out for my interests."

2. *Listen in ways that show you respect others and that you value their ideas.* Anyone around you is likely to have information and viewpoints that are of value to you and the organization. Be a magnet for facts. Listen especially for the frame of reference, the vision, the new way of looking at a situation that others bring. Don't tune out simply because you hear a minor error in fact or reasoning. (An occasional wild idea from someone with limited views and information might stimulate some fresh thinking on your part.)

This doesn't mean you have to lead an individual to think his or her ideas on everything are the absolute finest. Direct an individual's suggestion-generating efforts to areas where he or she truly has knowledge. A little coaching to get the individual's thinking on track will produce more useful ideas, and the attention you give will elevate that person's sense of worth.

3. *Practice openness—the critical value for team action.* Trust is based on perception as well as on fact. Mistrust comes from what people don't know as well as from what they do know. That means today's accelerating pace of tactical business maneuvers and corporate restructuring can cause misperceptions to snowball far more than usual.

Team members must share the openness with one another that leads to confidence and trust. Share information. Give it and take it. Share whatever information you have to improve your organization rather than hoarding it to boost your ego. In turn, expect others to share their facts and feelings with you.

Agree upon some rules of behavior that will permit the team to function at its best. When we know the people on our team, we can challenge the unseen. When we don't know them, we mistrust even what we do see.

4. **Speak your feelings.** In a team environment, people need to know your feelings as well as the hard facts. Sharing them is part of openness—of letting people know who you are.

Be real. Admit your weaknesses, concerns, fears.

When you disagree with someone, say so. Your peers and bosses are likely to have greater respect for you for openly disagreeing with them than for your saying you agree when you really don't. Let them know what stands in the way of your commitment.

When you are excited about something, tell why it's important to you.

5. **Explain what you understand and admit there are things you don't understand.** You don't have to be all-powerful or all-knowing to gain respect and trust. Tell people not only what you know but define what you don't know. When you lack information you need, go to the source—no matter how high or how low in the organization—and get it rather than wasting energy complaining to people who can't help you.

For as far ahead as we can see, we're in for change and uncertainty. Don't feel you have to present your subordinates a guaranteed future. When they believe you have their interests in mind, they will tolerate the many gaps in information that inevitably occur in a fast-moving organization. They will respect you for your defining what it is you don't know, and they'll see that you respect them if you ask them to share in the search for answers.

6. **Share as much as you know about where the organization is going.** An effective organization needs a sense of mission, a strategy for realizing it, and people who are well equipped and organized for executing smart tactics.

Whether your organization has or doesn't have a stated mission or a clear strategy, you owe your subordinates the best you can interpret as direction for your part of the organization. Sometimes the best you can present is: "This is how I see it."

You may have to go to upper management from time to time and point out: "It would help me if you would explain..."

Working from what's written or from what's implied, translate the general strategy so people understand the context in which they are working. And then work out the tactics with them. That's where you win or lose. After all, a mission or strategy is fairly generic; anyone can state the same things that your organization does. But it's the tactics, the execution, that makes it possible to be far better than others with the same strategy.

You have to explain the presence of seemingly conflicting values the organization plays as it proceeds where it wants to go. For instance, people may constantly be urged to reduce costs. When they see a relatively big investment made in a specific activity that doesn't follow standard practice, they ask: "Why the exception?" Someone needs to explain that sometimes a prime value has to be traded off for another that is also important such as speed of response in the marketplace.

Even with a formal mission statement and a grand strategy, an organization needs leaders at all levels who can give meaning to the day-to-day activity.

7. *Show consistency in the basic values that guide your decision making.* Mistrust comes from not knowing what to expect—not seeing any boundaries to or purpose for what you're doing. Don't put people in the position of saying, "You're honest, but you're liable to make a decision that I don't expect—and possibly don't even understand."

People want to know what values lie behind your decisions. What are you trying to accomplish and why is it important? Take the time to think about your values and beliefs and articulate them clearly. When you know your central purpose, your actions will follow within that framework, and they'll have a consistency that earns trust. You may have to zig and zag to get where you want to go, but, if you are following a purpose that others share, they will follow you because you are proceeding toward an agreed upon destination.

Inconsistency can arise from trying to do too many things. If you're getting into too many detailed decisions, you may lose sight of the big picture. You may be treading into so many areas that you do not understand all the ramifications of what you are doing. You raise the odds of making decisions that conflict with one another. If so, it's time to push decision-making responsibility down the line.

And there's a quick route to inconsistency: trying to please everyone and, thereby, wavering from your basic values. People will think you're changing your "story"—and you are!

8. *Make the right choices after viewing the alternatives that are before you.* Both your boss and your subordinates want to know you are well-informed and that you've considered all their inputs and weighed the options with concern and logic. They are likely to forgive wrong decisions based on "all the facts" and the best of intentions more readily than they'll trust your relying on luck or shooting from the hip.

On the other hand, don't expect to always have *all* the facts or people will come to trust you to miss the boat. The best leaders make good decisions without all the facts, but they don't disregard what's under their noses.

9. *Demonstrate awareness of all the key ramifications of your decision.* What are the side effects of a right decision? You need inputs from others to raise your awareness of the potential impacts of a decision you're weighing. Get inputs from others on what has to be done to deal with the ramifications.

Then, focus on the issues rather than on egos. Ask what will be accomplished for the business rather than who will be pleased. That's a tough one. It may lead to unpopularity more often than to mistrust.

10. *Explain why you are shifting management styles— from participative to more autocratic—when the situation calls for a shift.* Different management styles are appropriate for different situations. While participative management is an effective over-arching style today, there are times when a manager has to step in and make quick decisions and give directions. It's important, however, to let people know what you've decided and why. It's best to let them know in advance what the ground rules are for your various styles. People will understand the change and not distrust you if your actions are aligned with the values you have articulated to them.

11. *Let people know the downside, the negatives, as well as the good news.* Bad news travels fast. Don't let the grapevine beat you in informing your subordinates of bad news

that affects them. Help them get the straight story and put it into proper perspective. There's a good chance they are aware of it before you announce it, but they want your honest reports. If you're truly their leader, they want to know how your reaction compares with theirs.

One of the mysteries of the workplace is: Why do we often treat adults as children? Employees have homes, cars, investments, families; why should we patronize them with favors and feel we have to control them to get results? They are surrounded by illnesses, stresses, and death; why try to shield them from bad news in the workplace—news that may be relatively minor in terms of the big problems they shoulder off the job?

If people hear only the good news from you, they know you are not being fully open. They have grounds for not trusting you.

12. **Support your subordinates' decisions.** You're not perfect. Neither are your subordinates. Unless you want to make all the decisions down to the tiniest detail yourself, stand by their decisions. When a subordinate errs, follow up immediately to help him or her learn from the mistake. Get to work to study the decision-making process used to discover why he or she came up with the wrong answer. Was it lack of information? Was it lack of clear objectives? Because you're after results, focus the conversation on the future; make it one that leads to winning action, not to a feeling of loss or guilt.

Never stand aside washing your hands of all responsibility when a subordinate makes a public mistake. That's desertion— a fast route to mistrust. In some cases, you can step forward to present some additional evidence to prove the subordinate right. The least you can do is show that you aren't condemning the person for an error. Share responsibility for seeing the same mistake doesn't happen again.

13. **Show that you know how to work with and earn the support of upper management.** People are inclined to trust what you say and respect what you do when you seem to be able to work with and have the respect of top management.

Know what your senior management considers important— what the primary job is for you and your team. If you aren't in alignment with top management, your subordinates may perceive you as a person to be mistrusted.

It's not what you win for yourself in the way of awards,

raises, or promotions. It's a matter of getting the backing to take your team to new heights. Win management support of your needs for equipment, personnel, funding, whatever it takes to get the job done right. Ask for only what's necessary, and justify your requests.

14. **Signal an error, a breakdown, a missed objective that will affect other people's expectations.** People are depending on you. When you are accountable for doing something, don't try to hide the fact that you are missing the mark. Wave the yellow flag, ask for inputs, and call for a new agreement. People respect an honest person who admits he or she is human more than a proud one who needs to be right all the time.

Ask yourself "How do the changes I am making affect other people's plans?" That means telling not only your boss. In fast-moving, rapidly-changing organizations, you have to communicate with the entire team. Don't neglect horizontal communications with your peers.

15. **Respect old ideas while you dig for new ones.** Leaders help people make the transition from the present to the future.

Leaders thrive on new ideas, but you won't get followers to embrace them if they think you are trashing their ideas that built the present. None of us like to have our work disparaged or destroyed.

Take care in explaining how you would like to build on other people's good ideas of the past as you look for their new, more appropriate ideas for tomorrow.

Stewart Emery
is a senior organizational consultant at Human Factors, Inc. He
specializes in consulting to execu-
tives and senior managers on the ongoing challenge of creating sustainable economic value. He is an advocate of creating constituencies for
change, developing referent leadership and building spiritually healthy
organizations.

Emery is the author of the best-selling books, *You Don't Have to
Rehearse to be Yourself* and *The Owners Manual For Your Life*. Millions of
people in the United States and around the world have been touched by
his writing as well as his radio and television appearances. Tens of
thousands of people have attended his workshops, seminars, and speaking
engagements during the last two decades.

Emery studied economics, philosophy and psychology at the University of Sydney before pursuing a career in the advertising arts. He served
as a creative director of J. Walter Thompson's office in Sydney, Australia
and taught design at the University of New South Wales.

22

A Conversation with Norman Lear

Stewart Emery

The sun is settling into a layered sea of clouds that gently grace the seascape of the English Channel. Sitting in a lounge of the Grand Hotel, on the Isle of Jersey editing this manuscript on a computer about the size of a modest three-ring binder, I reflect on the day's edition of the *International Herald Tribune:* Israel and the Palestinians, having recognized each others right to exist, labor to realize a pledge of peace; Black South Africans will at last have seats in what has always been an exclusively white South African parliament; Boris Yeltzin appears to be consolidating his leadership of whatever remains of the Soviet Union after yet another political challenge; and the world's major economies struggle to post a semblance of economic growth.

I guess this is a "new" era; although having spent the end of the 1950s and all of the 1960s in the Australian advertising business, my response to the word "new" is somewhat tepid. On the other hand, the new millennium is clearly upon us. For the new millennium to become a new era, there has to be change at the most fundamental level. What follows are some thoughts about the nature of this change and about the kind of leadership required.

Salvation

Albert Einstein is quoted as saying: "We live in a world filled with problems that cannot be solved by the level of thinking that was used to create the problems." What level of thinking has created the realities of the 20th Century? Much of it has to do with our beliefs about salvation. Although the concept of salvation is probably more familiar in a theological context, the definition of the word encompasses "preservation from loss, calamity, etc.; the thing that preserves from these (be the salvation of)." The specifics of what we perceive we need to be saved from may vary as wildly as our imagination. Endemic to the human condition is the denial of self and the fear-driven pursuit of salvation through some separate and external source.

Medieval Europe was dominated by a belief in "faith" as the source of salvation. Resurrected during the Protestant Reformation, this belief system was dying by the middle of the 17th Century. The belief that religious faith could create heaven on earth was politically irrelevant by the middle of the 18th Century.

The decline of the belief in salvation through faith created a void that was filled by the rise of the belief in salvation by society. Between 1883 and 1888, in Germany, Chancellor Bismarck created national health insurance and compulsory old-age insurance. This marked the birth of the "Welfare State," and the expression of a promise that government should and could provide a risk-free existence for its constituents. Around this time, similar sentiments found expression in the United States as populism began—the first distinctly "anti-business" political movement. Populism demanded government control of the stock market, wages and hours of work, and agricultural prices.

And so began the 20th Century and the popular love affair with belief in salvation by society as practiced through the welfare state and totalitarianism, together with the assertion that the collective, the party, the state, is the absolute.

Soon ends are made to justify means and history becomes fiction masquerading as the truth.

This belief in salvation by society assumed a variety of forms; Auguste Comte and G.W.F. Hegel inspired Karl Marx, who set the stage for Lenin, Hitler, and Mao as "saviors of society." The power of totalitarianism was derived from the popular belief that the state could eliminate the fear of uncertainty and exploitation.

Belief and reality are often not the same as evidenced by the "reality" that totalitarianism governs through the exploitation of fear.

By the time Lyndon Johnson tried to sell Americans his Great Society, the idea of salvation by society had become a bitter joke. While the industrial revolution and the birth of technology are viewed as causal for the rise to dominance of the West, they were probably less causal than the promise of salvation by society in its various expressions. Now this promise is a shattered dream.

While we may have given up on the dream of a government guarantee of absolute salvation, we apparently have not given up on the idea of a risk free existence guaranteed by government regulation of the economic and social process. In the 20th Century, the great political debate did not center around whether or not governments should exercise power over the people, but around the breadth of that power. Today, the struggle over the degree of democratic and legal restraint of government power continues.

The need to believe in salvation through some separate and thus external source runs deep in the human psyche. Accompanying the historical procession of ideologies is our endless willingness to attribute that power to a charismatic leader. No century has borne witness to more leaders with more charisma than our 20th Century—and what carnage has ensued. Stalin, Hitler, General Tojo, and Mao possessed extraordinary charisma, developed an extraordinary ability to deny reality, and directed extraordinary destruction.

Must history continue to be the chronicles of what we can endure, and still learn nothing from? Too many dreams are shattered in a lifetime. Can innocence be lost and not replaced with cynicism?

These questions have been with me a long time. In Australia they led me away from a career in advertising. By 1969 it had become clear to me that advertising relentlessly peddled things to people who were all so eager for "sources of salvation." Until around this time I had believed that there were no wounds from my own anguished childhood that a little fame and fortune wouldn't heal. Then it occurred to me that I had accumulated enough of fame and fortune to have healed, if they hold the power

I had ascribed to them. Clearly they did not. I recalled my studies in psychology and philosophy and concluded that one cannot regulate the quality of internal experience through the apparent conquest of external sources of promised bliss. I decided that I did not want to live my life as a purveyor of broken dreams. So began my departure from advertising and an inner journey that led me to San Francisco in 1971.

Now, it is 1994. America is over-managed and under-led. Politics as a source of salvation has become another bad joke—although we continue to provide a constituency for the law makers who promise to legislate risk from our lives. The media, a pawn of advertising, continues at a maddening pace to promise salvation on behalf of its clients while promoting a parade of illusionary realities.

When a lunch with John Renesch yielded the desire to write this chapter, I knew I would like to develop the content in conversations with two men I hold in high regard: Norman Lear and Dr. Warren Bennis. Both have earned the right to be heard on the subjects of leadership, business, the media and politics.

As the sun rose to usher in one of those rare days of almost unlimited visibility that reveal the natural beauty of the Los Angeles basin, I set off to talk with Norman Lear.

The Conversation Begins

Norman Lear is a thoughtful man with a seemingly tireless generosity of spirit. He is uncomfortable with being considered a leader. "I consider myself a writer who loves to show real people in real conflict with all their fears, doubts, hopes, and ambitions rubbing against their love for one another," explains Lear, one of the most innovative and influential producers in television. It has been estimated that more than half the nation's population have watched the television shows of Norman Lear.

The focus of the morning's conversation was the current plight of American leadership, how we happen to be where we are and, of course, the prospects for leadership in a new era.

I find one of the benefits of having not grown up in the United States is that people are very willing to share with me their perceptions and insights about America's coming of age. In my conversations with Dr. Warren Bennis, who has devoted his life to the study of leadership, he consistently advocates that an essential function of leadership is the management of attention and meaning. "Leaders manage attention through a compelling vision that brings others to a place they have not been before. To make dreams apparent to others and to align people with them, leaders must communicate their vision. No matter how marvelous the vision, the effective leader must use a metaphor, a word or a model that makes that vision clear to others so they invest meaning and align to the vision"

This might easily be the *crucial* function of leadership. Certainly an excellent place to begin a conversation, so I asked Norman to offer his thoughts on the evolution of what Americans pay attention to and invest meaning in.

"A lot of years ago," responded Norman, "Walter Lippman was contemplating which of the institutions in American life had the most impact on Americans. He identified what he called the ancestral order of institutions based on their influence: the family being number one, religion being number two, civil authority being number three and education being number four. He called that the old ancestral order which we have seen, in our time, totally destroyed.

"Today the family has very little influence on the culture generally. People on the fringes are influenced by religion but the great mass of people no longer find religion a great influence. When we talk about leadership the whole question of civil authority is a joke. Unable to provide leadership to itself, it does not provide leadership to the American people. When I was a boy, if a mayor or a congressman or a senator were coming to town their reputations and their moral authority preceded them by minutes and miles because we had enormous respect for the office and for most of those individuals.

"There were the scandals that turned up now and again, but we invested, happily I think, and to our very great benefit, enormous moral suasion and authority to people in important civil jobs. All this is gone now. It is hard to believe that there is more chicanery among leaders today than ever before. This would indicate human nature has changed, which is unlikely. It seems to me, however, that human behavior has changed as a result of so many years of escalating self-involvement.

"Education is in disarray and certainly not the influence it once was. We talk a great deal about educating the underclass and the impoverished. We also need a really new education for the middle and upper class at large: an education in values. I don't see how we can develop a resource of leadership unless we develop spirit-led, values-driven sensibilities, which seem absent today. Instead we have cynicism and liberal well-meaning concerns about separation between church and state. There is both liberal and conservative cynicism about the soft issues in life; like what's it all about? and has life meaning? and what is meaning? We have developed a culture in which the discussion of that most enjoyable and fascinating of subjects, the one subject that more than any other has fascinated the human of the species from the very beginning of time, is an embarrassment, lest we get to the "G" word. God forbid people should talk about their thoughts on that subject. It seems to me that this is a very serious loss.

"I think because nature abhors a vacuum, we have seen the institution of business move in and take the place of the combination of all these institutions." I don't think business applied for the job of providing national or global leadership. That business is now considered in this role is problematical. It is too late to have the conversation about whether or not this is desirable, or whether corporate executives struggling to sustain the economic viability of their enterprises want leadership on this dimension added to their job descriptions. Things are as they are. Now the challenge is to recognize the current condition and respond usefully.

Norman offered this view of the current condition: "The corporate ethic, increasingly over a good many years, has been: give me a profit statement this quarter larger than the last and every thing else be damned. Because of businesses' enormous influence on the culture, this obsession with the short term has been described as the 'culture of narcissism' in one decade, the 'me generation' in another and the greed and avarice of the Reagan years, in the decade just passed. I am not trying to establish a villain here. This development wasn't planned. Businessmen didn't decide this is how things are going to be. Short-term thinking and America's addiction to numbers—SAT scores, Neilsen ratings, box office numbers, polls, polls, and more polls, simply 'happened' to us over time."

During the passing of these decades a profound change has

taken place in the equity ownership of American enterprise. Once upon a time the common stock of American corporations was held by thousands of individual men and women, many of whom fully expected to will their holdings to their children and grandchildren. Definitely a long-term strategy. Now it has come to pass that the great pension plans, investing billions of dollars, are the major equity holders. Certainly, they hold their positions on behalf of millions of Americans. However, they can exercise power that thousands of independent individuals cannot. "These pension plans do move hundreds of millions of dollars into this situation or that for two days or five to pick up a couple of dollars and then move on. The result is that business becomes more and more preoccupied with serving Wall Street and the numbers in the short term."

Norman Lear has started a new family at a time in life when most folks are happy to enjoy their grandchildren rather than young children of their own. I asked him to speak to the current state of the nation from his viewpoint as a father.

"I was a father at a very young age, twenty-three I guess...a long time ago...and shortly thereafter I started to think of life in terms of my daughter. Then there was a second daughter and then a third. I always thought about the future in terms of the youngest. Now that I have a five-year-old son and a grandchild, I look at the future and the world through their eyes. Now I ask: what is going to be good for them? What is going to be right for them? I'm forever hopeful, I wouldn't want to wake up in the morning if I didn't have hope, but I must say the future looks grim today.

"Consider that one-third of our tax money goes to pay the interest, not the principle, the interest, on our national debt. Everywhere we look, a burgeoning underclass. The infrastructure of our vital cities is disintegrating exponentially. Our nation, once the world's mightiest creditor, is now the biggest debtor nation of all time. The armies of homeless, no longer a sight reserved for the cities, are now stretching into suburbia. Our politics are a parade of scandal and shame. We have gang warfare and drug trafficking, children having children, racial and domestic violence, and the mess that is health care. The environment has become a slow motion apocalypse of acid rain, depletion of the ozone layer and global warming.

"The inferences we draw from all of this may vary, but rich or poor, liberal or conservative, Republican or Democrat, we all are looking at the same pictures provided by the media."

"Are you comfortable with the leadership provided by the media?" I asked him.

"No, not at all, I'm not comfortable with the leadership in America generally. I am a very disaffected Democrat. I hardly think of myself as a Democrat any more because I don't see any leadership. Let's talk about political leadership for a minute. We send those people to Washington. In Washington they talk about those people on The Hill, and The Hill suggests vision. A man or women seeks to get elected so that they can be sent to The Hill; so that they can report to us from their elevated point of vision what they are able to see that the rest of us, in our own busy lives, far away from politics and far away from Washington and certainly far from The Hill, cannot see.

"Leadership to me is somebody with the strength to say: you sent me here to The Hill and I see very clearly what direction we have to go in. Now I know it seems to you back home that this is a wrong direction but you sent me here to take a look for all of us, and I am looking for all of us, and this is the road I say we must take. With that, the leader has the guts to go with his or her conviction. I see very little of this kind of leadership today; everything seems to be about getting elected and then about getting re-elected.

"About the television media: for the longest time there hasn't been any real leadership in network television (I'm not talking about writers, producers, directors, and advertisers; I mean no real leadership at the head of the networks.) When television began, David Sarnoff's NBC had a symphony orchestra led by Toscanini, CBS did Playhouse 90 and there were all kinds of fine dramas. Ratings mattered to some degree, but what really mattered was taking pride in delivering something important to the American people. This pride was the essence of being a broadcaster and being a broadcaster had a special significance that carried with it special responsibilities. At the beginning, television leadership felt this. When network management began answering more and more to the Wall Street dictum that they had to do better in the short term, you could see ABC start to scramble to catch up with NBC and CBS. As soon as ABC began to catch up, NBC and CBS began to behave differently.

"When I came into television they were making thirty-nine shows and they didn't do repeats in the summer, they did summer replacements so the thirteen weeks in the summer was all organized around experimentation: new writers, new stars, new forms. Some wonderful things came out of the thirteen weeks summer replacement. Then came tape; then the notion: 'lets see if the public will take repeats'. So they tried thirteen weeks of repeats. Low and behold, the American public didn't turn off, so soon twenty-six, became the magic number: twenty-six episodes, twenty-six repeats. After that they cut to twenty-two so they could do something else with the other four weeks. Next they went to thirteen. "When I came on with 'All in the Family' in 1971, the order was for thirteen.

"We have made a world of mediocrity out of which mediocre leadership arises.

"I've come to believe that nothing moves forward in our society without the media. One of the great movements in our modern times has been the movement against tobacco. The fact that most rooms in which big dinners are held do not have a cloud of smoke over them by nine o'clock in the evening is fascinating to me. I find it quite stunning that it could have happened in so short a time. On the world scene, we see lurches to democratization. All of this is stirred and fanned by the media, so I think one president of the United States possessing great conviction and understanding, with the help of the media, could make a vast difference.

"The media is clearly a partner in the power base. I don't think it's a fifty-fifty partnership, however. For Ronald Reagan, a really strong president, the press was very much on his side. The fact that he slept in important meetings, the fact that he wasn't awakened to be told things, these were the small jokes and the stuff of legend. Reagan is called 'the Great Communicator.' One of his speech writers said that Reagan could read the phone book and make it interesting. President Reagan possessed a remarkable ability to manage attention and meaning.

"With Bill Clinton, even small transgressions are handled very differently, so it doesn't seem like a fifty-fifty partnership to me. I don't think this is the fault of the press. While the press has it's own failings, the problem is that Clinton has not had the strength to mold this press more to his image. I do think they are malleable and moldable. I believe we can make the case that the media, too, is looking for leadership, that it is willing to be led. I think this is just the way we are as human beings. Both individually and as groups, we are all looking for strong leadership.

"I'm tilting at the windmill of helping business to understand it has this enormous and unsought responsibility by virtue of the seven hours a day of television it sponsors into the average American home, in more than one room and even on the beach. Advertising has profoundly affected the American people and continues to do so on a daily basis.

"In recent years there have been ten to twenty commercials in a single half hour of prime time television and every single one of those imprints tell the same story: You are what you consume; You are successful with women if you smell this way or drink this beer. You are the envy of your peers if you drive this car; If your deodorant fails, your life will too. The terrible irony is that most Americans are faithful to the same messages, consume the same products, but don't have lives and experiences similar to those portrayed in the commercials. Because people can't find themselves in this implied place, they think that there must be something wrong with them.

"Relentlessly consistent, utterly single-minded and focused, the clear, dominating influence of commercial television is: "you are what you consume." Today, the truth is that which sells: if it doesn't sell it ain't reality and it ain't truth. We have to wake up to this and I am ever hopeful that we will".

Restated, Norman is saying that society has accepted the idea that 'salvation is to be found in consumption.' What is the deep motivation behind this relentless consumption? We seek a superior experience of being alive. Freud tells us that we are wired up to seek pleasure and avoid pain. Unfortunately, this diagnosis is as shallow as our culture. Our hearts yearn for a profound experience of spirit, and while this experience is a sublime pleasure, to simply proclaim that what we seek is pleasure is to promote our disease rather than heal it. The experience we so desperately seek is only to be found inside of us. It cannot be found in consumption of advertisers wares. We are quite simply 'looking for love in all the wrong places.'

Norman continued, "We have to develop a world that aspires to a great deal more than mediocrity and mindless consumption. We have to start with our values base, our code of ethics. We are way off in this regard. One of the great tragedies of modern life in America is that we have somehow ended up with a culture that allows only the people on the edges to discuss religion and such with impunity. It is left to the Pat Robertsons and the James Dobsons, along with New Age swamis and folks on the edges. For most people in ordinary daily life, whether sitting at their dinner table with half a dozen guests or as a guest at somebody else's dinner party, encouragement of a conversation about any aspect of religion or about the values that come from it just simply doesn't occur.

"There has to be a new terminology, because religion isn't really what I mean, and yet I find myself using the word because there isn't another. If I said 'spiritual', it would have another connotation—I'm satisfied to call it the 'what's it all about Alfie' question. I find there is no conversation that isn't tangential to some question that relates to higher meaning and all the unanswered questions.

"I sometimes wonder if this isn't the root cause of so much that is wrong on the surface of our society. We just may be the most well informed, yet least self-aware, people in history.

"As a part of tilting at the windmill, eighteen prominent Americans from the fields of business, media, labor and academia formed the Business Enterprise Trust in 1989. The mission of the trust is to honor acts of courage, integrity and social vision in business, and by this, to endorse the behaviors that the Trust considers critical to the future of American business and American society.

"I wanted this year, in conjunction with our Business Enterprise Trust Awards, to have a day long conference on the subject of values—based on spirit—in business. The idea was to have a conference at which business people would dare to talk about why they care to lead their companies in a values-driven fashion, and where that spirit stems from. I thought that would make for a fresh conference. The feedback was that business people weren't ready to step forward and declare publicly the experience they've held privately."

Conclusion

Norman strikes a chord within me. I remember reading somewhere "that all it takes for the forces of evil to win in the world is for enough good men to do nothing." The Founding Fathers gave us a declaration of "life, liberty and the pursuit of happiness." The pursuit of happiness part bothered me a little, living as I do in California, where the pursuit of happiness seems to be a mindless obsession. I wondered how the Founding Fathers could have intended this. A lawyer who loved language enlightened me in the matter. In 1776, when Thomas Jefferson penned the immortal words "Life, liberty and the pursuit of happiness," the word "pursuit" meant what the word "practice" means today. Hence we have "life, liberty and the practice of happiness" when the original is adjusted for modern word usage.

Life and liberty are privileges, perhaps entitlements. The experience of happiness is definitely not an entitlement. Happiness requires enlightened thinking, practice, and skill. Happiness is not something we experience as the effect of some external and separate source of salvation. It is not available simply because we consume some advertisers' ware. At the very least, happiness requires that we stop creating unhappiness through denial of the true nature of the self. Enduring happiness flows from a life that is values-based and spiritually correct.

In our consulting practice we have developed statistically "bullet proof" data demonstrating that, all other things being equal, values-based, spirit-directed organizations create superior long term economic value. We have developed considerable expertise at facilitating enterprises lead by men and women who have an appetite for fundamental change coupled with courage to be an advocate for business that is values-based and spirit-directed.

Recommended Reading & Resources

Adams, John D. (ed.). *Transforming Leadership*. Alexandria, VA: Miler River, 1986.

Adams, John D. *Understanding and Managing Stress: Instruments to Assess Your Lifestyle*. San Diego, CA: Pfeiffer and Co., 1989.

Argyris, Chris. *Knowledge for Action: A Guide to Overcoming Barriers to Organizational Change*. San Francisco, CA: Jossey-Bass Publisher, 1993.

Argyris, Chris & D. Schon. *Organizational Learning: A Theory-in-Action Perspective*. Reading, MA: Addison-Wesley, 1978.

Autry, James A. *Love and Profit: The Art of Caring Leadership*. New York, NY: Morrow, 1991.

Autry, James A. *Life and Work*. New York, NY: William Morrow, 1994.

Barrentine, Pat (ed.). *When The Canary Stops Singing: Women's Perspectives on Transforming Business*. San Francisco, CA: Berrett-Koehler, 1993.

Bennis, Warren. *On Becoming a Leader*. Reading, MA: Addison-Wesley, 1989.

Bennis, Warren & Burt Nanus. *Leaders: The Strategies for Taking Charge*. New York, NY: Harper Row, 1985.

Block, Peter. "Leadership and the Governance Revolution," *The New Leaders*, July/Aug. 1993.

Block, Peter. *Stewardship: Choosing Service Over Self Interest*. San Francisco, CA: Berrett-Koehler, 1993.

Breton, Denise & Christopher Largent. *The Soul of Economies: Spiritual Evolution Goes to the Marketplace*. Wilmington, DE: Idea House Publishing Company, 1991.

Brittain, Brian. "Prismatic Leadership: Leadership from the Inside Out," *The New Leaders*, Nov./Dec. 1991.

Brown, Juanita. "Corporation As Community: A New Image for a New Era." In *New Traditions in Business*, John Renesch (ed.). San Francisco, CA: Berrett-Koehler, 1992.

Cabezas, A. & G. Kawaguchi. "Empirical Evidence for Continuing Asian American Income Inequality: The Human Capital Model and Labor Market Segmentation." In *Reflections on Shattered Windows: Promises and Prospects for Asian American Studies*, G.Y. Okihiro, S. Hune, A.A. Hansen, & J.M. Liu (eds.). Pullman, WA: Washington State University Press, 1988.

Campbell, Susan. *Beyond the Power Struggle: Dealing with Conflict in Love and Work.* San Luis Obispo, CA: Impact Publishers, 1984.

Campbell, Susan. *Survival Strategies for the New Workplace: Personal Tools for Coping with Crisis, Change and Conflict.* New York, NY: Simon & Schuster, 1994.

Cannings, K. & C. Montmarquette. "Managerial Momentum: A Simultaneous Model of the Career Progress of Male and Female Managers," *Industrial and Labor Relations Review* 44, January 1991.

Covey, Stephen R. *Principle-Centered Leadership: Strategies for Personal & Professional Effectiveness.* New York, NY: Simon & Schuster Trade, 1992.

Covey, Stephen R. *The Seven Habits of Highly Effective People: Powerful Lessons in Personal Change.* New York, NY: Fireside, 1989.

DePree, Max. *Leadership Is an Art.* New York, NY: Currency Doubleday, 1989.

DePree, Max. *Leadership Jazz.* New York, NY: Currency Doubleday, 1992.

Eisler, Riane. *The Chalice & the Blade: Our History, Our Future.* New York, NY: Harper & Row, 1988.

Eisler, Riane & David Loye. *The Partnership Way.* New York, NY: Harper Collins, 1991.

"Ex-Pepsi Chairman Addresses Corporate Enlightenment," *The New Leaders,* Nov./Dec. 1991.

Fairholm, Gil. "Trust: Key to New Leadership," *The New Leaders,* Nov./Dec. 1993.

Fairholm, Gil. *Values Leadership: Toward a New Philosophy of Leadership.* New York, NY: Praeger, 1991.

Forrester, J.W., "A New Corporate Design," *Sloan Management Review.* Cambridge, MA: MIT Press, 1965.

Fox, Robert W. "The World's Urban Explosion," *National Geographic,* August 1984.

Gardner, John W. *On Leadership.* New York, NY: The Free Press, 1990.

"GE Boss Blasts Autocratic Leadership," *The New Leaders,* May/June 1992.

Gerhart, B. & S. Rynes. "Determinants and Consequences of Salary Negotiations by Male and Female MBA Graduates," *Journal of Applied Psychology,* 1991.

Goldin, C. *Understanding the Gender Gap: An Economic History of American Women.* New York, NY: Oxford University Press, 1990.

Graham, Jill W. "Servant-Leadership in Organizations: Inspirational and Moral," *Leadership Quarterly*, 1991.

Greenleaf, Robert K. *The Leadership Crisis: A Message for College and University Faculty*. Indianapolis, IN: The Greenleaf Center, 1987.

Greenleaf, Robert K. *Teacher as Servant*. Indianapolis, IN: The Greenleaf Center, 1987.

Greenleaf, Robert K. *Servant Leadership: A Journey Into the Nature of Legitimate Power and Greatness*. New York, NY: Paulist Press, 1977.

Hammerschlag, M.D. *The Dancing Healers*. San Francisco, CA: Harper & Row, 1989.

Handy, Charles. *The Age of Unreason*. London, England: Hutchinson, 1989.

Handy, Charles. *The Age of Paradox*. Boston, MA: Harvard Business School Press, 1994.

Harman, Willis. "21st Century Business: A Background for Dialogue," *New Traditions in Business* (ed.). John Renesch. San Francisco, CA: Berrett-Koehler, 1992.

Harman, Willis. *Global Mind Change*. Indianapolis, IN: Knowledge Systems, Inc., 1987.

Harman, Willis. "Sustainable Development: The Modern Challenge for Business," *The New Leaders*, Nov./Dec. 1991.

Harman, Willis & John Hormann. *Creative Work: The Constructive Role of Business in a Transforming Society*. Indianapolis, IN: Knowledge Systems, Inc., 1990.

Harris, Philip. *High Performance Leadership*, Glenview, IL: Scott Foresman, 1989.

Helgesen, Sally. *The Female Advantage: Women's Ways of Leadership*. New York, NY: Doubleday, 1990.

Henderson, Hazel. *Paradigms in Progress: Life Beyond Economics*. Indianapolis, IN: Knowledge Systems, Inc., 1991.

Henderson, Hazel. *Redefining Wealth and Progress: New Ways to Measure Economic, Societal, and Environmental Change*. Indianapolis, IN: Knowledge Systems, Inc., 1990.

Hesse, Herman. *Journey to the East*. New York, NY: Harper Row, 1985.

Imai, Masaaki. *Kaizen. The Key to Japan's Competitive Success*. New York, NY: McGraw-Hill, 1986.

Kiechel III, Walter. "The Leader as Servant," *Fortune*, May 4, 1992.

Kouzes, James M. & Barry Z. Posner. *Credibility: How Leaders Gain and Lose It, Why People Demand It*. San Francisco, CA: Jossey-Bass, 1993.

Kurtzman, Joel. *The Death of Money.* New York, NY: Simon & Schuster, 1993.

Land, George & Beth Jarman. *Breakpoint and Beyond.* San Francisco, CA: Harper Business, 1992.

"Leadership," as told to Rob Rabbin by Judith Skutch-Whitson, *The New Leaders,* Special Issue, Spring 1994.

Lee, Chris & Ron Zemke. "The Search for Spirit in the Workplace," *Training,* June 1993.

Liebig, Jim. *Merchants of Vision: People Bringing New Purpose and Values to Business.* San Francisco, CA: Berrett-Koehler, 1994.

Lulic, Margaret. *Who We Could Be At Work.* Minneapolis, MN: Blue Edge Publishing, 1994

Magaziner, Elemer. "New Thinking, Not Just New Insight," *The New Leaders,* Jan./Feb. 1994.

Maynard, Herman & Sue Mehrtens. *The Fourth Wave: Business in the 21st Century,* San Francisco, CA: Berrett-Koehler, 1993.

McCall, M.W., M. M. Lombardo Jr. & A. M. Morrison. *The Lessons of Experience: How Successful Executives Develop On the Job.* Lexington, MA: Lexington Books, 1988.

Morrison, Ann M. *The New Leaders: Guidelines On Leadership Diversity in America.* San Francisco, CA: Jossey-Bass, 1992.

Morrison, Ann M., R.P. White & E. Van Velsor. *Breaking the Glass Ceiling: Can Women Reach the Top of America's Largest Corporations?* Reading, MA: Addison-Wesley, 1992 (updated edition).

Morrison, Ann M., Marian N. Ruderman & Martha Hughes-James. *Making Diversity Happen: Controversies and Solutions.* Center for Creative Leadership, Greensboro, NC: 1993.

Morrison, Ann M. & Kristen M. Crabtree. *Developing Diversity in Organizations: A Digest of Selected Literature.* Center for Creative Leadership, Greensboro, NC: 1992.

Moskowitz, Milton and Robert Levering. *100 Best Companies to Work for In America.* New York, NY: Bantam, 1993.

Nair, Dr. Keshavan. "The Spirit of Leadership," *The New Leaders,* Nov./Dec. 1993.

Naisbitt, John. *Global Paradox: The Bigger the World Economy, the More Powerful Its Smallest Players.* New York, NY: William Morrow & Company, Inc., 1994.

Nelton, S. & K. Berney. "Women: The Second Wave," *Nation's Business,* May 1987.

"Norman Lear Stresses Need for Return to Spiritual Values, A Revival of the Human Spirit," excerpt from a speech to the National Education Association, *The New Leaders*, Jan./Feb. 1991.

Oakley, Ed & Doug Krug. *Enlightened Leadership: Getting to the Heart of Change*. New York, NY: Simon & Shuster, 1993.

Ohmae, Kenichi. *The Borderless World: Power and Strategy in the Interlinked Economy*. New York, NY: Harper Collins, 1990.

Ornstein, Robert and Paul Ehrlich. *New World New Mind: Moving Toward Conscious Evolution*. New York, NY: Doubleday, 1989.

Osborn, Susan. "The New Science of Leadership," *The New Leaders*, July/Aug. 1992.

Österberg, Rolf. *Corporate Renaissance: Business as an Adventure in Human Development*. Mill Valley, CA: Nataraj Publishing, 1993.

Pagonis, William. "The Work of Leadership," *Harvard Business Review*, Nov./Dec. 1992.

Pascarella, Perry. *The New Achievers*. New York, NY: The Free Press, 1984.

Pascarella, Perry & Mark Frohman. *The Purpose-Driven Organization*. San Francisco, CA: Jossey-Bass Publishers, 1989.

"Patagonia CEO Calls for Real Leadership—an End to 'White Noise and Mediocrity," *The New Leaders*, May/June 1993.

Peters, Tom & Nancy Austin. *A Passion for Excellence: The Leadership Difference*, New York, NY: Random House, 1985.

Rabbin, Rob. "Leadership as a Mystical Experience: Spiritual Awakening in the Board Room," *The New Leaders*, Jan./Feb. 1992.

Rasmussen, Tina "New Leaders: Anchors in Turbulent Waves," *The New Leaders*, Jan./Feb. 1994.

Ray, Michael and John Renesch (eds.). *The New Entrepreneurs: Business Visionaries for the 21st Century*. San Francisco, CA: New Leaders Press, 1994.

Ray, Michael & Alan Rinzler, (eds.).*Organizational Change*. New York, NY: Tarcher/Perigee, 1993.

Renesch, John, (ed.). *New Traditions in Business: Spirit and Leadership in the 21st Century*. San Francisco, CA: Berrett-Koehler, 1992.

Renesch, John and Dennis White. "Global Workplace Values Identified," *The New Leaders*, May/June 1994.

Renesch, John. "Walking the Talk: A Time for Impeccable Leadership," *The New Leaders*, March/April 1992.

Rockefeller, John D. *The Second American Revolution.* New York, NY: Harper & Row, 1973.

Russell, Peter. *The White Hole in Time.* San Francisco, CA: Harper, 1992.

Schmookler, Andrew. *Fools Gold: The Fate of Values in a World of Goods.* San Francisco, CA: Harper, 1993.

Schwartz, Peter. *Art of the Long View: The Path to Strategic Insights for Yourself & Your Company.* New York, NY: Doubleday, 1991.

Scovel, K. "The Relocation Riddle," *Human Resource Executive,* June 1990.

Senge, Peter M. *The Fifth Discipline: The Art and Practice of the Learning Organization.* New York, NY: Doubleday, 1990.

Senge, Peter M., Charlotte Roberts, Richard Ross, Bryan Smith and Art Kleiner. *The Fifth Discipline Fieldbook.* New York, NY: Currency Doubleday, 1994.

Spears, Larry C. "Robert K. Greenleaf: Servant-Leader," *Friends Journal,* Aug. 1991.

Spears, Larry C. "Trustees as Servant-Leaders," *International Journal of Values-Based Management,* Volume Six, Number One, 1993.

Spears, Larry C. , (ed.). *The Greenleaf Legacy.* New York, NY: John Wiley & Sons, Inc., (scheduled) 1995.

Terry, Robert W. *Authentic Leadership: Courage in Action.* San Francisco, CA: Jossey-Bass, 1993.

Thompson, B.L. "Training's Salary Survey," *Training,* November 1990.

Tichy, N.M. & M. Devanna. *The Transformational Leader.* New York, NY: John Wiley & Sons: 1986.

Tichy, Noel & Stratford Sherman. *Control Your Destiny Or Someone Else Will.* New York, NY: Doubleday, 1993.

Vaill, Peter. *Managing as a Performing Art.* San Francisco, CA: Jossey-Bass, 1989.

Van Velsor, E. & M.W. Hughes. *Gender Differences in the Development of Managers: How Women Managers Learn From Experience.* Greensboro, NC: Center for Creative Leadership, 1990.

Wheatley, Margaret J. *Leadership and the New Science: Learning About Organization from an Orderly Universe.* San Francisco, CA: Berrett-Koehler, 1992.

Wiesbord, Marvin. *Discovering Common Ground.* San Francisco, CA: Berrett-Koehler, 1992.

Zweig, Connie & Jeremiah Abrams. *Meeting the Shadow.* Los Angeles: New York, NY: Tarcher, 1991.

Periodicals

The New Leaders:
The Business Newsletter for
Transformative Leadership
(bimonthly newsletter)
New Leaders Press
1668 Lombard Street
San Francisco, CA 94123
800/928-5323

World Business Academy Perspectives
(quarterly journal)
Berrett-Koehler Publishers, Inc.
155 Montgomery St.
San Francisco, CA 94104-4109
800/929-2929

At Work: Stories of Tomorrow's Workplace
(bimonthly newsletter)
Berrett-Koehler Publishers, Inc.
155 Montgomery St.
San Francisco, CA 94104-4109
800/929-2929

Business Ethics:
The Magazine of Socially Responsible Business
(bimonthly magazine)
Mavis Publications, Inc.
52 South 10 St., #110
Minneapolis, MN 55403-2001
612/962-4700

The Systems Thinker
(newsletter, 10x/year)
Pegasus Communications, Inc.
P.O. Box 120
Kendall Square
Cambridge, MA 02142
617/576-1231

Institutes and Centers

Business for Social Responsibility
1850 M Street N.W., #750
Washington, DC, 20036
202/842-5400
or
P.O. Box 28370
San Francisco, CA 94128
415/931-1795

Center for Creative Leadership
Greensboro, NC; Colorado Springs, CO; San Diego, CA
8910 University Center Lane, Suite 1000
San Diego, CA 92122
619/453-4774

Center for Developmental Systems
Sante Fe, NM; Battle Ground, WA; Portland, OR
28036 NE 212th Ave.
Battle Ground, WA 98604-7514
206/687-1408

Robert K. Greenleaf Center
1100 W. 42nd Street, Suite 321
Indianapolis, IN, 46208
317/925-2677

USC Leadership Institute
Graduate School of Business Administration
University of Southern California
Los Angeles, CA 90089-1421
213/740-3618

World Business Academy
433 Airport Blvd., #416
Burlingame, CA, 94010
415/342-2387

Index

How to Contact Authors

JOHN D. ADAMS
Eartheart Enterprises, Inc.
84 Camino De Herrera
San Anselmo, CA 94960
415/258-0367

BARBARA R. HAUSER
Gram, Plant, Mooty, et. al.
3400 City Center 33 S. 6th St.
Minneapolis, MN 55403-3796
612/343-3949

JAMES A. AUTRY
Senior Management Associates
P.O. Box 12069
Des Moines, IA 50312
515/279-1245

CHARLES F. KIEFER
Innovation Associates, Inc.
3 Speen St., # 140
Framington, MA 01701
508/879-8301

WARREN BENNIS
U.S.C. Business School
University of Southern California
Los Angeles, CA 90089-1421
213/740-0767

PETER K. KREMBS
1606 W. 28th St.
Minneapolis, MN 55408
612/872-6419

ELEMER MAGAZINER
2675 W. Hwy. 89A, #1028
Sedona, AZ 86336
602/282-1804

SUSAN M. CAMPBELL
256 Bayview Ave.
Belvedere, CA 94920-2404
415/435-8021

MAX DEPREE
2967 Lakeshore Dr.
Holland, MI 49424
616/399-0967

CAROL MCCALL
World Institute for Life Planning
191 University Blvd., #303
Denver, CO 80206
800/999-9551

STEWART EMERY
Human Factors, Inc.
3301 Kerner Blvd., Suite 200
San Rafael, CA 94901
415/459-6060

ANN M. MORRISON
New Leaders Institute
P.O. Box 1110
Del Mar, CA 92014
619/792-5922

ED OAKLEY
Enlightened Leadership
International
7100 E. Belleview
Englewood, CO 80111
800/798-9881

PERRY PASCARELLA
Penton Publishing, Inc.
1100 Superior Ave.
Cleveland, OH 44114
216/696-7000

ROBERT RABBIN
Hansa Institute
20 Sunnyside Ave. Suite A-118
Mill Valley, CA 94941
415/389-0214

TINA RASMUSSEN
P.O. Box 363
Moraga, CA 94556
510/631-9485

CAROL SANFORD
Spring Hill Publications
28036 N.E. 212th Ave.
Battle Ground, WA 98604
206/687-1408

BARBARA SHIPKA
4600 Colfax Ave. S.
Minneapolis, MN 55409
612/827-3006

LARRY C. SPEARS
Greenleaf Center
1100 W. 42nd St., #321
Indianapolis, IN 46208
317/925-2677

MARTHA SPICE
Growth Dynamics
6701 Democracy Blvd., #300
Bethesda, ND 20817
301/469-4890

KATE STEICHEN
P.O. Box 303
Crestone, CO 81131
719/256-4290

MARGARET J. WHEATLEY
Kellner-Rogers & Wheatley
3857 N. 300 W
Provo, UT 84604
801/221-0044

How to Contact the Editor

JOHN RENESCH
Sterling & Stone, Inc.
1668 Lombard Street
San Francisco, CA 94123
415/928-1473

314

Additional copies of

LEADERSHIP
in a NEW ERA

can be purchased from
the organizations listed below

ARIZONA
Project Linguistics Int'l., Sedona   602/282-1804

CALIFORNIA
Advantage Consulting, Moraga   510/631-9485
Eartheart Enterprises, Inc., San Anselmo   415/258-0367
Hamsa Institute, Mill Valley   415/389-0214
New Leaders Institute, Del Mar   619/792-5922
Susan Campbell, Consultant, Belvedere   415/435-8021

COLORADO
Enlightened Leadership Int'l., Englewood   303/694-4644
Natural Leadership™, Crestone   719/256-4290
World Institute for Life Planning, Denver   800/999-9551

INDIANA
Robert K. Greenleaf Center, Indianapolis   317/925-2677

MARYLAND
Growth Dynamics Inc., Bethesda   301/469-4890

MASSACHUSETTS
Innovation Associates Inc., Framingham   508/879-8301

MINNESOTA
Barbara Shipka, Consultant, Minneapolis   612/827-3006
Gray Plant Mooty Mooty & Bennett, Minneapolis   612/343-3949
Management Development Strategies, Minneapolis   612/872-6419

OHIO
Penton Publishing Inc., Cleveland   216/696-7000

WASHINGTON
Spring Hill Publications, Battleground   206/687-1408

OTHER BUSINESS ANTHOLOGIES
developed by New Leaders Press

The New Entrepreneurs: Business Visionaries for the 21st Century.
Authors include Anita Roddick, Peggy Pepper, Betsy Burton, Greg
Steltenpohl, Ron Kovach, Jeff Sholl, Jacqueline Haessly, David P.
Jasper, Richard B. Brooke, Sharon Gadberry, John H. Stearns, Cheryl
Alexander, Marjorie Kelly, Chris Manning, Paul Hwoschinsky, William
B. Sechrest, Nicholas P. LiVolsi, Bill Veltrop. Edited by Michael Ray and
John Renesch.
*Available in hardcover from New Leaders Press at $29.95 (U.S.);
call 1.415.928.1473.*

New Traditions in Business: Spirit & Leadership in the 21st Century. Authors include Willis Harman, Michael Ray, Herman Maynard,
Jim Channon, William Miller, Peter Senge, Terry Mollner, Robert Rosen,
Juanita Brown, Cynthia Barnum, David Gaster, Charles Kiefer, Carol
Sanford, John Thompson, and Ken Blanchard; edited by John Renesch.
*Available in paperback from Berrett-Koehler Publishing at $17.95 (U.S.);
call 1.800.929.2929.*

When the Canary Stops Singing: Women's Perspectives on Transforming Business. Author's include Riane Eisler, Carol Frenier, Kathleen
Keating, Marie Kerpan, Barbara Shipka, Kim McMillen, Jacqueline
Haessly, Jan Nickerson, Anne L. Rarich, Jeanne Borei, Hope Xaviermineo,
Cheryl Harrison, Mitani D'Antien, Barbara Fittipaldi, and Sabina Spencer; edited by Pat Barrentine.
*Available in hardcover from Berrett-Koehler Publishers at $24.95 (U.S.);
call 1.800.929.2929.*

FORTHCOMING COLLECTIONS (as of July, 1994):

**Learning Organizations: Developing Cultures for Tomorrow's
Workplace** (est. pub. date: 1995). Authors include Peter Senge and
Fred Kofman, Charles Handy, Rosabeth Moss Kanter, and over thirty
other authors. Edited by Sarita Chawla and John Renesch.

Community Building: Renewing Spirit & Learning in Business
(est. pub. date: 1995). Authors include John Gardner, George Land and
Beth Jarman, Jordan Paul, Michael Ray, Marvin Weisbord, and over
twenty others. Edited by Kazimierz Gozdz.

Rediscovering the Soul of Business: A Renaissance of Values
(est. pub. date: 1995). Authors are expected to include Thomas
Moore, Gary Zukav, Anita Roddick, Thomas Chappell, Elaine Gagné,
and more than a dozen others. Edited by Bill DeFoore and John
Renesch.

FROM THE PUBLISHERS OF *LEADERSHIP in a NEW ERA*

THe NeW LeaDeRS

THE ONLY BUSINESS NEWSLETTER ON TRANSFORMATIVE LEADERSHIP

- Profiles of exemplars in business
- Articles by visionary business scholars
- News of transformation at work

SUBSCRIBE TODAY & SAVE!!!

☐ 1 year/6 issues, now only $89
☐ 2 years/12 issues, now only $159
(note: foreign subscribers, please add $15/year)

CALL 1-800/928-LEADers for credit card orders
(1-800/928-5323)
FAX 1-415/928-3346
MAIL your order with payment to:
THE NEW LEADERS
1668 Lombard Street
San Francisco, CA 94123

* * * * *

Also receive up to six issues/year of
our companion newsletter
The New Leaders DIALOGUES
at no extra charge!